MATTHEW AS STORY

Other Books by Jack Dean Kingsbury

The Parables of Jesus in Matthew 13

Matthew: Structure, Christology, Kingdom

Matthew (Proclamation Commentary)

Jesus Christ in Matthew, Mark, and Luke
(Proclamation Commentary)

The Christology of Mark's Gospel

JACK DEAN KINGSBURY

MATTHEW AS STORY

88-320

FORTRESS PRESS   PHILADELPHIA

To
John Schmidt †

Library of Congress Cataloging in Publication Data

Kingsbury, Jack Dean.
 Matthew as story.

 Bibliography: p.
 Includes index.
 1. Bible. N.T. Matthew—Criticism, interpretation, etc. I. Title.
 BS2575.2.K48 1986 226'.206 85–16204
 ISBN 0–8006–1891–2

1825H85 Printed in the United States of America 1–1891

Contents

Preface

THIS book is a study in literary, or narrative, criticism. It is one of the first such books on Matthew to be written. The object is to explore the world of Matthew's thought with an eye to the flow (plot) of the gospel-story that is being told. Chapter 1 explains the method that informs the other chapters. It likewise contains a great deal of material that is meant to supplement and enrich the further discussion. Chapters 2—4 trace the story-line of Matthew as it pertains to Jesus, and chapter 6 does the same with reference to the disciples. Chapter 5 focuses on the use in Matthew of the title "the Son of man." Chapter 7 takes the reader outside the world of Matthew's story and deals with the community for which the first evangelist wrote. Chapter 8 rounds out the book with concluding remarks.

This book is fundamentally different in character from my volume on the Book of Matthew in the Proclamation Commentaries series. That volume, published in 1977 and now revised, is a study in composition criticism, which is a refinement of the method of redaction criticism. It treats the thought of Matthew in topical fashion as it first defines the center of this thought and then discusses questions of christology (the figure of Jesus), of theology (the notion of the Kingdom of Heaven), and of ecclesiology (discipleship and the church of Matthew). This book, as a product of literary criticism, sets forth the thought of Matthew as it finds expression in the very story of Jesus being narrated. Moreover, the analysis of this story is carried out in terms of categories that literary-theorists employ in their investigation of works such as the novel.

True as it unquestionably is that both methods, the composition-critical and the literary-critical, have their legitimacy, it cannot be overlooked that the way in which each one leads the interpreter to read and, in many cases, to assess Matthew is vastly different. When viewed from different angles, the same Gospel admits to different analyses. But different though these analyses are, they need not on this account be wholly incompatible or without areas of contact. The reader who has perused my book of 1977 and who also takes this one in hand will be able to spot places where he or she encounters what is familiar; on this score, chapter 7, which moves outside the world of Matthew's story, is a special case in point. But this notwithstanding, the present volume lays just claim to being a fresh contribution to Matthean studies. The application of a new method has cast the contents of Matthew in a strikingly new light.

Three factors prompted the writing of this book. The idea itself originated in conjunction with work on my inaugural professorial address, "The Figure of Jesus in Matthew's Story: A Literary-Critical Probe," which was delivered during Sprunt Lectures Week in February 1983 at Union Theological Seminary in Virginia and has subsequently been published in the *Journal for the Study of the New Testament* 21 (June 1984): 3–36. Further impetus came from the preparation of a second address, "The Parable of the Wicked Husbandmen and the Secret of Jesus' Divine Sonship in Matthew: Some Literary-Critical Observations," which was delivered at the annual meeting of Studiorum Novi Testamenti Societas in August 1984 at Basel, Switzerland, and is to appear in the *Journal of Biblical Literature*. The burden of this address was to argue that in Matthew's gospel-story (and not just in Mark's) the notion that Jesus is the Son of God is treated as a secret. And third, yet another factor motivating the writing of this book was the desire on my part to ascertain to what extent literary criticism might commend itself as an approach for writing the commentary on Matthew which has been commissioned for the Hermeneia series.

As authors are wont to do, I, too, have taken advantage of speaking invitations to deliver portions of this book to clergy conferences and to students and professors at various seminaries, divinity schools, and universities. I have benefited greatly from the discussions that attend such addresses, and these discussions have not been without impact on the final manuscript. In this connection, I would like to say a special word of thanks to those at North Park Theological Seminary in Chicago who invited me to deliver the Lund lectures for 1985. In other respects, I should also like to thank John A. Hollar of Fortress Press for guiding this book to publication and Mark A. Powell, my graduate assistant, for preparing the index. Last but by no means least, my heartfelt thanks likewise go to my wife, Barbara, for assisting me in this project in all those unheralded ways that deserve, but always seem to escape, mention.

JACK DEAN KINGSBURY
Union Theological Seminary in Virginia
Epiphany, 1985

Abbreviations

AnBib	Analecta biblica
BETL	Bibliotheca ephemeridum theologicarum lovaniensium
BEvT	Beiträge zur evangelischen Theologie
BJRL	*Bulletin of the John Rylands University Library of Manchester*
BU	Biblische Untersuchungen
BWANT	Beiträge zur Wissenschaft vom Alten und Neuen Testament
CBA	Catholic Biblical Association of America
CBQ	*Catholic Biblical Quarterly*
CBQMS	Catholic Biblical Quarterly—Monograph Series
ConBNT	Coniectanea biblica, New Testament
FRLANT	Forschungen zur Religion und Literatur des Alten und Neuen Testaments
GBS	Guides to Biblical Scholarship
HNTC	Harper's New Testament Commentaries
HTKNT	Herders theologischer Kommentar zum Neuen Testament
HUCA	*Hebrew Union College Annual*
IR	*The Iliff Review*
IDB	G. A. Buttrick, ed., *Interpreter's Dictionary of the Bible* (Nashville: Abingdon Press, 1962)
Ign. *Eph.*	Ignatius, Letter to the Ephesians
Pol.	Ignatius, Letter to Polycarp
Smyrn.	Ignatius, Letter to the Smyrnaeans
IRT	Issues in Religion and Theology
JAAR	*Journal of the American Academy of Religion*
JBL	*Journal of Biblical Literature*
JR	*Journal of Religion*
JSNT	*Journal for the Study of the New Testament*
LXX	Septuagint

NLH	*New Literary History*
NovT	*Novum Testamentum*
NovTSup	Novum Testamentum, Supplements
NT	New Testament
NTAbh	Neutestamentliche Abhandlungen
NTL	New Testament Library
NTS	*New Testament Studies*
OBO	Orbis biblicus et orientalis
OT	Old Testament
PRS	*Perspectives in Religious Studies*
RRel	*Radical Religion*
SANT	Studien zum Alten und Neuen Testament
SBL	Society of Biblical Literature
SBLDS	SBL Dissertation Series
SBS	Stuttgarter Bibelstudien
ScrMin	Scripta minora
SNTSMS	Society for New Testament Studies Monograph Series
ST	*Studia theologica*
TDNT	G. Kittel and G. Friedrich, eds., *Theological Dictionary of the New Testament* (Grand Rapids: Wm. B. Eerdmans, 1964–76)
TI	Theological Inquiries
TS	*Theological Studies*
ZTK	*Zeitschrift für Theologie und Kirche*

1
Understanding Matthew:
A Literary-Critical Approach

THE goal of this book is to explore the story that is found in the Gospel according to Matthew. To guide this exploration, the method to be used is that known as literary criticism. Since literary criticism has many guises, the method itself begs to be discussed in some detail (chap. 1). This discussion, in turn, stands in the service of the principal task of the book: to trace the flow of Matthew's story and to show how, in conjunction with this, its portrait of Jesus (chaps. 2—4) and of the disciples (chap. 6) emerges. In addition, there are also special topics that call for attention. These pertain to such matters as Jesus' designation of himself as the Son of man (chap. 5) and the social and religious circumstances in which the Christian community that stood behind Matthew's Gospel apparently lived (chap. 7).

As presently practiced, literary criticism focuses on the Gospels as narratives. It involves a study of the content of these narratives and of the rhetorical techniques by means of which they are told. One literary theorist, Seymour Chatman, has provided a useful outline for discussing the constituent parts of narrative,[1] and David Rhoads has shown with what profit this outline can be employed in investigating a Gospel such as that of Mark.[2] The present investigation of Matthew's Gospel will also draw from Chatman's outline, and supplement it as well with the work of others.

The Gospel of Matthew is a unified narrative, and recognition of this is essential to its literary-critical study.[3] It is on this point, in fact, that literary criticism stands apart from the historical-biographical, the form-critical, and the redaction-critical approaches to Matthew. Scholars taking one or the other of these approaches have tended to scrutinize Matthew not so

1. Cf. Chatman, *Story and Discourse*.
2. Cf. Rhoads, "Narrative Criticism," 411–34; also Rhoads and Michie, *Mark as Story*.
3. Petersen, *Literary Criticism*, 20–23, 28, 40; Rhoads, "Narrative Criticism," 412–14.

much to understand the gospel-story it relates as such, but in order to obtain from it information that will enable them to gain insight into historical or theological realities that, properly, lie behind or beyond this story. Thus, uppermost in the minds of the nineteenth- and early twentieth-century proponents of the historical-biographical approach to Matthew was the use of it to establish a factually sound portrait of the life and ministry of the historical Jesus. As for the form critics following World War I, Matthew was of interest to them as a source of individual sayings or stories that could be made to provide a sketch of the rise and development of the gospel tradition between the time of Easter and the time of the writing of the Gospels themselves. And as far as the redaction critics in the years since World War II are concerned, they have largely investigated Matthew so as to reconstruct the theology or social situation of the evangelist and of the community that stood behind the Gospel.

To approach Matthew's Gospel as a unified narrative, however, is to concentrate on the very story it tells. When one reads the Matthean narrative, one temporarily takes leave of one's familiar world of reality and enters into another world that is autonomous in its own right. This world, which possesses its own time and space, is peopled by characters and marked by events that, in varying degrees, are extolled or decried in accordance with this world's own system of values. By inhabiting this world one experiences it, and having experienced it, one leaves and returns, perhaps changed, to one's own world.[4]

THE STORY OF THE NARRATIVE

Like other narratives, Matthew's Gospel may be said to comprise two parts. These two parts Chatman designates as the "story" and its "discourse."[5] The "story" of Matthew is the life of Jesus from his birth to his death and resurrection. The "discourse" of Matthew is the means whereby this story of the life of Jesus is told. In simple terms, the "story" is "what" is told, whereas the "discourse" is "how" the story is told.

Events

The story of a narrative such as that of Matthew's Gospel encompasses, according to Chatman, three elements, namely, "events," "characters," and "settings."[6] "Events" are the string of incidents, or actions, which stretches the length of a story. They comprise the "plot," or flow, of a story. To create a "plot," the author arranges the events of a story in a particular order or sequence so as to elicit from the reader some desired response. In chapters

4. Cf. Uspensky, *Poetics of Composition*, 137.
5. Chatman, *Story and Discourse*, 19–27.
6. Ibid., 26 (chap. 2).

2—4 of this book, the plot of Matthew's story will be traced in detail. The concern here is to discuss the element of conflict.

The element of conflict is central to the plot of Matthew.[7] As the royal Son of God in whom God's end-time Rule is a present, albeit hidden, reality, Jesus is the supreme agent of God who "thinks the things of God" (3:17; 12:28; 16:23). The conflicts in which he becomes embroiled are with Satan (4:1–11), demons (12:28), the forces of nature and of illness,[8] civil authorities (such as Herod and Pilate),[9] Gentiles (including Roman soldiers),[10] and Israel,[11] above all its leaders.[12] On those occasions when the disciples, too, "think the things not of God, but of men," Jesus likewise enters into conflict with them.[13] In one instance, in Gethsemane, he even struggles with himself (26:36–46). The thing to observe is that whereas Jesus freely employs his incomparable authority to vanquish Satan, demons, and the forces of nature and of illness, he chooses not to compel humans to do his bidding (26:53; cf. 11:27a).[14] On the contrary, he calls humans to repentance in view of the gracious nearness of God's kingly Rule (4:17). The upshot is that the conflict on which the plot of Matthew's story turns is that between Jesus and Israel.

The Israel Jesus confronts comprises the Jewish crowds and their leaders. Until the passion, however, the crowds are generally well disposed toward Jesus, so that his conflict with them is over whether he can win them to his side. At the same time, "warning passages" such as 2:3; 8:10–12; 10; 11:16–24; and 13:10–13 occur, leading the reader to anticipate that Jesus will not, finally, be successful. Nevertheless, not until the arrest of Jesus do the crowds become his adversaries (26:47–56). Moreover, this change of attitude on their part occurs so abruptly that it occasions surprise. At 22:33 it is yet reported of the crowds that they react to Jesus' teaching with amazement. At 23:1, they are the recipients, along with the disciples, of Jesus' words of woe against the scribes and Pharisees. And at 21:45–46, they are even made out to be a source of fear for the Jewish leaders, who see in them a threat to their guileful plans to capture Jesus and kill him (cf. 26:3–5). But despite this, at Jesus' arrest the same crowds

7. Rhoads ("Narrative Criticism," 415) discusses this point with reference to Mark, but it is, of course, no less true of Matthew.

8. Cf. 4:23–24; 8—9; 11:5; 12:9–14, 15, 22; 14:14, 15–21, 22–33; 15:21–28, 29–31, 32–38; 17:14–21; 19:2; 20:29–34; 21:14–16, 18–22.

9. Cf. Matthew 2; 27; also 14:1–12.

10. Cf. 8:28–34; 27:27–31, 32–37.

11. Cf. 11:16–19, 20–24, 25; 13:10–13.

12. Cf. 9:3, 11, 34; 12:2, 10, 15, 24–37, 38–45; 13:10–15; 16:1–4; 19:3; 21:12—23:39; 26—27.

13. Cf. 8:21–22, 23–27; 14:28–32; 16:5–12, 21–23; 17:14–20; 19:13–15; 20:20–28; 26:30–35, 36–46; 26:25.

14. This observation, made by Rhoads ("Narrative Criticism," 415) relative to Mark, applies also to Matthew.

whom he had daily been teaching in the temple, armed with swords and clubs, suddenly appear with Judas in order to seize him on behalf of the chief priests and the elders (26:47, 55). Indeed, what is still more ironic is that these people, the very ones to whom God had sent Jesus as Shepherd and King (2:6), should also shout aloud to Pilate, the Roman governor, "His blood be on us and on our children!" (27:25). The repudiation of Jesus by the people of Israel is complete.

The implacable adversaries of Jesus, however, are the Jewish leaders. They stand forth as the guardians of the law and the tradition on the one hand and of the temple cult on the other, the factors that make Israel distinct as a nation. In Matthew's story, they are the epitome of what it means to "think the things not of God, but of men" (15:6–8, 13). From the outset, they are resolutely opposed to Jesus, for the first offense with which they charge him, namely, blasphemy against God, is at the same time the offense for which they finally condemn him to death (9:3; 26:65–66). But true as it is that there is no appreciable change in the gravity of Jesus' conflict with the Jewish leaders, what does change, and considerably so, is the level of tension. This increases, and such increase is due to two factors in particular: (a) The initial conflict Jesus has with the Jewish leaders is still preparatory in nature and serves the purpose of readying the reader for the more intense conflict soon to follow. (b) And in Jesus' last great confrontation with the Jewish leaders prior to his passion, he becomes involved in continual debate with an ever-expanding circle of opponents.

The sharp increase in tension in Jesus' conflict with the Jewish leaders corresponds neatly with the development of the plot of Matthew's story. The second part of the story (4:17—16:20) comprises two sections, with 4:17—11:1 telling of Jesus' ministry to Israel of teaching, preaching, and healing and 11:2—16:20 telling of Israel's response to Jesus, which is that of repudiation. In the narration of Jesus' ministry of teaching, preaching, and healing, the emphasis is on the fact that Jesus calls Israel to repentance and proffers it salvation (cf. 4:17). In line with this emphasis, the conflict between Jesus and the Jewish leaders which flares toward the end of this section (Matthew 9) is not yet irreconcilably hostile. Instead, it functions mainly to prepare the implied reader for the more intense conflict to come. Three things give clear indication of this: (a) The conflict of Matthew 9 is not so acutely confrontational as that which follows, for Jesus is not himself directly attacked for something he himself does. (b) This conflict does not have to do with the Mosaic law as such. (c) And this conflict does not provoke the Jewish leaders to make the fateful decision that they must kill Jesus.

To demonstrate especially the first of these points, observe how "indirect" is this initial conflict between Jesus and the Jewish leaders. The first charge the Jewish leaders lodge against Jesus, that he is guilty of commit-

ting blasphemy against God, is one that some scribes make "within themselves," so that Jesus must discern their thoughts (9:3). The second charge,
that Jesus eats with toll-collectors and sinners, the Pharisees address to the
disciples (9:11). The third charge, which pertains to the practice of fasting
and is a view shared by the Pharisees, is raised with Jesus by the disciples
of John but concerns Jesus' disciples (9:14). And the fourth charge, that
Jesus is in collusion with the prince of demons, is one the Pharisees express
either to themselves alone or only in the hearing of the crowds (9:34). To
repeat, this initial conflict Jesus has with the Jewish leaders, as grave as it
surely is, is nonetheless "preparatory" in nature.

In 11:2—16:20, Israel is depicted as responding to Jesus' ministry of
teaching, preaching, and healing by repudiating him (11:6, 16–24; 13:57).
Correlatively, Jesus' conflict with the Jewish leaders now becomes an integral part of this motif of repudiation, and it rapidly escalates to the point of
irreconcilable hostility. This heightening of tension comes to expression in
the following ways: (a) Debate becomes increasingly confrontational,[15] that
is, for the first time in Matthew's story Jesus is himself directly attacked for
an act he himself intends to perform (12:9–13). (b) Debate concerns the
Mosaic law itself (12:1–8, 9–13). (c) And debate gives rise to such rancor in
the Jewish leaders that they conspire to take Jesus' life (12:14).

To sketch this development, Jesus, after giving answer to the Baptist's
question from prison (11:2–6) and censuring the crowds for not having
repented (11:16–24), again enters into conflict with the Jewish leaders
(12:1–8, 9–14). Unlike in earlier conflict, the object of controversy is the
Mosaic law itself, namely, violation of the command to rest on the sabbath
(Exod. 20:8–11; Deut. 5:12–15). In the two debates at issue, a noticeable
shift occurs as one moves from the first debate to the second in terms of
how acutely confrontational each is. In the first debate, the Pharisees
confront Jesus, but the charge they make is against the disciples: in plucking, or "reaping," grain to eat, the disciples have "worked," and this the
Pharisees adjudge to be unlawful (Matt. 12:1–2). In the second debate, the
Pharisees again confront Jesus, but this time the accusation they make in
the question they raise has to do with an act Jesus himself is about to
perform: if Jesus heals a man on the sabbath who is not in danger of dying,
he will have broken the command of Moses which enjoins rest (12:10). In
the case of both charges, Jesus rebuts the Pharisees by asserting that
meeting human need in these instances is not unlawful but in line with
God's will that mercy be shown or that good be done (12:3–8, 11–12). In
immediate response to Jesus' setting himself against the law of Moses as

15. Dewey (*Markan Public Debate*, 109–22) has called attention in her study of Mark to this
same kind of movement toward conflict that is more keenly confrontational, the great differ-
ence being that in Mark it occurs solely in the tightly knit section of 2:1—3:6.

they interpret it, the Pharisees take leave of Jesus and consult on how to destroy him (12:14). With this sharp turn of events, Matthew's story has arrived at that juncture where the conflict between Jesus and the Jewish leaders has become "mortal." Then, too, the circumstance that Jesus "withdraws" in the face of danger (12:15) is corroboration of this.

Once reached, this high level of tension between Jesus and the Jewish leaders abates no more, as is clear from the ensuing encounters Jesus has with the Jewish leaders in 11:2—16:20.[16] Beginning with 16:21, the third part of Matthew's story recounts Jesus' journey to Jerusalem and his suffering, death, and resurrection (16:21—28:20). As is apparent, Jesus' conflict with the Jewish leaders is likewise integral to the dominant motif of this part of the story. In keeping with this, the conflict in this part, too, reflects features such as these: (a) Debate remains acutely confrontational, so that it is consistently Jesus who is himself directly challenged over issues that pertain to what he himself teaches or does (19:3; 21:12—22:40). (b) Debate continues to focus on questions of critical importance, like the matter of "authority" or the correct way to read and interpret scripture or the law (19:3–9; 21:12—22:46). (c) Debate also continues to be carried out in an atmosphere of "mortal" struggle (21:45–46). In addition to these, however, another feature also stands out in Jesus' conflict with the Jewish leaders in this part: the two times Jesus visits the temple in Jerusalem, debate with the Jewish leaders occurs unremittingly, as one after another the various groups that make up the Jewish leadership face Jesus so as to call him to account, or to best him in argument, or, at the last, even to be put on the spot by him (21:12–17; 21:23—22:46).

To illustrate this flow of events, at 16:21 Jesus announces to the disciples that it is God's will he go to Jerusalem and suffer many things at the hands of the Jewish leaders and be killed. In the course of the journey to Jerusalem itself, Jesus engages in debate with the Jewish leaders only once, over the question of divorce, and the purpose this debate serves is the instruction of the disciples (19:3–12). Nevertheless, once Jesus enters Jerusalem and the temple, he is continually approached by various groups that, taken together, represent the whole gamut of Jewish officialdom. Previously in Matthew's story, Jesus has had to do only with the scribes and/or Pharisees[17] (once with the Pharisees and Sadducees; 16:1). By contrast, he now confronts such as the following, and all are bent on reprimanding him or besting him in debate: the chief priests and the scribes (21:15), the chief priests and the elders of the people (21:23), the chief priests and the Pharisees (21:45), the disciples of the Pharisees with the Herodians (22:15–16), the Sadducees (22:23), and a lawyer who is spokesman for the Phar-

16. Cf. 12:24–37, 38–45; 15:1–9; 16:1–4.
17. Cf. 8:19; 9:3, 11, [14], 34; 12:2, 14, 24, 38; 15:1, 12; 19:3.

isees (22:34–36). In encounter with these respective groups, the result is always the same: Jesus scores a striking victory, and the Jewish leaders suffer a humiliating defeat. Indeed, at the last Jesus himself seizes the initiative and asks the Pharisees a question about David's son for which they have no answer (22:41–45). In so doing, he shows that he has effectively reduced all his opponents to silence. In consequence of this, the whole series of debates in the temple between Jesus and the Jewish leaders ends on this comment by Matthew: "And no one was able to answer him a word, nor from that day did any one dare to ask him any more questions" (22:46). This comment signals the departure of the Jewish leaders. Unencumbered by their presence, Jesus turns to the disciples and the crowds still remaining in the temple, and in a scathing speech of woes he excoriates the scribes and Pharisees (Matthew 23). With this, no more exchange between Jesus and the Jewish leaders is possible, and the leaders fix their minds on one objective, the death of Jesus (26:3–5).

What is the resolution in Matthew's story of the conflict between Jesus and the Jewish leaders? Excluded is the notion that the story of Matthew holds out hope to the reader for believing the Jewish leaders can be won over to Jesus' message of the Kingdom (4:17). Before the first confrontation has even taken place, the reader has already been exposed to a whole series of negative images of the Jewish leaders: pejorative statements by John the Baptist, by Jesus, and by Matthew as narrator; and deprecatory scenes. As early as 2:4–6, the Jewish leaders, in the persons of the chief priests and scribes, make their debut in the story as ones who do the bidding of king Herod the Great. At 3:7–12, John the Baptist denounces the Pharisees and Sadducees as a "brood of vipers" and pictures them as standing before the Coming One (i.e., Jesus) as before their judge. In the Sermon on the Mount, Jesus predicts persecution for the disciples after the manner of the prophets (5:10–12); depicts the scribes and Pharisees as practicing a righteousness that falls short of what is necessary for gaining entrance into the Kingdom of Heaven (5:20); and assails the "hypocrites" in the synagogues for performing their acts of piety not in worship of God but so as to win public acclaim for themselves (6:1–18). Following the Sermon, Matthew remarks, with a side-glance to the scribes, that they, unlike Jesus, are "without authority" in their teaching (7:29). Later, implored by a centurion to heal his slave, Jesus declares in view of the centurion's faith that whereas the "sons of the Kingdom" will be cast into the darkness outside, Gentiles will sit at table in the future Kingdom with Abraham, Isaac, and Jacob (8:11–12). And in the scene of 8:19–20, a scribe who would arrogate to himself the authority to become a disciple is turned away by Jesus. Virtually on the heels of this series of negative images, Jesus clashes with the Jewish leaders. In his initial controversy with them, he accuses them of thinking "evil" in their hearts (9:4), the trait in Matthew's story which the devil himself personifies (6:13; 13:38–39). In two additional controversies, Jesus furthermore attacks the Jewish leaders as being an "evil and adulterous generation" (12:39; 16:4)—that is to say, a generation that takes after the devil and is faithless to God. Correlatively, it is likewise said three times of the Jewish leaders that they "test," or "tempt," Jesus (16:1; 19:3; 22:34–35), which is Matthew's way of attributing to them affinity with the devil, since he is "the Tempter" (4:1, 3). In short, the impression the reader gets is that there is virtually a complete impasse throughout Matthew's story between Jesus and the Jewish leaders.

The death of Jesus, of course, constitutes the primary resolution of his conflict with the Jewish leaders. From the standpoint of the leaders, Jesus' death signifies the rejection by God himself of the "deception," or "fraud," that Jesus has perpetrated (27:41–43, 63–64). From the standpoint of Jesus, his death serves as the central event of the mission for which God has chosen and sent him (3:16–17; 16:21; 21:37–39). Before he was born, God had announced through the angel that he should be called "Jesus," which means "God saves," or "God is salvation" (1:20–21). Through his death, Jesus accomplishes the promise that inheres in his name, for he effects the salvation of all people from their sins (26:28; cf. 1:21). Because the viewpoints of the Jewish leaders and of Jesus are diametrically opposed as regards the meaning of Jesus' death, it is God who ultimately decides the conflict between Jesus and Israel. By raising Jesus from the dead and investing him with all authority in heaven and on earth (28:6, 9–10, 18), God vindicates Jesus and decides the conflict in his favor. Then, too, God's investiture of Jesus with absolute authority also prefigures the resolution of a further conflict that is still pending—namely, the one that the risen Jesus and his missionary church enter into with all the nations of the world including Israel (28:19–20). The resolution of this latter conflict will come only at the consummation of the age, when Jesus Son of God will return in his role as the Son of man of OT prophecy and carry out the final judgment that signals the coming of God's splendid Kingdom in the sight of all people everywhere.

It was stated that the conflict on which the plot of Matthew's story turns is that between Jesus and Israel, especially the Jewish leaders. Nevertheless, because the disciples, too, "think the things not of God, but of men" (16:21–25), Jesus also enters into conflict with them. Still, the conflict between Jesus and the disciples is of a fundamentally different order from that between Jesus and the Jewish leaders. The disciples, after all, are not enemies of Jesus but his followers. The source of their conflict with Jesus is their periodic failure to comport themselves in a manner that befits sons of God (5:9, 45) and disciples of Jesus (10:1, 24–25) who live in the sphere of God's end-time Rule (13:11, 38). In like fashion as Jesus calls them to come after him, entrusts them with a mission to Israel, and makes of them the recipients of divine revelation (4:17—16:20), so he must also engage them in conflict as they show themselves to be persons of "little faith,"[18] or fail at once to grasp his words (15:15–16; 16:5–12), or do not avail themselves of the authority he has imparted to them (14:16; 15:33; cf. 17:16, 19). Moreover, as Jesus journeys to Jerusalem and embarks on his passion (16:21—28:20), his conflict with the disciples intensifies, for they do not, and in fact will not, perceive the truth that servanthood is the essence of discipleship. The resolution of Jesus' conflict with the disciples is that he does finally lead them to comprehend that servanthood is the essence of discipleship, and thus he readies them for the worldwide ministry to which he commissions them (28:16–20; 24—25). Because the Matthean portrait of the disciples is the subject of chapter 6 in this book, further comment on Jesus' conflict with the disciples can await that discussion.

In summary of the preceding, the "events" of a story have been defined as the incidents that occur throughout the story, and the "plot" of a story has been said to be the peculiar way in which the author has arranged the events. Central to the plot of Matthew is the element of conflict. The principal conflict is that between Jesus and Israel, and the primary resolution of this conflict is to be found in the death of Jesus. On another level, Jesus also struggles with the disciples, and here the conflict is to bring them to understanding, or to enable them to overcome their "little faith," or to invite them to avail themselves of the great authority Jesus has given them, or, above all, to lead them to perceive that the essence of discipleship is servanthood.

Characters

In Chatman's scheme, the story of a narrative encompasses not only "events" and the "plot" to which events give rise but also "characters."[19] Typically, "characters" are the persons who appear in a narrative work such as Matthew's Gospel.[20] Groups of persons, like the "crowds," for example, may function as a single character. "Characterization" has to do with the way in which an author brings characters to life in a narrative.[21] To bring characters to life, an author has at least two methods available to him or her:[22] (a) The author can "show" the reader the characters by letting them speak and act for themselves or by having other characters talk about them or react to them; or (b) the author can arrange to have a narrator simply

18. Cf. 8:26; 14:31; 16:8; also 6:30; 17:20.
19. Chatman, *Story and Discourse*, 107–38.
20. This definition is basically that of Abrams (*Glossary of Literary Terms*, 20). Chatman (*Story and Discourse*, 108) believes it is stating the obvious; he defines a "character" as a "paradigm of traits" (ibid., 126–27).
21. Cf. Rhoads, "Narrative Criticism," 417.
22. Cf. Abrams, *Glossary of Literary Terms*, 21; Rhoads and Michie, *Mark as Story*, 101.

"tell" the reader about them. In Matthew's story both methods are used, but "showing" is preferred to "telling."

One can distinguish among kinds of characters on the basis of the traits they possess. Chatman defines a "trait" as a personal quality of a character that persists over a part or the whole of a story.[23] Thus, Jesus is described in Matthew as being "obedient" toward God (3:15; 4:1–11; 26:36–46) and "compassionate" toward the crowds (9:36; 14:14; 15:32). But although both traits are clearly ascribed to him, the fact that he is compassionate is explicitly stated, whereas the fact that he is obedient must be inferred. But if there are some character traits that the reader must infer, what is to prevent the type of unwarranted "psychologizing" of characters in the gospel-stories which was so prevalent in nineteenth-century lives of Jesus? The answer Chatman would give is that the traits attributed to characters must be reflective of the narrative work in question and the contemporary culture in which it arose.[24] As far as kinds of characters are concerned, E. M. Forster[25] posits the first two of the following three categories and M. H. Abrams[26] makes mention of the third. (a) "Round" characters are those who possess a variety of traits, some of which may even conflict, so that their behavior is not necessarily predictable; round characters are like "real people." In Matthew's story, Jesus and the disciples count as round characters. (b) "Flat" characters are those who possess few traits and are therefore highly predictable in their behavior. In Matthew's story, the Jewish crowds and the Jewish leaders prove to be flat characters. (c) And "stock" characters are those who possess only one trait. In Matthew's story, the minor characters rate as stock characters. A case in point is the "leper" whom Jesus cleanses, for he exhibits the single trait of "faith" (8:1–4).

As was just indicated, the principal characters of Matthew's story are Jesus, the disciples, the Jewish leaders, the crowds, and the minor characters. Since the protagonist, or leading character, is of course Jesus, the task of characterizing these figures or groups best begins with him.

Jesus

The importance Matthew confers on Jesus conspicuously sets him apart from all other characters. Within the world of his story, Matthew establishes God's system of values as normative. In corresponding fashion, he presents Jesus as God's supreme agent who is in complete accord with God's system of values. Other than God himself, therefore, Jesus is the one major character whom Matthew always puts in the right. The attitude Jesus takes toward characters and events determines to what extent the reader,

---

23. Chatman, *Story and Discourse*, 125.
24. Cf. ibid., 119–20, 124–26.
25. *Aspects of the Novel*, 103–18.
26. Cf. *Glossary of Literary Terms*, 185.

too, gives them his or her approval. Hence, more than any other character or group of characters, Jesus influences the plot, or flow, of Matthew's story. For example, even as a babe in the infancy-account it is around him that the story revolves.

Jesus reveals through his words and deeds how he understands himself, his relationship to God, and his place in the history of salvation. He knows God to be his Father (11:25) and himself to be God's unique Son (11:27; 21:37–38a). As God's Son, he is aware of himself as being the decisive figure in the history of salvation (21:33–43); the one who is the "builder" of the church, the eschatological people of God (16:18–19); and who is of ultimate significance for Israel (12:41–42; 15:24; 21:43) and the Gentiles alike (25:31–46).

How do other characters react to Jesus in Matthew's story? To get some indication of this, one might consider how various characters construe his identity. Though not a character, Matthew, as narrator, announces that he holds Jesus to be Christ, Son of David, Son of Abraham (1:1), and also Emmanuel (1:23) and Son of God (2:15). For his part, Joseph, the husband of Mary, does as the angel has commanded and gives "Jesus" his name (1:21, 25). The Magi regard Jesus as the King of the Jews and worship him as such (2:2, 11). Conversely, Herod the Great and, later, Pilate take King of the Jews to mean that Jesus is an insurrectionist (2:6, 13; 27:37). John the Baptist thinks of Jesus as the Coming One, that is, the Messiah, who is to carry out at once the final judgment (3:11–12; 11:2–3). At Jesus' baptism and transfiguration, God affirms him to be his unique Son (3:17; 17:5). Satan, too, knows Jesus to be the Son of God and tempts him as such (4:3, 6). Demons recognize Jesus as the Son of God and hence as their tormentor (8:29). The Jewish leaders look upon Jesus as being a deceiver and one who is in collusion with Satan (9:34; 12:24; 27:63). The Jewish crowds, although they twice name Jesus Son of David only to dismiss the idea in the first instance (12:23) and to explain it away in the second (21:9, 11), settle on taking him to be a prophet: John the Baptist, Elijah, Jeremiah, or some other prophet (16:14; 21:11, 46). Like one segment of the crowds, Herod Antipas, too, thinks of Jesus as being John the Baptist raised from the dead (14:2). By contrast, the people of Nazareth cannot imagine that Jesus is anyone other than the son of the carpenter (13:55). Again, several of the minor characters address Jesus as the Son of David (9:27; 15:22; 20:30–31; 21:15). And in a different vein, the disciples confess Jesus to be the Son of God (14:33; 16:16), as do the Roman soldiers at the foot of the cross as well (27:54).

As a barometer of the way characters react to Jesus, what do such diverse views suggest? They suggest that Jesus is an extraordinary personage toward whom others are unable to remain neutral: he evokes fervid responses that run the gamut from ardent confession to abject repudiation.

They also suggest that whereas transcendent beings, such as God, Satan, and demons, all know Jesus to be the Son of God, human characters diverge widely in their perceptions of him. Jesus' identity, therefore, is not immediately apparent to humans, which means that if the reader is to grasp the meaning of Matthew's story, he or she must be able to understand and evaluate the basis on which any given human character decides who Jesus is and therefore what he is about.

Which traits does Jesus possess in Matthew's story and how do they manifest themselves in his interaction with others? Because of the multiplicity of traits ascribed to Jesus, he is in Forster's terms a "round" character. Here, however, only those traits can be cited which appear to be crucial: (a) In relation to his mission, Jesus is "saving," "authoritative," and utterly "certain" that he is accomplishing God's purposes. The single most fundamental character trait ascribed to Jesus is the power to save, as the angel declares to Joseph: ". . . you shall call his name Jesus, for he will save his people from their sins" (1:21). Correlatively, with incomparable authority Jesus teaches, preaches, heals, calls disciples, and bests his opponents in debate.[27] And in the sure conviction that he is doing God's will, Jesus journeys to Jerusalem to suffer, die, and be raised (16:21). (b) In relation to God, Jesus is "perfect" (5:48), that is to say, he loves God wholly with heart, soul, and mind (22:37).[28] Jesus loves God with his whole heart, for he is blameless in his fealty to God (4:1–11). Jesus loves God with his whole soul, for he is prepared to surrender his life should God so will (26:36–46). And Jesus loves God with his whole mind, for he lays claim for himself neither to the prerogatives of worldly power[29] nor to the security of family, home, and possessions (8:20; 12:50). (c) In relation to himself, Jesus possesses "integrity." The operative principle in this connection is the affirmation that "by their fruits you will know them" (7:16, 20; 12:33). When Jesus is judged by this principle, no discrepancy is found between what he says and what he does. (d) In relation to the disciples, Jesus is "enabling" and "faithful." The disciples have forsaken all to be with Jesus (19:27–29), and Jesus promises them that to the consummation of the age, they can rest assured of his sustaining and abiding presence (18:20; 28:20). (e) In relation to the Jewish crowds and the minor characters, Jesus is "compassionate." The crowds in Jesus' eyes are like shepherdless sheep, harassed and helpless, and in his loving concern for them he would gather them to him (9:36; 14:14; 15:32). A number of the minor characters approach Jesus for healing, and with rare exception he readily and mercifully grants them their requests (20:29–34). (f) In relation to the Jewish leaders, Jesus is "confronta-

27. Cf. 3:16; 7:29; 9:6; 11:27; 21:23–27 to 4:18–22, 23; 9:9, 35; 11:1.
28. Cf. Gerhardsson, "Hermeneutic Program," 129–50.
29. Cf. 20:25, 28; 21:5.

tional." In Jesus' view, the Jewish leaders are evil (12:34), and they take after the one with whom they have affinity, namely, the devil or the Evil One (13:38–39). (g) And in relation to his death, Jesus is "self-giving." The essence of righteousness is love toward God and toward the neighbor. Love toward the neighbor means serving others, not lording it over them. In his death, Jesus serves all others, for he gives his life to redeem the world (20:25–28).

Accordingly, Jesus, the protagonist, stands forth in Matthew's story as the supreme representative of God's system of values who understands himself to be God's unique Son and the decisive figure in the history of salvation; who evokes a multiplicity of perceptions from others concerning his identity as well as fervid responses that range from confession to repudiation; and who is in his interactions with others "saving," "authoritative," "enabling" and "faithful," "compassionate," "confrontational," and utterly "self-giving" even while proving himself to be a person of "integrity" whose "perfect fealty" is to God. How are such other persons as the disciples, the Jewish leaders, the crowds, and the many anonymous individuals to be characterized? To ascertain this, one will want to pay special attention to the attitudes that Matthew as narrator and Jesus take toward these characters and that the characters take toward themselves.

The Disciples

Though a group, the disciples may be treated as a single character. Like Jesus, they are "round," but whereas this is the case with Jesus because of the great number of traits ascribed to him, this is the case with the disciples because they possess not only numerous traits but also traits that conflict. Except for Judas' act of betrayal[30] and the climactic resurrection scene in Galilee (28:16–20), the disciples do not greatly influence the plot, or flow, of Matthew's story. This is not to deny, of course, that there are not also scenes and speeches involving the disciples which have crucial significance for the time that is envisaged following the death and resurrection of Jesus.[31]

Because the disciples possess conflicting traits, the reader is invited, depending on the attitude Matthew as narrator or Jesus takes toward them on any given occasion, to identify with them or to distance himself or herself from them. It is through such granting or withholding of approval on cue, therefore, that the reader becomes schooled in the values that govern the life of discipleship in Matthew's story.

Matthew divides the second part of his story (4:17—16:20) into two major sections (4:17—11:1; 11:2—16:20). Within the first section, he recounts the call of the disciples and their ministry to Israel (4:17—11:1). In so doing, he

---

30. Cf. 26:14–16, 20–25, 47–49.
31. Cf., e.g., 10:16–42; 16:18–20; 17:24—18:35; 23—25; 26:26–29; 28:16–20.

likewise identifies the fundamental marks of discipleship. For example, the disciples, summoned by Jesus to come after him, are "followers" who give him their total allegiance and embrace the task of becoming fishers of men.[32] Having forsaken home, family, and goods, they become "brothers" of Jesus and of one another.[33] As disciples, they are "learners" (23:10)—attending to Jesus' words, including all his discourses, and bearing witness to his deeds. They are likewise "sons of God," for Jesus teaches them to know God as Father and to do his will.[34] And because in summoning them Jesus invites them to live in the sphere of God's end-time Rule,[35] he furthermore graciously enables them to share in his "authority" (10:1) and instructs them in a "ministry" in Israel in which they, too, will preach the nearness of the Kingdom and heal every sickness and every infirmity (10:1, 5, 7). Conversely, through their association with Jesus, they also become "vulnerable" to attack from outside enemies.[36]

Such character traits as are associated with these marks—being "loyal," "loving," "attentive" and "observant," "obedient" and "trusting," "authoritative," "servantlike," and "vulnerable"—all cast the disciples in a positive light. Nevertheless, conflicting traits also surface in 4:17—11:1. The scribe whom Jesus turns away from following him is "presumptuous": he pridefully believes he can surmount the rigors of discipleship on the strength of his own resolve (8:19–20). The man who is already a disciple and whom Jesus commands to follow him at once is "irresolute": he fails to recognize that discipleship brooks no divided loyalty (8:21–22). And the disciples on the stormy sea fall prey to "little faith": not realizing that their faith will sustain them in the peril they face, they give in to cowardice (8:23–27).

In the section 11:2—16:20, the disciples are characterized in the main by contrasting them with Israel: while Israel is darkened and without understanding, the disciples are "enlightened." Thus, what the Father conceals from the wise in Israel, he reveals through Jesus to "infants," that is, to the disciples (11:25–27). Whereas all segments of Israel repudiate Jesus, the disciples become his new family called to do the will of his heavenly Father (Matthew 11—12). To the Jewish crowds "it is not given" to know the mysteries of the Kingdom of Heaven, but to the disciples "it is given" (13:11). If the Jewish public and Herod Antipas mistakenly perceive Jesus to be a prophet of whatever note (16:13–14), the disciples rightly confess him to be the Messiah, the Son of the living God (16:16). And if the leaders of the Jews believe Jesus to be in collusion with Satan (12:24), provoke him to

32. Cf. 4:19–20, 21–22; 8:22; 9:9; also 19:27.
33. Cf. 10:2–4; 12:49; 18:35; 23:8; 25:40; 26:10; also 19:27.
34. Cf. 5:45; 13:38; 6:9; 7:21.
35. Cf. 4:17, 23; 9:35; 10:7; 13:38.
36. Cf. 9:14; 10; 12:1–2; 15:2; 24—25.

controversy,[37] and plot his death (12:14), the disciple Peter stands forth as the "rock" on which Jesus will build his church (16:18).

But again, conflicting with this trait of being enlightened are other, unfavorable traits. On two occasions the disciples, faced with a challenging situation, become "distraught": although Jesus has given them to share in his authority, they do not undertake to feed the crowds but despair of their resources (14:16–17; 15:33). Out on the water, the disciples lose the courage of faith and become exceedingly "fearful": when confronted with what they think is an apparition they cry out in terror (14:26), and Peter, having received permission to walk on the water, is suddenly overcome by doubt (14:30–31). And instead of availing themselves of their gift of understanding, the disciples stand "perplexed" before a parable of Jesus and Peter asks that it be explained to them (15:15–16; cf. also 16:5–12).

In the third part of Matthew's story (16:21—28:20), the characterization of the disciples develops principally through a direct comparison of their values with the values of Jesus. To be sure, the disciples also evince some of the same traits in this part which they did earlier. On a positive note, they continue to be "learners";[38] and they are "obedient" as well, as when they carry out Jesus' instructions for obtaining the donkey and the colt (21:2–7) or in making preparations for the celebration of the Passover (26:18–19). Negatively, the disciples likewise remain susceptible to bouts of "little faith," as when they are unable to heal the demoniac boy (17:14–20); and because they do not realize that faith to perform miracles is also theirs simply for the asking, they are unwarrantedly "surprised" when the fig tree Jesus curses suddenly withers (21:18–22).

But central to this part of Matthew's story is the contrast of Jesus' view of his passion to that of the disciples. Jesus announces to the disciples that it is God's will he should suffer and be killed, but Peter takes issue with this and asserts, to the contrary, that God should forbid such from happening to him (16:21–22). This sharp exchange constitutes a clash of two systems of values: that grounded in "thinking the things of God," and that grounded in "thinking the things of men" (16:23). Since Jesus thinks the things of God, he is "self-giving" and construes his passion in terms of rendering to others self-sacrificial service (20:28). Since Peter and the disciples think the things of men, they are "self-concerned," bent on saving their lives and avoiding suffering and death (16:25).

On the journey to Jerusalem, the disciples reflect in their behavior this latter system of values. To their credit, they do understand Jesus' predictions of his passion (26:2), and it is said, following the second one, that they are "saddened" by it (17:22–23). Nevertheless, they also show that they

37. Cf. Matthew 12; 15:1–20; 16:1–4.
38. Cf. Matthew 18; 24—25.

are "status-conscious" (19:13–15), "enamored of wealth" (19:23–26), "anxious about their future" (19:27), and "desirous of power and position" (20:20–24).

The upshot is that when Jesus actually enters on his passion the disciples, although they want to stand by him (26:41), are totally unable to cope with events and end up by failing him. At first they show that they are "imperceptive" to the true meaning of what is taking place: when the woman pours ointment on Jesus' head, they indignantly label as wasteful what is in reality the preparation of his body for burial (26:8, 12). Later, they show that they are "self-deluded" and Judas shows that he is "deceitful." Thus, Judas, although he has already sold himself to the chief priests (26:14–16), asks Jesus whether he will be the one to betray him in such a manner as to anticipate that Jesus' answer will be no (26:25). And the other disciples boldly express false confidence in their ability to remain loyal to Jesus: they all insist that if need be, they will die with him rather than deny him (26:30–35). In Gethsemane, too, yet another example of this same "self-delusion" occurs: Peter and the two sons of Zebedee, though confident that they possess the fortitude to face death with Jesus, cannot even muster the strength to watch with him but instead fall asleep (26:36–46). Indeed, indicative of how "futile" are the thoughts and actions of the disciples relative to Jesus' passion is the attempt by one of them on Jesus' arrest to defend him by drawing a sword (26:51–53). But be that as it may, the sober result is that following the arrest of Jesus, all the disciples in one way or another desert him: (a) Most become "disloyal" to him by breaking their bond of allegiance and fleeing (26:31, 56). (b) Judas, who has already been "deceitful" (26:25) and "treacherous" (26:47–49), soon becomes "self-destructive" as well (27:3–10). (c) And Peter, by denying Jesus, becomes "apostate" (26:69–75). The disciples had wanted to stand by Jesus in his passion, but they could not; as Jesus had said, ". . . the spirit indeed is willing, but the flesh is weak" (26:41). In relation to the passion of Jesus, the disciples exhibit many traits that spring from a system of values that is not that of Jesus.

The narrator's last word on the eleven disciples, however, is not one of failure. On the mountain in Galilee, the risen Jesus reconciles them to himself. Although they can still fall victim to "little faith" (28:17), they nonetheless undertake the worldwide missionary task to which he commissions them on the "authority" he grants them and "confident" of his sustaining presence to the consummation of the age (28:16–20).

Perhaps the preceding characterization of the disciples can best be summarized by relating it to the following word Jesus speaks to the disciples in his missionary discourse: "It is sufficient for a disciple to be like his teacher . . ." (10:25). By inviting the reader to approve of some of the traits of the disciples and to disapprove of others, Matthew brings the reader to a realization of what this rubric means. Summoned by Jesus, the disciples become "followers" who live in the sphere of God's end-time Rule; "learners" and "sons of God"; "brothers" of Jesus and of one another; ones who share in Jesus' "authority" and "ministry" to Israel and are consequently "vulnerable" to attack; and ones who are, in contrast to Israel, the recipients of divine revelation and hence are "enlightened." On the one hand, therefore, the disciples are "like" their teacher.

But on the other hand the disciples are also "unlike" their teacher. The one or the other of them can be "irresolute," or they can be susceptible to bouts of "little faith," or they can become "distraught" or "fearful." In respect to the passion of Jesus, they even operate with a system of values which is oriented toward "self-concern" and "saving one's life" and is therefore diametrically opposed to that of Jesus. The result is that they show themselves, on the way to Jerusalem, to be "status-conscious," "enamored of wealth," "anxious about their future," and "desirous of power and position"; and, during the passion, to be "imperceptive," "self-deluded," "futile" in thought and action, and "disloyal." For his part, Judas becomes "deceitful," "treacherous," and "self-destructive"; and Peter becomes, through his denial of Jesus, "apostate." In the thought of Jesus, the disciples are "willing" in spirit but "weak" in flesh. Nonetheless, the final word on the disciples is that Jesus reconciles them to himself and, although they will continue to be beset by "little faith," they nevertheless undertake the worldwide mission with which Jesus entrusts them, "empowered" by him and "confident" of his sustaining and abiding presence.

The Jewish Leaders

The Jewish leaders comprise the Pharisees, the Sadducees, the chief priests, the elders, and the scribes.[39] Although the Matthean picture of these several groups does not always square with what is known of them historically, the rhetorical effect of the way they are presented is to make of them a monolithic front opposed to Jesus.[40] Because of this they, too, may be treated as a single character. Except for Jesus himself, it is the Jewish leaders who influence most the development of the plot of Matthew's story. Their characterization is, in fact, shaped through their conflict with Jesus. But if Jesus is a "round" character, the Jewish leaders are a "flat" character, for the many traits ascribed to them are in essence manifestations of a single "root trait," and they give no evidence of undergoing change in the course of the story. The attitudes of Jesus and of Matthew as narrator

39. In 22:16, mention is made of the "Herodians" in conjunction with the disciples of the Pharisees, but how the reader is to think of them is far from certain (cf., e.g., Sandmel, "Herodians," 2:594–95).

40. Cf., e.g., Hummel, *Auseinandersetzung*, 12–22; Walker, *Heilsgeschichte im ersten Evangelium*, 11–33; Van Tilborg, *Jewish Leaders*, 1–6.

toward the Jewish leaders consistently cause the reader to distance himself or herself from them. On this score, it is not different with such figures as Herod the Great, Archelaus, Herod Antipas, Pilate, the Roman soldiers who abuse Jesus, and the guard of soldiers ordered to stand watch over Jesus' tomb.

Presented though these groups are as a monolithic front, some few distinctions among them can nevertheless be observed. For example, the stereotyped phrase by which reference is made to the High Council, or Sanhedrin (26:59), is "the chief priests and the elders (of the people)."[41] Other members of the Sanhedrin are the scribes;[42] and the high priest, who is the presiding officer, is Caiaphas (26:3, 57). Historically, until the fall of Jerusalem in A.D. 70 the Sanhedrin exercised broad powers in Palestine of a religious, political, and judicial nature.[43] Necessarily, however, it was obliged to defer to the authority of the respective procurators Rome appointed to Palestine.[44] In Matthew's story, the Roman procurator of note is of course Pilate, so that it is only with his approval and under the auspices of his office that the sentence of death the Sanhedrin gives Jesus can legally be carried out (26:65–66; 27). In other respects, whereas the chief priests and the elders are associated more particularly with Jerusalem and the temple,[45] the scribes and the Pharisees are closely linked to the synagogue[46] and very frequently mentioned in connection with matters of the law[47] and of the tradition of the elders (cf., e.g., 15:1–2).

How do Jesus and Matthew as narrator view the Jewish leaders, and what do the latter disclose of themselves? Although the Jewish leaders exhibit numerous character traits, close scrutiny shows that the many traits are in reality manifestations of a single "root trait." The first major appearance the Jewish leaders in the persons of the Pharisees and Sadducees make in Matthew's story is in the pericope on the ministry of John the Baptist, and the first words John directs at them are the epithet with which he denounces them, namely, "brood of vipers!" (3:7). The idea this epithet conveys is that the Jewish leaders are "evil." It is because they are evil that they are, as John says, ripe for eschatological judgment (3:7–10) or, as Jesus says, headed for Gehenna (23:33). In yet another word, Jesus captures the meaning of the epithet even more pointedly: "Brood of vipers! How can you speak good, when you are evil?" (12:34).

41. Cf. 21:23; 26:3, 47; 27:1, 3, 12, 20; 28:11-12.

42. Cf. 26:57; also 16:21; 27:41.

43. Cf. Reicke, *New Testament Era*, 142–52.

44. Cf. ibid., 138, 144.

45. Cf., e.g., 16:21; 21:23; 26:3, 47; 27:1, 3,12, 20; 28:11–12; also 2:3–4; 20:18; 21:15; 26:14, 59; 27:6, 41, 62.

46. Cf. 23:6, 34; also 6:2, 5; 10:17; 12:2, 9, 14.

47. Cf., e.g., 23:2; also 5:20; 9:11; 12:2; 19:3; 22:15, 17, 34–36; 23:16–22, 23–24.

The notion that "evilness" is the root trait characterizing the Jewish leaders is in full accord with the tenor of Matthew's story. In the dualism of this world of thought, the one who is "good" is God himself (19:17), and the "Evil One" is the devil (13:38–39). As the supreme agent of God, Jesus raises up in the world "sons of the Kingdom" (13:38), whereas the devil raises up "sons of the Evil One" (13:38–39). As persons who are evil, the Jewish leaders have affinity with the devil (12:34), and their place is within his sphere of influence (cf. 12:26). Because they "think evil in their hearts" (9:3–4), they are the epitome of "an evil and adulterous generation," that is, a generation that does the devil's will and is faithless to God (12:39, 45; 16:4).

If the root trait characterizing the Jewish leaders in Matthew's story is that they are "evil," such evilness manifests itself in a variety of other character traits. These other character traits, in turn, are descriptive of the Jewish leaders both as "leaders" and as a character-group that interacts with such other characters as Jesus, the disciples, and the crowds.

As "leaders," the Jewish leaders evince their evilness most prominently in the fact that they show themselves to be "hypocritical." Hypocrisy in Matthew's story is the opposite of being "perfect." To be perfect is to be wholehearted, or single-hearted, in the devotion with which one serves God (5:48; Deut. 18:13). To be hypocritical is to be "divided" in one's fealty to God. Thus, hypocrisy is a form of inner incongruity, and cases in point are such as the following: paying honor to God with the lips while the heart is far from him (Matt. 15:7–8); making pronouncements about what is right while not practicing them (23:3c); and appearing outwardly to be righteous while being inwardly full of lawlessness (23:28).

The hypocrisy that typifies the Jewish leaders as "leaders" gives rise in its own right to two further character traits: being "lawless," and being "in error" (i.e., being "false teachers"). "Lawlessness" in Matthew's story is not doing the will of God,[48] which is epitomized as loving God with heart, soul, and mind and loving the neighbor as the self (22:37–40). Evidence that the Jewish leaders do not love God is adduced from their practice of piety: as they give alms, pray, and fast, they act not in worship of God but ostentatiously, out of eagerness to be seen by people (6:1–18; 23:5). And their lack of love for the neighbor reveals itself in the fact that they have been faithless in looking after Israel, the trust committed to their care (9:36), and, in line with this, willfully impervious to the truth that what God desires most of them in their treatment of others is "mercy" (9:13; 12:7).

Along with being lawless, being "in error" is likewise an expression of the hypocrisy that betokens the Jewish leaders (22:29). As errorists, the Jewish leaders are "false teachers." Esteeming themselves to be expert in

48. Cf. e.g., 12:50 to 13:41; also 7:21, 23; 23:27–28.

matters of law, scripture, and religion, they are in reality unable to "read" scripture and discern its meaning.[49] For example, although they know from scripture where the Messiah is to be born (2:4–6) and that they are to expect the coming of Elijah (17:10–11), when Elijah does appear in the person of John the Baptist they refuse him repentance (17:12–13; 21:31–32) and presage thereby that they will also cause Jesus Messiah to suffer (17:12). Entrusted though they are with the task of teaching Israel, the teaching they deliver is "without authority" and, like leaven, "corrupting" (7:29; 16:11–12). A case in point is the Pharisaic "tradition of the elders" (15:2). With a view to the manner in which it is applied, Jesus decries it as "teaching as doctrines the precepts of men" (15:9), and charges that because of it the very word of God is rendered void (15:6). Still, with respect to the whole matter of the way in which the Jewish leaders relate to God's word in scripture, the stark irony is that while they are indeed instrumental in bringing this word to fulfillment, they do so as ones who falsify it[50] and who appeal to it with perverse intent;[51] who repudiate the Son whom God has promised in it to Israel (27:43); and who consequently bring divine judgment on both themselves (21:41) and the nation (21:43; 22:7).

As hypocrites who are both lawless and false teachers, the Jewish leaders are furthermore depicted as being "spiritually blind" ("blind guides"; 15:14). In their blindness, they can be observed either to give no leadership to the people (9:36), or ineluctably to lead them into a "pit" (15:13–14). It is in Jesus' speech of woes that illustrations abound as to what it means for the Jewish leaders to be blind guides.[52] Accorded the privilege and responsibility of providing access to God's Kingdom through the right teaching of his will, they in fact so teach as to gainsay Jesus and to bar entry to God's Kingdom (23:13). When they proselytize, they make of the convert twice as much a child of Gehenna as themselves, for they bind the convert to their practice of the law (23:15). In drawing punctilious distinctions between oaths that are binding and oaths that are not, they succeed only in showing themselves to be false teachers (23:16–22). While they go beyond what the law requires and tithe the most insignificant of the garden herbs, they neglect in the process those matters that are the very essence of the law (23:23–24). Although they scrupulously concern themselves with minor things, such as the cleansing of the outside of vessels, they overlook the circumstance that they ought to be concerned with major things, such as the moral integrity of the inner person (23:25–26). Outwardly they appear to people to be righteous, that is, those who know and do God's will, but

49. Cf. 9:13; 12:3–4, 5–7; 19:4–9; 21:16, 42; 22:31–32.
50. Cf. 15:3–13; 22:29.
51. Cf. 22:17–18, 35; 27:6–10.
52. Cf. 23:16, 17, 19, 24, 26. For a thorough treatment of the seven woes of Matthew 23, cf. Garland, *Matthew 23*.

inwardly they are full of pretension and lawlessness, for they are blind to the will of God (23:27–28). And even though they seemingly honor the prophets, the fact of the matter is that they are no different from their fathers, who did not shrink from shedding the blood of the prophets (23:29–31).

Accordingly, the evilness that characterizes the Jewish leaders in Matthew's story in their capacity as "leaders" manifests itself in such other character traits as that they are "hypocritical," and by extension also "lawless" and "in error" ("false teachers"), and "spiritually blind" ("blind guides"). How does this same evilness manifest itself in the interaction of the Jewish leaders with Jesus, the disciples, and the crowds?

Through their interaction with Jesus, the Jewish leaders show that they are "implacably opposed" to him. As they see it, Jesus is not the Son of God who speaks and acts on the authority of God so as to call Israel to repentance and to life in the sphere of God's eschatological Rule. Instead, they understand him to be a "fraud" or false messiah who acts in collusion with Satan and threatens to usurp their authority as Israel's rightful leaders and to subvert the nation through the overthrow of law, tradition, and temple cult.[53] In their dealings with Jesus, their implacable opposition to him comes to the fore in any number of character traits they exhibit, such as the following: (a) They are "malicious," charging Jesus with blasphemy for forgiving sins (9:3–4), demanding of him a sign to prove that he is not in collusion with demonic forces (12:39; 16:1–4), and repeatedly putting him to the test in ways that place them in the service of Satan, the fountainhead of all temptation.[54] (b) They are "legalistic," insisting on formal observance of the law and tradition even though this results in lovelessness in the face of human need or inattentiveness to the deeper intention of the law.[55] (c) They are "slanderous," defaming Jesus by attributing his exorcisms to the power of Beelzebul (9:32–34; 12:22–24). (d) They are "conspiratorial," plotting the death of Jesus (12:14; 26:3–4; 27:1). (e) They are "fearful," determining to arrest Jesus, held by the public to be a prophet, in a manner that will not stir the crowds to action against them (21:46; 26:5). (f) They are "deceptive," scheming to entrap Jesus in argument so that he will be led to discredit himself by advocating either opposition to, or collaboration with, "Caesar" (22:15). (g) They are "cunning," enlisting the services of Judas, the crowds, and Pilate in bringing about the death of Jesus.[56] (h) They are "unjust," striving at Jesus' trial for false testimony by which to condemn him to death (26:59–62). (i) They are "blasphemous," turning the truth of

53. Cf. 27:63–64; 9:34; 12:24; 7:28–29; 9:8; 15:12–14; 22:29; 23; 27:64; 12:2, 10; 9:11, 14; 15:1–2; 21:12–13.
54. Cf. 4:1, 3; 16:1; 19:3; 22:18, 35.
55. Cf. 9:10–13; 12:1–8, 9–13; 15:1–20.
56. Cf. 26:4, 14–16; 27:2, 11–26; 27:20.

Jesus' claim to be the Messiah Son of God into the lie that it is an offense against the majesty of God (26:63–66; 27:41–43). (j) They are "apprehensive of the future," concerned that not even the death of Jesus will succeed in purging Israel of the "fraud" he has perpetrated (27:62–66). (k) And they are "corrupt" and "mendacious," bribing the soldiers following the resurrection to spread the lie that Jesus' disciples came by night and stole his body (28:11–15).

Should the Jewish leaders evince their evilness in interaction with Jesus by showing themselves to be "implacably opposed" to him, the same is true of them as regards the disciples. From the standpoint of the Jewish leaders, the disciples, as followers of Jesus, are likewise enemies of Israel, for they, too, violate law and tradition (9:14; 12:1–2; 15:1–2). Although on the whole the Jewish leaders have relatively little to do with the disciples, their opposition to them finds expression in character traits like these: (a) They are "accusatory," charging the disciples with breaking the sabbath law by working and with transgressing the tradition of the elders by eating with unwashed hands (12:1–2; 15:1–2). (b) They are "guileful" and "callous," purchasing the services of Judas to betray Jesus yet leaving Judas to his own devices in coming to terms with his burden of guilt (26:14–16; 27:3–4). (c) They are "calumnious," concocting the lie following the resurrection that the disciples were guilty of stealing the body of Jesus (27:64; 28:13). (d) And in the future they will be "hostile," inflicting verbal and physical abuse on the disciples and persecuting them even to the point of putting them to death (5:11–12; 10:17, 23; 23:32–36).

Finally, the Jewish leaders also attest to their own evilness in the way in which they relate to the crowds, revealing in this respect that they are "faithless" to their trust. In the leaders' view, the crowds, although they do not believe in Jesus, are nevertheless susceptible to the deceit he practices, for they follow him (e.g., 4:25), are amazed at his teaching and search him out for healing,[57] glorify God over his works,[58] toy with but reject the idea that he might be the Son of David (12:22–23), and hold him to be a prophet (16:14; 21:11, 46). In their own relationship to the crowds, the Jewish leaders reveal that they do not attend to the crowds as a trust committed to their care by exhibiting such character traits as the following: (a) They are culpably "remiss" as leaders, leaving the crowds "harassed and helpless, like sheep without a shepherd" (9:36). (b) They are "pitiless," obligating the crowds to observe a welter of precepts while neglecting to provide them with the necessary guidance (23:4). (c) They are "pretentious," drawing attention to themselves for purposes of gaining public acclaim and personal honor (23:5–12). (d) They are "fearful," unwilling to arrest Jesus in public

57. Cf. 5:1; 7:28–29; 21:23; 26:55; 4:23–25; 8:16; 12:15; 14:14; 15:30; 19:2.
58. Cf. 9:8, 33; 15:31.

lest this arouse the crowds, seeing in him as they do a prophet (21:11, 46; 26:5). (e) And in their guile they are "manipulative," persuading the crowds to demand of Pilate that Jesus be put to death (26:4; 27:20).

To sum up, the Jewish leaders in Matthew's story are fundamentally characterized as being "evil," and this root trait, in turn, manifests itself in other character traits they exhibit both in their capacity as "leaders" and in their interaction with Jesus, the disciples, and the crowds. As "leaders," the Jewish leaders prove themselves to be "hypocritical," which also results in their being "lawless" and "in error" ("false teachers"), and they are "spiritually blind" ("blind guides"). In terms of the way they interact with Jesus, they show themselves to be "implacably opposed" to him, and they demonstrate this in that they are "malicious," "legalistic," "slanderous," "conspiratorial," "fearful," "deceptive," "cunning," "unjust," "blasphemous," "apprehensive of the future," "corrupt," and "mendacious." As far as the disciples are concerned, the Jewish leaders reveal that they are likewise "implacably opposed" to them, and they give evidence of this in that they are "accusatory," "guileful," "callous," "calumnious," and potentially "hostile." And in the manner in which they relate to the crowds, the Jewish leaders show that they are "faithless" to them as their trust, and they attest to this by the fact that they are culpably "remiss," "pitiless," "pretentious," "fearful," and "manipulative."

The Crowds

If the characterization of the Jewish leaders is wholly negative, the same cannot be said of the Jewish crowds. Like the leaders, the crowds, too, may be dealt with as a single, "flat" character. They are not rich in traits, and the ones they possess tend not to change until the end of Matthew's story, when they suddenly appear with Judas to arrest Jesus (26:47, 55). The characterization of the crowds develops along two lines: through their interaction with Jesus, and through their being contrasted to their leaders. Until Jesus' arrest, the reader's attitude toward the crowds is largely one of approval and sympathy.

Through their interaction with Jesus, the crowds show that they are "well disposed" toward him. Jesus himself looks on the crowds with compassion, for they are "harassed" and "helpless," being "leaderless" (9:36). They for their part follow him[59] and throng about him.[60] He teaches them,[61] and they are "amazed"[62] at his teaching. He heals their sick,[63] and they witness his miracles and become "frightened" (9:8) or "astonished" (9:33; 15:31). In

59. Cf. 4:25; 8:1; 12:15; 14:13; 19:2; 20:29; 21:9.
60. Cf. 8:18; 12:46; 13:2; 17:14.
61. Cf. 11:7; 12:46; 15:10; 23:1.
62. Cf. 7:28; 22:33.
63. Cf. 4:23–24; 9:35; 11:5; 14:14; 15:30; 19:2.

two instances crowds become "hungry" while with Jesus, and he feeds them (14:15–21; 15:32–38). On occasion, however, a crowd can also become "obstructionist," as when the people ridicule the notion that the daughter of the ruler is not dead but sleeping (9:23–25a) or attempt to hush the two blind men who appeal to Jesus for healing (20:31).

But despite their amicability, the crowds are "without faith" in Jesus. True, they once raise the question of whether he is the Son of David (12:23), and they also hail him as such on his entry into Jerusalem (21:9). But the grammatical form in which they put their question anticipates a negative answer (12:23), and when asked who this Jesus is whom they have hailed as the Son of David, they reply that he is the prophet from Nazareth (21:11). Indeed, "prophet" is exactly what the crowds take Jesus to be,[64] and this is in Matthew's story a misguided conception, for Jesus is in reality the Messiah Son of God (3:17; 16:16). In more sinister fashion, it is also the crowds whom Jesus decries as "this generation" that repudiates both himself and John (11:7, 16–19), and it is the crowds who stand before his parables as those who are "blind, deaf, and without understanding" (13:1–2, 10–13).

But although the crowds are without faith in Jesus and see in him only a prophet, in being generally well disposed toward him they contrast sharply to their leaders, and this contrast is highlighted in several instances. The rhetorical effect of highlighting this contrast is to show the reader that if the crowds are not disciples of Jesus, neither are they his inveterate enemies. Thus, in the case of the paralytic, some of the scribes regard it as blasphemy that Jesus forgives sins, but the crowds witness the absolution and healing of the man and are awe-struck by this and glorify God (9:2–8). Following an exorcism by Jesus, the crowds marvel and say, "Never was anything like this seen in Israel," but the Pharisees retort, "He casts out demons by the prince of demons" (9:32–34). In response to another exorcism of Jesus, the crowds at least raise the question whether he might be the Son of David, but the Pharisees flatly assert once again that it is only with Satan's help that he casts out demons (12:22–24). In debate over the resurrection, at the same time Jesus reduces the Sadducees to silence the crowds react to his teaching with astonishment (22:23–33, 34). And in two further instances, Jesus either delivers teaching to the crowds which the Pharisees find offensive (15:10–12) or utters woes in the presence of the crowds and his disciples against the scribes and Pharisees (Matthew 23).

On balance, then, the Jewish crowds are "well disposed" toward Jesus but "without faith" in him. In being without faith in Jesus, they contrast to the disciples. And in being well disposed toward Jesus, they contrast to their leaders.

64. Cf. 16:13–14; 21:11, 46.

The Minor Characters

The minor characters are the persons who dot the pages of Matthew's story and, except for one like "Joseph" (1:18—2:23), appear briefly in a scene and then vanish. Most of these persons do not so much as bear a name, passing before the reader merely as the "Magi" (2:1–12), "a leper" (8:2), "a centurion" (8:5), "the mother-in-law [of Peter]" (8:14), "two demoniacs" (8:28), the men who bring Jesus a paralytic (9:2), "a ruler" (9:18), "a woman" (9:20), "two blind men" (9:27), the townspeople of Nazareth (13:54), "the men of that place [Gennesaret]" (14:35), "a Canaanite woman" (15:22), "a man" (17:14), "a child" (18:2), "children" (19:13), "the young man" (19:22), "the mother of the sons of Zebedee" (20:20; 27:56), "two blind men" (20:30), "the children" in the temple (21:15), "a woman" (26:7), "[Pilate's] wife" (27:19), "the centurion" (27:54), "those who were with him [the centurion]" (27:54), and "many women" (27:55). Others are indeed introduced by name, but they, too, make sudden appearances only to vanish again just as quickly: "Joseph" (1:18—2:23), "Mary" (1:18; 13:55), "Barabbas" (27:15–23), "Simon [of Cyrene]" (27:32), "Mary Magdalene" (27:56, 61; 28:1), "Mary the mother of James and Joseph" (27:56, 61; 28:1), and "Joseph [of Arimathea]" (27:57). Almost without exception, these persons are "stock" characters—that is, they possess one trait only. But in contradistinction to the disciples, the Jewish leaders, and the crowds, they cannot be treated as though they were all alike. The respective trait of any one or group of these persons is what determines to what extent the reader approves or disapproves of that person or group.

Those just listed are not the only persons to appear in Matthew's story. Others do so as well, but the purpose they serve is such that they can scarcely be said to exhibit traits.[65] Some, for instance, simply facilitate the action of a scene. Examples are "the herdsmen" (8:33), the "disciples of John" (11:2), "such a one" (26:18), "a servant girl" (26:69), "another [servant girl]" (26:71), and "the bystanders" (26:73). Others function as mere catalysts, creating opportunities for yet other characters to exhibit the traits they possess. Cases in point are the "dumb demoniac" in 9:32–34 or the "man with a withered hand" in 12:9–15. The healing of the demoniac provides the crowds and the Jewish leaders with an opportunity to show, respectively, that they are well disposed or intensely hostile toward Jesus. And the restoration of the man's hand provides Jesus with an opportunity to show that he "does good" on the sabbath, whereas this prompts the Jewish leaders to show that they do evil, even plotting death. Additional persons who seem to function in Matthew's story along these lines are the "paralytic" (9:2), the "toll-collectors and sinners" (9:10), "the girl" (9:25), "a

65. Such "persons" as these Chatman (*Story and Discourse*, 138–42) does not regard as bona fide "characters" but consigns to the "setting" of the narrative.

blind and dumb demoniac" (12:22), "the daughter [of the Canaanite woman]" (15:22, 28), "[Jesus'] mother and his brothers" (12:46), "the son [of a man]" (17:15, 17), and "the collectors of the half-shekel tax" (17:24). Finally, there are also those persons in Matthew's story who seem to meld completely with the setting of which they are a part. Examples of such are the brothers of Jesus ("James," "Joseph," "Simon," and "Judas"; 13:55), "[Jesus'] sisters" (13:56), and "Simon the leper" (26:6).

But these aside, the principal way the reader discovers "what kinds of persons" the minor characters are is by observing them as they serve as "foils"[66] for other characters in the story, that is, as contrasts to other characters. The "Magi" (2:1) and the "centurion" (8:5) serve as foils for Israel: the faith of these Gentiles contrasts with the unbelief of Israel (2:1–12; 8:5–13). The "two blind men" (9:27), the "Canaanite woman" (15:22), the other "two blind men" (20:30), and the "children" in the temple (21:15) also serve as foils for Israel: these no-accounts see and confess what Israel cannot, namely, that Jesus is its Davidic Messiah. Pilate's "wife" (27:19) serves as a foil for Pilate himself: her warning to Pilate not to have anything to do with that innocent man (Jesus) contrasts to Pilate's decision to accede to the Jewish demand that Jesus be put to death. "Barabbas" (27:15–26) serves as a foil for Jesus: a notorious prisoner is set free, whereas an innocent man is delivered up to be crucified.

In most cases, however, it is for the disciples that the minor characters serve as foils. The faith of many of them—such as the "leper" (8:2), the men who bring the paralytic to Jesus (9:2), the "ruler" (9:18), the "woman" with a hemorrhage (9:20), the "men of Gennesaret" (14:35), and the "man" whose son is an epileptic (17:14), contrasts to the little faith the disciples display at points throughout Matthew's story (8:26; 14:31; 17:20). The humble station of the "child" in the one instance (18:2) and of the "children" in the other (19:13) contrasts to the disciples' concern for greatness and privilege (18:1; 19:3). The choice of the "young man" (19:22) to prefer wealth over discipleship contrasts to Jesus' word for the disciples to choose the attainment of the Kingdom over riches (19:23–30). And in the passion-narrative, several minor characters serve as foils for the disciples in the sense that they minister to Jesus in ways the disciples could have been expected to do but do not:[67] a "woman" (26:7) anoints Jesus, preparing him for burial; "Simon of Cyrene" (27:32) carries Jesus' cross; the "Roman soldiers" (27:54) make public confession of Jesus; "Joseph of Arimathea" (27:57–60) requests the body of Jesus and gives it proper burial; the "many women" (27:55–56) who had followed Jesus from Galilee do not desert him at the cross but stand at a

66. Rhoads ("Narrative Criticism," 419) notes that in Mark the minor characters serve as "foils," and this observation is valid also with respect to Matthew.

67. Rhoads and Michie (*Mark as Story*, 132–33) make this point relative to Mark, and it proves to be true of Matthew as well.

distance watching; and after the sabbath, the "two Marys" (28:1) go as mourners to see Jesus' sepulchre. Perhaps "Joseph" (1:18—2:23) ought also to be seen as rendering service to Jesus in the infancy-narratives in like fashion as these minor characters do in the passion-narrative: through his acts of obedience to the commands of the angel during a similarly critical period, Joseph takes the pregnant Mary to be his wife, gives Jesus his name, saves him from death by fleeing to Egypt, and returns him to Israel but settles him in Nazareth outside the jurisdiction of Archelaus. With few exceptions, therefore, the minor characters are exemplary figures in Matthew's story and exhibit traits that reflect the system of values which both Jesus and Matthew as narrator advocate.

This completes our survey of the characters of Matthew's narrative. Jesus is the protagonist; the other major characters are the disciples, the Jewish leaders (and other authorities), and the Jewish crowds. Rounding out the list are numerous minor characters. The task now is to look briefly at some of the important settings in Matthew's narrative.

Settings

The story of a narrative, observes Chatman, is made up not only of "characters" and "events" but also of "settings."[68] A "setting" is the place or time or social circumstances in which a character acts.[69] The purpose settings may serve varies considerably. In some instances, a setting simply makes action possible. In the case of the pericope on the question about fasting, for example, the setting is as minimal as the temporal adverb "then" (9:14). By contrast, in other instances the setting may be highly charged with meaning. For example, when Matthew reports as Jesus hangs upon the cross, "Now from the sixth hour there was darkness over all the land until the ninth hour" (27:45), he conveys a strong sense of impending disaster.

Within the context of Matthew's story, particular times and places are of no little significance. Thus, the conception, birth, and naming of Jesus mark the end of the time of prophecy and the beginning of the "time of fulfillment" (1:22–23). Indeed, the so-called "formula quotations,"[70] which are peculiar to Matthew, highlight some ten occurrences associated with the life of Jesus as being special examples of the fulfillment of prophecy. And other key temporal references are, respectively, Jesus' announcements that God's Rule "has drawn near" (4:17) or "has come upon you" (12:28); his statements concerning the "hour" of his betrayal (26:45) or the "hour" or

68. Chatman, *Story and Discourse*, 138–45.
69. Abrams, *Glossary of Literary Terms*, 175.
70. Cf. 1:22–23; [2:5–6]; 2:15, 17–18, 23: 4:14–16; 8:17; 12:17–21; [13:14–15]; 13:35; 21:4–5; [26:56]; 27:9–10.

"day" that connotes the end or the final judgment;[71] and his frequent use of such idioms as "those [i.e., final] days"[72] or "the consummation of the age."[73]

As for places, "Bethlehem" is the lowly town in which prophecy dictates that the royal Messiah shall be born (2:4–6). "Egypt" is the land of refuge: just as Israel, who was God's son, found refuge in the person of Jacob in Egypt and was later called out, so Jesus Son of God finds refuge in Egypt and is later called out (2:13–15).[74] "Nazareth" is the village from which Jesus comes by virtue of his having grown up there,[75] and "Capernaum," which is "his own city" (9:1) and where he may have a "house,"[76] is where he resides during his ministry (4:13); nevertheless both, along with "Chorazin" and "Bethsaida," become emblematic of Israel's repudiation of Jesus as its Messiah (11:20–24; 13:53–58). "Galilee" is the region in which Jesus discharges his ministry to Israel of teaching, preaching, and healing (4:23) and where he returns following his resurrection to commission his disciples to their worldwide missionary task (28:16–20; cf. 4:15).[77] Gentile cities or lands, such as the "country of the Gadarenes" (8:28) or "Tyre and Sidon" (15:21), lie beyond the purview of Jesus' own mission to the lost sheep of the house of Israel (15:24); Jesus' visit to them, however, portends the Gentile mission to come. And "Jerusalem," the "holy city"[78] and the "city of the great King" (5:35), is the city of repudiation[79] and of death[80] for Jesus, the place where his enemies are at home.[81]

Other locations, too, are of significance in Matthew. The "desert" is at once a place of end-time expectation, where John the Baptist prepares Israel for the coming of its Messiah (3:1–12), and a place of testing, where Satan would have Jesus break faith with God (4:1–4). It is also the place where Jesus would have the disciples realize that they already possess the requisite authority to feed the hungry crowds (14:16; 15:33). The "synagogue" is a local center of worship, teaching, and court proceedings under the authority of such Jewish leaders as the scribes and Pharisees.[82] Here Jesus

71. Cf. 24:36, 42, 44, 50; 25:13; 7:22; 10:15; 11:22, 24; 12:36.
72. Cf. 24:19, 21, 29, 38; also 3:1.
73. Cf. 13:39, 40, 49; 24:3; 28:20.
74. Cf. Bourke, "Literary Genus," 160–75; for a different view, cf. Brown, *Birth of the Messiah*, 213–19.
75. Cf. 2:23; 21:11; 26:71.
76. Cf. [8:14]; 9:1, 10, 28; 13:1, 36; 17:25.
77. As an example of how important the element of "setting" can be perceived to be in a narrative such as Matthew, Farmer (*Jesus and the Gospel*, 138–40) regards the passage 4:12–16, in which "Galilee" and other locations or areas figure prominently, as providing the "conceptual outline" for the whole of Jesus' ministry (4:12—20:16).
78. Cf. 4:5; 27:53.
79. Cf. 2:3; 23:37.
80. Cf. 16:21; 20:17–19.
81. Cf. 15:1; 16:21; 20:17–19.
82. Cf. 4:23; 9:35; 10:17; 12:9; 13:54; 23:1–7; 5:20; 6:2, 5.

confronts Israel with his message;[83] but here his opponents also try to ensnare him in his speech so as to bring accusation against him (12:9–10), and his disciples, as missionaries, are in danger of being subjected to severe persecution.[84] The "sea" is a place of great peril and destruction: in it humans and animals perish,[85] and although Jesus has mastery over it, it evokes feelings of cowardice, fear, and little faith in the disciples.[86] The "temple" is the house of God (21:13) which is under the control of the Jewish leaders, especially the chief priests,[87] and which is not serving its intended purpose as a place of worship (21:13). For the brief time Jesus teaches and heals there, he imparts God's benefactions to the people;[88] but once he leaves it, it is deserted (23:38) and ripe for destruction (24:1–2). In point of fact, Jesus himself supplants the temple as the "place" where God mediates salvation to people.[89] And the "mountain" is a site of end-time revelation:[90] here God declares Jesus to be his unique Son (9:7), and here Jesus Son of God, unlike Israel son of God of old, resists temptation and keeps faith with God (4:8–10). Here Jesus also performs such end-time acts as teaching the will of God (5:1–2); healing the people (15:29–31); foretelling the events that will lead up to the close of the age (24:3); disclosing through the act of prayer the unique relationship he has to God (14:23); and, following his resurrection, commissioning his disciples to their end-time ministry (28:16).

Settings, then, are temporal, geographical, or social in nature and serve to "set the character off."[91] Together with events and characters, settings make up the story of a narrative. Still, the story is only the one part of a narrative; the discourse is the other part, and it is this part that must now be discussed.

THE DISCOURSE OF THE NARRATIVE

If the "story" of a narrative such as Matthew is "what" is told (the life of Jesus from conception and birth to death and resurrection), the "discourse" is, in Chatman's terminology,[92] "how" this story is told, that is, the means the author uses in order to put the story across. The discourse of the Matthean narrative encompasses such matters as the "implied author" and the "narrator," the "point of view" espoused by the narrator or any char-

83. Cf. 4:23; 9:35; 13:54.
84. Cf. 10:17; 23:34.
85. Cf. 8:32; 18:6; also 21:21.
86. Cf. 8:23–27; 14:24–33.
87. Cf. 21:15, 23, 45; 27:3–10.
88. Cf. 21:14–16; 26:55.
89. Cf. 1:21; 26:28; 27:51.
90. On the motif of the mountain, cf. Donaldson, "Jesus on the Mountain."
91. Chatman, *Story and Discourse*, 138.
92. Cf. ibid., 19–22.

acter, and the "implied reader."[93] In addition, the kind and style of the language used to tell the story and the rhetorical techniques employed are also important elements of the discourse of Matthew. The latter will be dealt with in subsequent chapters to the extent that they present themselves in the course of the investigation of the gospel-story of Matthew itself. In what follows, it is the former that will receive attention.

The Implied Author and the Narrator

Literary theorists distinguish in analyzing a narrative among the "real author," the "implied author," and the "narrator."[94] The "real author" of Matthew is the historical person who created this narrative, the one scholars call the first evangelist. In the act of creating this narrative, the first evangelist also created a literary version of himself, a second self, which the reader comes to know through the process of reading the story of the narrative. This second self is the "implied author." The "narrator," in turn, is the voice, or invisible speaker, the reader hears as he or she moves through the story, the one who tells the reader the story. It is the narrator, for example, who intones the first words, "The book of the origin of Jesus Christ, Son of David, Son of Abraham" (1:1).

One of the reasons literary theorists distinguish between the "implied author" who stands behind the whole of a narrative work and the "narrator" who tells the story is that a narrator can prove himself or herself to be "unreliable." The "unreliable narrator" is one found to be at odds with the implied author.[95] This occurs when the narrator does not espouse the same system of ideas, values, or beliefs which sustains and informs the story. In the case of Matthew, however, the reader has to do only with a "reliable narrator," one who is in full accord with the implied author. For this reason, the need to distinguish rigorously between the narrator and the implied author is not so pressing. In this study, at any rate, both narrator and implied author will be designated as "Matthew"; in this way, a familiar nomenclature can be retained. By the same token, where it is desirable for the sake of the discussion to differentiate between Matthew as narrator and Matthew as implied author, this will be done. Along these same lines, the term "(first) evangelist" will also be reserved throughout the rest of this study to denote the real author of the First Gospel.

Despite the recognition that the narrator throughout Matthew's Gospel is but the reliable voice of the implied author, it is nonetheless imperative, if one is to understand the kind of narrator Matthew is, to take notice of the characteristics he exhibits. The one characteristic he exhibits has already

93. On these matters, cf. ibid., chaps. 4—5.
94. Cf. Booth, *Rhetoric of Fiction*, 70–76; Chatman, *Story and Discourse*, 147–51; also Rhoads, "Narrative Criticism," 420–22.
95. Cf. Chatman, *Story and Discourse*, 226–28, 233–37.

been mentioned, namely, that he is "reliable." Other characteristics are that he is "omnipresent" and "omniscient" as far as the world of his story is concerned; speaks in the "third person"; directs "comments" to the reader which provide inside information most often not available to the characters in the story; and indicates that the vantage point from which he involves himself in the story lies, temporally, between the resurrection and the Parousia.[96]

Thus, Matthew as narrator is "omnipresent" in relation to the world of his story, for he is able to be in any place at any time in order to inform the reader what is taking place. Not a character himself, he is the invisible speaker who is both above and beyond the story, since he is the one who tells it, and also within the story, since there is no scene from which he is absent. Whether with Jesus in the desert (4:1) or with John in prison (11:2) or with the disciples in the boat (4:1) or with Peter weeping bitterly by himself (26:75), Matthew is ever-present.

Matthew as narrator is likewise "omniscient," for there is nothing in the world of this story of which he does not have full knowledge. For example, he knows the thoughts the scribes express "to themselves" (9:3) or the words of the prayer Jesus utters in private in Gethsemane (26:39). Similarly, he is aware of the feelings any given character is experiencing, as when Herod the Great becomes frightened (2:3), or Jesus has compassion on the crowds (9:36), or the Jewish leaders or the disciples become indignant (21:15; 26:8). And he is also aware of what characters in his story sense— that is, what they may hear (2:22; 4:12) or see (3:16; 9:11) on this or that occasion.

As narrator, Matthew's mode of narration is that of the "third person" as opposed to the "first person."[97] In first-person narration, the narrator speaks as "I" and is himself or herself one of the characters in the story. In third-person narration, the narrator assumes the detached posture of an invisible "observer" of the action in the story and refers to the characters either by "name" or as "he," "she," or "they." The pericope on the baptism reflects well Matthew's use of third-person narration: "Then *Jesus* came from Galilee to the Jordan to *John*, to be baptized by *him*. But *he* would have prevented *him*, saying ..." (3:13–14).

In the course of telling his story, Matthew as narrator directs comments to the reader which provide him or her with inside information most often not available to the characters in the story. By means of such commentary, Matthew explains certain matters or, more significantly, interprets characters and events and renders judgment on them. By making the reader the

96. The groundbreaking article by Petersen on " 'Point of View' in Mark's Narrative" is also instructive for gaining insight into the narrator the reader encounters in Matthew.
97. Cf. Abrams, *Glossary of Literary Terms*, 143.

recipient of such inside information, Matthew places him or her in the privileged position of being better informed than the characters in the story. For instance, through such narrative comments as Matt. 1:1 and 2:15 (cf. 1:23), the reader knows far in advance of any human character in the story that Jesus is Israel's Davidic Messiah, God's Son. What is equally important, by feeding the reader inside information Matthew as narrator is also urging the reader to appropriate his judgments concerning characters and events. Striking examples of narrative commentary in Matthew's story are the genealogy (1:1–17); the formula-quotations;[98] the explanation of terms (1:23; 27:33) or translation of foreign words (27:46); remarks that are addressed directly to the reader (24:15; 27:8; 28:15); and the many statements that apprise the reader of the thoughts (21:25–27), feelings (2:10, 22), perceptions (21:45; 22:18), and intentions (21:46) of characters.

The final characteristic of Matthew as narrator to be mentioned at this juncture is, in reality, a characteristic of Matthew as implied author. In three passages the reader is addressed by a voice, but the nature of the comment in each case is such that it bursts the bounds of the story-world of Matthew. Clearly, in these passages the implied author disrupts the story in order to speak directly to the reader. In disrupting the story in this fashion, the implied author gives indication of the place in time he would assign himself. The first two passages are the comments found in 27:8 and 28:15: "Therefore that field [purchased with the money paid Judas] has been called the Field of Blood to this day"; and "... this story [that the disciples stole the body of Jesus] has been spread among the Jews to this day." And the third passage is the "aside" found in 24:15 in the eschatological discourse: "let the reader understand." On the basis of these three passages, it is obvious that the place Matthew, the implied author, assigns himself lies at some remove from the event of the resurrection (28:1–15) and is situated in the time of the messianic woes and of the church's mission to the nations which will conclude only with the consummation of the age (24:8, 14–15). It is from this particular place that Matthew as implied author oversees the whole of the story of the life and ministry of Jesus and also involves himself, through his voice as narrator, in every aspect of this story.

Point of View

Another facet of the "discourse" of Matthew, that is, the way in which the first evangelist has chosen to put his story across, is that of "point of view."[99] Major aspects of point of view are the "evaluative" (often called the ideological), the "phraseological," the "spatial and temporal," and the "psychological."[100]

98. Cf. above, n. 70.

99. Chatman, *Story and Discourse*, 151–58. Also Rhoads, "Narrative Criticism," 421–22.

100. Cf. Uspensky (*Poetics of Composition*) and Lanser (*Narrative Act*, 184–222). As far as Matthew's Gospel itself is concerned, an instructive study of "point of view" which draws on the work of Uspensky is that of Anderson ("Point of View in Matthew").

"Evaluative point of view" has to do with some conception of reality. It denotes a particular way of looking at things which also involves rendering some judgment on them in terms of the degree to which they are "good" or "bad," "right" or "wrong." To the extent divulged by a story, the narrator and the various characters all have their respective evaluative points of view. Typically, these evaluative points of view give rise to conflict.

Characteristic of a gospel-story such as that of Matthew is that the many conflicting evaluative points of view expressed by the various characters can fundamentally be reduced to two, the "true" and the "untrue."[101] The measuring rod for distinguishing truth from untruth is, as Matt. 16:23 indicates, "thinking the things of God" (as opposed to "thinking the things of men"). Within the world of the Matthean story, therefore, it is God's evaluative point of view which Matthew the implied author has made normative. What this means, in turn, is that the evaluative point of view which Matthew ascribes to himself as narrator or to any given character is to be judged true or false on the basis of whether it aligns itself with, or contravenes, the evaluative point of view of God. Because Matthew as implied author reliably places his voice as narrator in the service of the evaluative point of view which he has made normative—that is, God's evaluative point of view, and because Jesus is the supreme agent of God, it is plain that the reader is to regard the evaluative points of view of both Matthew as narrator and Jesus as being in complete alignment with the evaluative point of view of God. Accordingly, there is only one true way in which to view things in Matthew—namely, the way established by God, and this is the way in which both Matthew as narrator and Jesus also view things.

By contrast, as one moves, respectively, from the disciples to the Jewish crowds and to the Jewish leaders, the degree to which each group deviates from "thinking the things of God" and "thinks the things of men" becomes ever greater. Whereas the disciples are blessed with the capacity to think the things of God, there are glaring instances where they think the things of men. The Jewish crowds, though destined to think the things of men,[102] nevertheless on occasion appear to think the things of God (cf. 9:33; 15:31). The Jewish leaders, however, seem never, except unwittingly, to think the things of God and always to think the things of men.

"Phraseological point of view" concerns the "speech," or "diction," that typifies and distinguishes Matthew as narrator or any given character. The "speech" of Matthew or a character, in turn, is a good indicator of the evaluative point of view he or a character espouses. For example, the formula-quotations are all spoken by Matthew himself, and a key compo-

101. Cf. Lotman, "Point of View in a Text," 343.
102. Cf. 13:2, 10–13; 27:20, 25.

nent in each is the citation of OT scripture. Because OT scripture counts as the word of God,[103] the result of the fact that the formula-quotations make up an important part of Matthew's speech is that this makes of him as narrator an exponent of God's evaluative point of view in assessing the salvation-historical significance of various events in the life of Jesus.[104] Again, also typical of Jesus' speech throughout Matthew's story is the citation of OT scripture. What this indicates, as passages such as 15:4 and 22:31–32 demonstrate, is that Jesus, too, is a thoroughly reliable exponent of God's evaluative point of view. And to take a third example, the words "if you are the Son of God" are first associated in Matthew's story with Satan, who utters them in order to test Jesus (4:3, 6). Later, therefore, when Jesus hangs upon the cross and the passersby shout at him, "... if you are the Son of God, come down from the cross" (27:40), the reader recognizes from the phraseology of the passersby that they, like Satan previously, are testing Jesus and consequently have aligned themselves with him who is the fountainhead of all evil.

"Spatial and temporal point of view" pertains to the position in time and space from which characters or events are observed or described. As I have stated, the place Matthew as implied author assigns himself relative to the world of his story lies beyond the event of the resurrection but short of the Parousia (24:15; 27:8; 28:15). From this vantage point, Matthew oversees all time and space in his story-world and, through his voice as narrator, involves himself in them. Spatially, Matthew as narrator is omnipresent in relation to the story he tells, for he moves about freely to report the action, taking up positions outside or within any particular scene. Concomitantly, once Jesus makes his appearance in the story as an adult, Matthew as narrator "accompanies" him, with few exceptions,[105] from baptism to death (3:13—27:56). Prior to the baptism and following the death of Jesus, Matthew tracks a series of less prominent characters,[106] but always in the interest of conveying information to the reader about Jesus. Still, when Matthew as narrator closes his story with the Great Commission, he is again present with Jesus (28:16–20; cf. 28:9–10).

With respect to temporal point of view, Matthew as narrator first surveys in the genealogy the history of Israel (1:1–17) and then tells the story of the life of Jesus from conception and birth to death and resurrection (1:18—28:20). Because his is the voice of one who looks back on the life of Jesus, he recounts events in past time (cf., e.g., 2:1: "Now after Jesus *had been born* in Bethlehem of Judea in the days of Herod the king, behold, wise men from the East *came* to Jerusalem ..."). But this notwithstanding, in some eighty

103. Cf. 1:22; 2:15; 15:4; 22:31.
104. Cf. above, n. 70.
105. Cf. 14:3–12; 27:58, 69–75.
106. Cf. 1:18—3:12; 27:57—28:8, 28:11–15.

instances Matthew as narrator shifts from past time and employs the historic present[107] (cf., e.g., 3:1: "Then Jesus *comes* from Galilee to the Jordan to John …"). Matthew's use of the historic present has the effect of eliminating any distance in time between himself as narrator and Jesus or other characters, so that he reports the action as Jesus or the characters experience it. Then, too, more often than not Matthew thus makes himself contemporary with the characters in his story in order to focus on the words Jesus is speaking on any occasion. Through such focus Matthew enables Jesus to address directly not only other characters in the story, but also the reader. Temporally, therefore, Matthew as narrator fundamentally relates the story of Jesus' life in past time but frequently makes himself contemporary with Jesus or other characters through his use of the historic present for the dual purpose of making the action more vivid and especially of having Jesus speak directly not only to other characters but also to the reader.

"Psychological point of view" refers to knowledge on the part of Matthew as narrator or of a character about what some (other) character thinks, intends, feels, sees, or otherwise experiences. Omniscience of this kind is predicated both to Matthew and to Jesus, who provide the reader as a matter of course with inside views into the inner workings of others.[108] Thus, Matthew as narrator knows that Jesus "marvels" at the centurion's faith (8:10), or that the Pharisees approach Jesus with the "intent of testing him" (19:3), or that the disciples become "very sorrowful" when Jesus predicts his suffering and death a second time (17:23). Similarly, Jesus, too, knows or sees that the Pharisees have "taken counsel against him, how to destroy him" (12:14), or that the disciples have become "indignant" at the woman who has poured expensive ointment on his head (26:8, 10), or that the men who have brought him a paralytic have "faith" that he can heal him (9:2). The reason the reader is provided with inside views of characters is to shape his or her attitude toward them. Through the inside views that Matthew as narrator gives of Jesus, he portrays him sympathetically,[109] and through the inside views he and Jesus give of other characters, they portray the characters either sympathetically or unsympathetically. The upshot is that whereas the reader is led never to disapprove of Jesus, he or she is led in some scenes to view characters with approval but in others to view them with disapproval.

In summary, then, the major aspects of point of view are the evaluative, the phraseological, the spatial and temporal, and the psychological. "Thinking the things of God" is the evaluative point of view that Matthew,

---

107. On the manner in which Matthew employs the historic present, cf. Anderson, "Point of View in Matthew," 11–14; also Hawkins, *Horae Synopticae*, 148–59.

108. Cf. Anderson, "Point of View in Matthew," 17–22.

109. Cf. esp. 9:36; 14:14; 20:34; 26:37.

the implied author, has established as normative for his story, and the ones who are constantly in alignment with this point of view are himself as narrator and Jesus. Phraseologically, therefore, what Matthew as narrator says is "reliable," and what Jesus says is "truth," not "untruth." Spatially and temporally, Matthew as narrator, by "accompanying" Jesus through his ministry and by enabling him, through the use of the historic present, to confront directly not only other characters but also the reader, underscores the fact that Jesus is the supreme exponent of God's evaluative point of view. And psychologically, Matthew, again as narrator, by leading the reader, through the use of inside views, always to regard Jesus sympathetically and to regard other characters sympathetically or unsympathetically depending on whether they draw close to Jesus or oppose him, furthermore enhances Jesus' stature as the supreme exponent of God's evaluative point of view.

The Implied Reader

Just as literary theorists like Chatman, in discussing the "discourse" of a narrative, distinguish among the real author, the implied author (the real author's "second self"), and the narrator (the "voice" that tells the story), so they also distinguish among the "real reader," the "implied reader," and the "narratee."[110] With respect to Matthew's Gospel, the term "real reader" denotes any flesh-and-blood person who has actually heard it or read it, whether it be the Christian of the first century for whom it was originally written or anyone in the twentieth century who takes it to hand. By contrast, the term "implied reader" denotes no flesh-and-blood person of any century but an imaginary person who is to be envisaged, in perusing Matthew's story, as responding to the text at every point with whatever emotion, understanding, or knowledge the text ideally calls for. Or to put it differently, the implied reader is that imaginary person in whom the intention of the text is to be thought of as always reaching its fulfillment. And third, the term "narratee" denotes, most simply, whoever it is to whom the narrator (the "voice" that tells the story) is to be construed as addressing his many remarks. Thus, it is to the narratee that Matthew as narrator is speaking when in 1:1 he utters the words "The book of the origin of Jesus Christ, Son of David, Son of Abraham." But as correct technically as it may be to say this, the fact of the matter is that in this instance the narratee proves to be but a stand-in for the implied reader. One can simplify matters, therefore, and merely construe Matthew the narrator as addressing himself to the implied reader.

Accordingly, the important thing to keep in mind is that it is the implied

---

110. Cf. Chatman, *Story and Discourse*, 147–51, 253–62; Prince, "Fictional 'Narratees,' " 100–106; Iser, *Act of Reading*, 27–38; Lanser, *Narrative Act*, 179–84.

reader who is silently and invisibly present throughout Matthew's story to attend to every word. Now as regards the implied reader, he or she also has, like the implied author, a place or position of his or her own in relation to the world of Matthew's story. This position lies, as the passages 24:15; 27:8; and 28:15 reveal, at some distance from the resurrection but short of the Parousia and is, in fact, identical with that of Matthew as implied author. From this vantage point in time, the implied reader, too, can oversee the story of the life and ministry of Jesus as Matthew conveys this through his voice as narrator, and he or she can comprehend the whole of this story.

This insight, that the implied reader not only is present throughout Matthew to hear the whole story but also has a position of his or her own which lies between the resurrection and the Parousia, is of no little significance, especially for understanding the great discourses of Jesus (Matthew 5—7; 10; 13; 18; 23; 24—25). Consider, for example, the missionary discourse in 9:35—10:42. In 10:5–6 Jesus enjoins the disciples, "Go nowhere among the Gentiles, and enter no town of the Samaritans, but go rather to the lost sheep of the house of Israel." For the implied reader this injunction occasions no surprise, because it dovetails neatly with the story of Jesus' ministry to Israel as recounted thus far in Matthew (4:17—9:34; 4:17, 23; 9:35–36). In 10:17–18, however, Jesus suddenly tells the disciples about persecutions that will befall them and that envisage not solely a mission to Israel, but also a mission aimed at Gentiles: "Beware of men; for ... you will be dragged before governors and kings for my sake, to bear testimony before them and the Gentiles." For the implied reader, this sudden reference in Matthew 10 to a Gentile mission comes as unexpected. From the perspective of the flow of Matthew's story, these words of Jesus in v. 18 do occasion surprise for the implied reader.

But from another perspective, namely, that of the temporal position beyond the resurrection which also distinguishes the implied reader (24:15), the movement in the text of Matthew 10 from an exclusive mission to Israel (vv. 5–6) to a mission that includes Gentiles as well (v. 18) merely parallels the movement within the wider story of Jesus. This movement portrays Jesus, on the one hand, as being sent only to the lost sheep of the house of Israel (15:24) but, on the other hand, as initiating a universal mission to the Gentiles immediately after his resurrection (28:18–20). From his or her peculiar vantage point beyond the resurrection, the implied reader is fully able to comprehend, and to relate to each other, the particularism of 10:5–6 concerning Israel and the universalism of 10:18 concerning the Gentiles. Accordingly, the same saying or event that occasions surprise for the implied reader when he or she approaches it in terms of the flow of Matthew's story is comprehensible and occasions no surprise when he or she views it in terms of a special position in the time following the resurrection. In similar fashion, other passages in other discourses of Jesus which likewise occasion surprise for the implied reader in light of the flow of Matthew's story—because they seem so clearly "out of place" with respect to the earthly ministry of Jesus (cf. 5:11–12; 13:38; 18:19–20; 23:34)—are perfectly intelligible when viewed from the perspective of a special position beyond the resurrection in the time of the risen Jesus and of the universal mission (24:15).

With these observations, the discussion of the implied reader may be brought to a close and, with it, also the larger discussion regarding the "discourse" of a narrative. If the "story," with its events, characters, and settings, constitutes the one part of a narrative, the "discourse," which has to do with how the story is told and concerns such matters as the implied author, the narrator, point of view, and the implied reader, constitutes the other part of a narrative. To set the stage for an examination of the gospel-story of Matthew itself, two issues must yet be dealt with which have thus far been withheld from consideration, namely, the structure of Matthew's Gospel and its view of the history of salvation.

THE STRUCTURE OF MATTHEW AND ITS VIEW
OF THE HISTORY OF SALVATION

Matthew's story of the life of Jesus unfolds in three broad segments, or parts.[111] To signal the beginning of each new part, Matthew employs a formula, or stereotyped phrase: "From that time on Jesus began to preach [to show his disciples] ..." (4:17; 16:21). The thing to note is that each time this formula occurs, it introduces a new phase in the ministry of Jesus. When taken as the cue, it gives rise to this broad outline of the story of Matthew: (I) The Figure of Jesus Messiah (1:1—4:16); (II) The Ministry of Jesus Messiah to Israel and Israel's Repudiation of Jesus (4:17—16:20); and (III) The Journey of Jesus Messiah to Jerusalem and His Suffering, Death, and Resurrection (16:21—28:20). As this outline suggests, Matthew tells the story of the life of Jesus first by presenting him to the implied reader and then by describing, respectively, his public ministry to Israel and his journey to Jerusalem where he suffers, dies, and is raised.

In treating the element of time in a narrative, Chatman speaks of "story-time" and "discourse-time."[112] "Discourse-time" has to do with the order in which the implied reader is actually told about the events that make up a story. For instance, it is the discourse-time of Matthew which dictates that the implied reader is not told of the death of John the Baptist until Matthew 14, at which juncture John's death is presented as having already taken

---

111. On the structure of Matthew, cf. Kingsbury, *Matthew: Structure, Christology, Kingdom,* 1–25. For an excellent, thorough treatment of this topic, cf. Bauer, "Structure of Matthew's Gospel."
112. Chatman, *Story and Discourse,* 62–63.

place. By contrast, "story-time" simply refers to the chronological order in which all the events cited in a narrative occur. In Matthew's Gospel, story-time extends from creation on the one hand to consummation on the other (19:4, 8; 25:31–46), though the greater interest lies with the time that extends from Abraham to the consummation (1:1–17; 28:20). In any case, Chatman's story-time approximates what biblical scholars have customarily termed the "history of salvation." In terms of this history, the point to be made is that Matthew, in telling of the life of Jesus, is careful to situate it within the broad context of God's dealings with his people. Inasmuch as the time involved stretches from Abraham to the end of the age, Matthew divides this time into distinct epochs and periods.

The two epochs Matthew distinguishes in the history of salvation are the age of prophecy, or the "time of Israel (OT)," and the eschatological age of fulfillment, which is the "time of Jesus (earthly—exalted)."[113] To stress the passing of the first and the arrival of the second, Matthew makes liberal use of formula-quotations to call attention to the fulfillment in the life of Jesus of some aspect of OT prophecy.[114]

For its part, the age of fulfillment, or the "time of Jesus (earthly—exalted)," runs from Jesus' birth (1:16, 22–23) to his return at the consummation in his role as the Son of man (25:31–46). Within this epoch, Matthew differentiates among several periods through his use of the respective expressions "the Kingdom of Heaven is at hand" and "the gospel of the Kingdom." Specifically, he employs these expressions to divide the "time of Jesus (earthly—exalted)" into the ministries to Israel of John (3:1–2), of Jesus (4:17), and of the pre-Easter disciples (10:7) and the ministry to the nations of the post-Easter disciples, or church (24:14; 26:13).

Accordingly, Matthew both knits together, and differentiates among, the ministries of John, Jesus, the pre-Easter disciples, and the post-Easter church. Nevertheless, it is the ministry of Jesus that is decisive in this sequence. John is the forerunner of Jesus (17:10–13), and the pre-Easter and post-Easter disciples carry out their ministries only on the commission of Jesus (10:5; 28:18–20). This is why the "time of fulfillment" is indeed the "time of Jesus (earthly—exalted)."

This survey of both the topical outline of Matthew's life of Jesus and the salvation-historical context within which it has been situated raises the question of the fundamental message of Matthew's story. The key passages 1:23 and 28:20, which stand in a reciprocal relationship to each other, highlight this message. At 1:23, Matthew quotes Isaiah in saying of Jesus: in "Emmanuel ... God [is] with us." And at 28:20 the risen Jesus himself

---

113. On Matthew's understanding of salvation-history and the scholarly discussion of this topic, cf. Kingsbury, *Matthew: Structure, Christology, Kingdom*, 25–37.

114. Cf. above, n. 70.

declares to the disciples: "I am with you always, to the close of the age." Strategically located at the beginning and the end of Matthew's story, these two passages "enclose" it. In combination, they reveal that the message the story of Matthew proclaims is that *in the person of Jesus Messiah, his Son, God has drawn near to abide to the end of time with his people, the church, thus inaugurating the eschatological age of salvation.*

Embedded in this message is a claim and a call to commitment. As a word of prophecy, 1:23 shows that in the birth of "Emmanuel," that is, Jesus Son of God, the hope of Israel has at last come to fulfillment. Hence, the affirmation this passage makes is that Jesus is of decisive significance for the salvation of Israel. In 28:18–20, the risen Son of God commissions his followers to "make disciples of all nations." Hence, the affirmation this passage makes is that Jesus is of decisive significance for the salvation of the Gentiles. Together, therefore, these passages set forth the bold claim that the story of Matthew advances on behalf of Jesus: for the salvation of both Jew and Gentile, Jesus Son of God is of decisive significance. Then, too, because the story of Matthew ends with Jesus' enjoining the disciples, and with them the implied reader, to engage in mission, it consequently ends by issuing the disciples and the implied reader the call to commit themselves without reserve to the carrying out of this mission.

This completes our consideration of a literary-critical approach to Matthew. The task now is to undertake an investigation of the gospel-story itself. Subsequently I shall treat, in turn, the figure of Jesus, his ministry to Israel, his journey to Jerusalem and passion, his role as the Son of man, his disciples, and the community of Christians for whom this story was written.

2

The Presentation of Jesus (1:1—4:16)

THE plot of Matthew's story revolves around Jesus, and integral to this plot is the element of conflict. By and large, two conflicts dominate: that between Jesus and Israel, especially the Jewish leaders; and that between Jesus and the disciples. Whereas the first conflict turns out tragically for Israel, the second ends in reconciliation for the disciples. In this chapter and in chapters 3 and 4, the aim is to focus both on the overall flow of Matthew's story and on Jesus' conflict with Israel. In chapter 6, the focus will be on Jesus' conflict with the disciples.

I stated in the last chapter that Matthew's story divides itself into three parts and that 1:1—4:16 constitutes the first part. There is a scholarly tradition, however, that holds that Matthew 1—2 forms the first part of Matthew's story. As proof of this, reference is often made to the break in time between the years of Jesus' infancy (1:1—2:23) and the appearance of John and Jesus as adults (3:1—4:16). To trace properly the flow of Matthew's story, it is necessary to recognize that 1:1—4:16 does in fact constitute a major segment.

Four factors indicate the unity of 1:1—4:16.[1] The most important is that the climactic statement regarding the identity of Jesus, the motif that dominates the beginning of Matthew's story (cf. 1:1), does not occur until the baptism (3:13-17). In the baptismal pericope, God himself enters the world of Matthew's story and declares Jesus to be his beloved Son (3:17). In making this declaration, God expresses to Jesus, and to such transcendent beings as Satan as well (4:3, 6), his evaluative point of view concerning Jesus' identity—that is, how he "thinks" about Jesus. To be sure, prior to the baptism Matthew does indeed mention the truth that Jesus is the Son of God. But he does so as narrator and in the form of private comments to

---

1. Cf. Kingsbury, *Matthew: Structure, Christology, Kingdom*, 7–17; Bauer, "Structure of Matthew's Gospel."

which no human character within the story has access but only the implied reader (1:22–23; 2:15). Accordingly, God's baptismal declaration at 3:17 reveals itself to be climactic within the context of 1:1—4:16 because this is the place where God's understanding of Jesus as his Son ceases to be of the nature of private information available only to the implied reader and becomes instead an element within Matthew's story that henceforth influences the shape of events.

A second factor that calls attention to the unity of 1:1—4:16 is the formula-quotations in 2:23 and 4:12–16. It is generally held that the travels of Jesus prior to his public ministry come to an end when Joseph brings Mary and the infant Jesus from Egypt and settles in Nazareth (2:23). But these formula-quotations prove that the travels of Jesus do not in reality end until he takes up residence in Capernaum, which becomes "his own city" (cf. 9:1). It is to make this point that the passage 4:12–14 has been shaped in such fashion as to take up flawlessly from the earlier passage 2:22–23. These passages read as follows:

> . . . he [Joseph, with Mary and the infant Jesus] went and dwelt in a city called Nazareth, that what was spoken by the prophets might be fulfilled . . .
> . . . he [Jesus] left Nazareth and went and dwelt in Capernaum by the sea, in the regions of Zebulun and Naphtali, that what was spoken by the prophet Isaiah might be fulfilled . . .

A third factor that attests to the unity of 1:1—4:16 is the presence in the Greek text at 3:1 of the particle *de* ("now," "then"). The context reveals that this particle frequently appears in the opening line of a pericope in order to connect that pericope with preceding narrative (cf., e.g., 1:18; 2:1, 13, 19; 4:12). By employing *de* at 3:1, Matthew shows that the interpreter is not to posit a fundamental break in the text between chapters 2 and 3 but is, on the contrary, to view the materials of the two chapters as belonging together.

A fourth and last factor betokening the unity of 1:1—4:16 is that all the pericopes making up this larger section narrate events *preliminary* to Jesus' ministry to Israel. In the temptation scenes (4:1–11), Jesus faces the devil in private encounter. At the baptism, Jesus is, as will be shown, the only human character in Matthew's story to see the Spirit descend upon him and to hear God's baptismal declaration (3:16–17). And as for the ministry of John, its sole purpose is to ready Israel for the time when Jesus will come and commence his public activity (3:11–12; 4:17). Consequently, these events, too, and not just those surrounding Jesus' infancy, can be seen as preliminary to the beginning of Jesus' public ministry in Israel (cf. 4:17). To repeat, the whole of 1:1—4:16, and not merely chapters 1—2, form the first part of Matthew's story.

THE DAVIDIC MESSIAH-KING

The Genealogy

Jesus is God's supreme agent in Matthew's story, and the purpose of the genealogy with which Matthew begins is to advance this claim. The genealogy asserts God's direct control of Israel's history and sets forth in the listing of Jesus' forebears an initial evaluative point of view concerning his identity. Through the use of the expression *biblos geneseōs* ("book of the origin") in the introduction of the genealogy (1:1), Matthew echoes such OT passages as Gen. 2:4 and 5:1 (LXX).[2] These passages are themselves introductions to genealogies, and these genealogies bear witness to the governance of human history by God (Gen. 2:4—4:26; 5:1—6:8). Add to this observation the interpretive clues provided by the key verse Matt. 1:17, and the message of the genealogy is plain: the whole of Israel's history has been so guided by God that the promises made to Abraham and to king David which ostensibly had come to naught in the Babylonian captivity have attained their fulfillment in the coming of the heir of Abraham and David, namely, the Messiah. Consequently, Jesus is, as Matthew says in 1:1, "Christ" ("Messiah"), "Son of David," and "Son of Abraham."

Through this string of names and titles placed at the head of his story, Matthew sounds the theme of the "identity of Jesus" and makes of each designation a vehicle for becoming acquainted with him. To these, other designations will shortly be added. The question is: How does each designation enrich the implied reader's understanding of Jesus?

As 1:16 of the genealogy indicates, "Jesus" is the personal name of the protagonist of Matthew's story. Although Joseph is the one who gives Jesus his name (1:25), he does so on instructions from the angel of the Lord (1:20). Ultimately, therefore, God himself is the source of Jesus' name. As to meaning, "Jesus" denotes that "God [is] salvation," and the angel touches on this as he tells Joseph that Jesus "will *save* his people from their sins" (1:21). Accordingly, the force of the name "Jesus" is that in the one thus called, God is active to save. Hence, of all the traits Matthew ascribes to Jesus in the course of his story, the one most fundamental is that he is "saving."

Despite the fact that "Jesus" is a personal name and occurs no fewer than 150 times in Matthew's story, it is striking that human characters never make use of it in direct address to Jesus. Indeed, only five times do humans even utter this name so as to refer to Jesus in conversation with other characters.[3] Overwhelmingly, "Jesus" is the name Matthew as narrator reserves for his own use. In thus reserving the use of this name for himself, Matthew forges the closest possible association between himself as narrator

2. Cf. Johnson, *Biblical Genealogies*, 149, 186.
3. Cf. 21:11; 26:69, 71; 27:17, 22; also 27:37.

and Jesus. What this reveals, in turn, is that Matthew's evaluative point of view as narrator, that is, his conception of reality, coincides with that of Jesus. Because the name "Jesus" alludes to the circumstance that God is active in Jesus to save, the name itself attests to Jesus' being God's supreme agent who espouses God's evaluative point of view in discharging the mission God has set for him (1:21). Since Matthew, through his own use of Jesus' name, closely associates himself with Jesus, he gives the implied reader to understand that both he, as narrator, and Jesus will reliably advocate God's evaluative point of view, his conception of reality, as this is explicated in the gospel-story.

Beyond the genealogy (1:1–25), Jesus' name identifies him, in relation to his origins, as the one who is born in "Bethlehem of Judea" (2:1, 5–6) but is raised in "Nazareth of Galilee" (2:23; 21:11; 26:71). To the villagers of Nazareth, he is the "son of the carpenter," his mother is "Mary," and he has both "sisters" and "brothers" ("James," "Joseph," "Simon," and "Judas"; 13:55–56). As an adult, Jesus moves from Nazareth to "Capernaum" (4:13), which becomes "his own city" (9:1) and where he may have a "house."[4] In Jerusalem to the south, he can be recognized as one who hails "from Galilee" (26:69, 73; 21:11).

If the genealogy is that of "Jesus," the protagonist of the story, Matthew nonetheless refers to him in 1:1 by means of the full name "Jesus Christ." In this verse, the Greek term *christos* ("Anointed One," "Christ," "Messiah") is a personal name ("Jesus Christ") that is likewise a title ("Jesus [who is] Messiah"). Among the major titles ascribed to Jesus in Matthew's story, *christos* is the most general. This explains why one must always look to the context, immediate or wider, in order to know how to construe it. Thus, if in 1:1 *christos* is interpreted in terms of "Son of David" and "Son of Abraham," elsewhere it also points to Jesus as the "Coming One" (11:2–3) or as the "King of the Jews" (2:2, 4) or as the "Son of God" (16:16, 20; 26:63, 68). Ask, therefore, what the title *christos* says of Jesus in Matthew's story, and the answer is that it rather summarily characterizes him as God's Anointed, the King and Shepherd of Israel (2:2, 4, 6). As the one foretold by the prophets (2:6), he has ardently been awaited by Israel (11:2–3). By his coming, he brings the long history of Israel, begun in Abraham, to its fulfillment (1:1–17). As to origin and pedigree, he is miraculously conceived by the Spirit and adopted into the line of David (1:18–25). As to his ministry, it will issue at the last in salvation or damnation for people (3:11–12; 11:2–6).

Matthew affirms in 1:1 not only that Jesus is the Christ, or Messiah, but also that he is "Son of David" and "Son of Abraham." In what sense is Jesus the "Son of Abraham"? He is the Son of Abraham both because it is in him

4. Cf. 9:10, 28; 13:1, 36; 17:25.

that the entire history of Israel, which had its beginning in Abraham, attains to its goal (1:17) and because he is the one through whom God will extend to the nations his blessing of salvation (8:11; 28:18–20).

To affirm that Jesus is the Son of Abraham seems to be no problem in Matthew's story. But the same cannot be said as regards the title "Son of David."[5] In fact, Matthew goes to some lengths in chapter 1 to show not only "that" but also "how" Jesus can legitimately be designated in v. 1 as the "Son of David." In recounting the final link of the genealogy (1:16), Matthew permits it to be "broken." Instead of stating, in line with the pattern he has established, ". . . and Jacob fathered Joseph, and Joseph fathered Jesus," he states, ". . . and Jacob fathered Joseph the husband of Mary, of whom Jesus was born" (1:16). The problem Matthew thus incorporates into the genealogy is this: How can Jesus legitimately be designated the Son of David (1:1) when Joseph son of David (1:20) is not his father and Mary, his mother, is not said to be from the line of David? Matthew's answer to this problem is found in 1:18–25: Jesus can legitimately be designated the Son of David because Joseph son of David obeys the instructions he receives from the angel of the Lord and gives Jesus his name (1:20–21, 25). In other words, Jesus, born of Mary but not fathered by Joseph, is legitimately Son of David because Joseph son of David adopts him into his line.

Later in his story, Matthew portrays Jesus as acting in his capacity as the Son of David and hence fulfilling in his ministry the eschatological expectations associated with David (21:9, 15). As the Son of David, Jesus enters Jerusalem and "takes possession" of it, yet shows himself in so doing to be not a warrior king, but the humble King of peace (21:4–5). In the main, however, Jesus performs acts of healing as the Son of David. Those directly or indirectly linked with these acts are people who count for nothing in Israel's society: the "blind"[6] and such "disenfranchised persons" as a Gentile woman (15:21–28) and children (21:15). Just as the title "Son of Abraham" characterizes Jesus as the one in whom the Gentiles will find blessing, so the title "Son of David" characterizes Jesus as the one in whom Israel will find blessing. Because these blind and disenfranchised persons "see" and "confess" that Jesus is Israel's Davidic Messiah, they play a not insignificant role in the conflict Jesus has with Israel. In that "Son of David" constitutes for them their evaluative point of view concerning Jesus' identity, they call attention to the guilt that is Israel's for not receiving Jesus as its Davidic Messiah.

To sum up, Matthew employs the genealogy to assert that God has guided the whole of Israel's history so that it might culminate in the birth of "Jesus," the protagonist of his story, who is "Messiah," "Son of David," and

---

5. Cf. Kingsbury, "Son of David," 591–602.
6. Cf. 9:27–31; 12:22; 20:29–34; 21:14.

"Son of Abraham." This is the initial evaluative point of view concerning Jesus' identity which Matthew advances, and in the rest of 1:1—4:16 he augments it considerably.

The Magi and the Flight to Egypt

Following the birth of Jesus in Bethlehem, Matthew reports that Magi from the East arrive in Jerusalem and inquire after him (2:1). "Where," they ask, "is he who is born King of the Jews?" (2:2). "King of the Jews" is consequently the evaluative point of view of the Magi concerning Jesus' identity. And because the Magi have come to offer Jesus their sincere worship (2:2,11), Matthew urges the implied reader to accept this title, too, as correctly applying to Jesus. As Matthew will later show, Jesus is indeed the King of the Jews, yet not as one who restores to Israel its national splendor or foments rebellion against Rome, but as one who saves others by willingly submitting to suffering and death (27:27–31).

In contrast to the Magi, Herod the Great and all Jerusalem react with fear to the news that the Messiah, the King of the Jews, has been born (2:2–4). Not only this, but also Herod proves in Matthew 2 to be prototypical of other human characters with whom Jesus will become embroiled in conflict in the course of his ministry—namely, Pilate and the Jewish leaders. As the Messiah, the King of the Jews, Jesus looms in Herod's eyes as a threat to assume the throne of Israel. This is why Herod plots to have Jesus killed (2:8, 13). According to Herod's evaluative point of view, Jesus is an insurrectionist. Similarly, Pilate also deals with Jesus on the presumption that the Messiah, the King of the Jews, is one who lays political claim to the throne of Israel (27:11–14). Since Pilate accedes to the charge that Jesus is the King of the Jews, he permits Jesus to be crucified (27:37). According to Pilate's evaluative point of view, too, Jesus is an insurrectionist.

The manner in which Herod reacts to the perceived threat the infant Jesus poses anticipates the manner in which the Jewish leaders will later respond to the adult Jesus. Both Herod and they reveal themselves to be "spiritually blind" (2:3; 27:63); "fearful" (2:3; 21:46); "conspiratorial" (2:7; 12:14); "guileful" and "mendacious" (2:8; 26:4; 28:13–14); "murderous" (2:13; 12:14); "wrathful" (2:16; cf. 21:15); and "apprehensive of the future" (2:16; 27:62–64).[7] In Matthew's story, Herod is the precursor of the Jewish leaders, and his opposition to Jesus foreshadows theirs.

God himself foils the plot of king Herod. He directs the Magi through a dream not to return to Herod (1:12) and dispatches an angel to Joseph to instruct him, again in a dream, to flee to Egypt and to remain there until Herod dies (2:13–14). In obeying at once this command from God and the other commands that follow, Joseph's righteousness (1:19) casts Herod's

---

7. Cf. also Fiore, "Characterization in Matthew," 5.

wickedness in ever sharper relief. After Herod's death, the angel of the Lord again comes to Joseph in a dream and orders him to return to Israel (2:19–21). Then, warned by God through still another dream, Joseph settles in Nazareth (2:22–23).

THE SON OF GOD

The Figure and Ministry of John

To prepare the way for the ministry of Jesus, John the Baptist appears in his appointed role of "forerunner" (3:3; 11:10). As forerunner, John is "Elijah" in the sense that he fulfills the eschatological expectations associated with the prophet (Matt. 11:14; 17:10–13). As regards these expectations, Malachi had prophesied that before the terrible day of the Lord came, Elijah would be sent in order to ready Israel for the judgment this day would bring (Mal. 4:5–6). In John's ministry, this prophesy becomes reality, but in altered fashion: John is the forerunner not of God, but of Jesus Messiah; and he prepares the way not for the final judgment as such, but for the ministry of Jesus (Matt. 11:10, 14; 17:10–13).

While the ministry of John precedes that of Jesus, the term "forerunner" connotes more than mere temporal precedence. As the forerunner of Jesus, John foreshadows in his person and work the person and work of Jesus. Both John and Jesus are the agents of God sent by God (11:10; 10:40). Both belong to the time of fulfillment (3:3; 1:23). Both have the same message to proclaim (3:2; 4:17). Both enter into conflict with Israel: in the case of the crowds, a favorable reception ultimately gives way to repudiation (3:5–6; 4:24–25; 11:16–19); in the case of the leaders, the opposition is implacable from the outset (3:7–10; 9:3). Both John and Jesus are "delivered up" to their enemies (4:12; 10:4). And both are made to die violently and shamefully (14:3–12; 27:37). To know of John is to know in advance of Jesus.

The mission of John is to "restore all things" (17:11). To accomplish this, he proclaims to Israel from the desert of Judea, "Repent, for the Kingdom of Heaven is at hand!" (3:1–2). At the heart of this summons lies the notion that Israel has lost its way. What is required is that Israel turn from evil, place its trust in God, and obey him. Urgency is also of the essence, for God has already set in motion the events that will issue in judgment. Indeed, the Coming One is soon to appear, and when he does he will, with incomparable authority, carry out the final judgment to salvation or damnation (3:11–12).

The crowds in Israel give ear to John's proclamation. Matthew records: "Then went out to him Jerusalem and all Judea and all the region about the Jordan" (3:5). Submitting to John's baptism, the crowds confess their sins and show themselves to be a repentant people ready for the arrival of the Coming One and the final judgment (3:6, 11–12).

Along with the crowds, the Jewish leaders also go out to John for baptism (3:7). For them, however, John has only scathing words (3:7–10). He describes them as a "brood of vipers," which is to say he likens them to venomous snakes that are evil to the core. He likewise challenges them to demonstrate by their deeds that they have not rejected his summons to repentance, warning them that they cannot rely on descendancy from Abraham in order to persevere in the approaching judgment.

John, then, is the divinely sent forerunner who readies Israel for the imminent arrival of Jesus. But this notwithstanding, John's conception of Jesus' ministry, though it is correct, is also insufficient. To John's way of thinking, Jesus is the Coming One (= Messiah; 11:2–3) who will appear in order to carry out the final judgment to salvation or damnation (3:11–12). "Already," John exclaims, "the ax is laid to the root of the trees; every tree therefore that does not bear good fruit is cut down and thrown into the fire!" (3:10). According to John's evaluative point of view, Jesus is the Coming One whose arrival on the scene of history portends the end-time judgment.

This evaluative point of view of John concerning the person and ministry of Jesus explains why John, in prison, sends disciples to Jesus to ask whether he is in fact the Coming One or whether they are to await another (11:2–3). John has heard of the "works of [Jesus] Messiah," but they have not issued in the final judgment (11:2; 3:11–12). In giving reply to John's query, Jesus refers to his ministry of word and deed in such manner as to show that it fulfills OT expectation and consequently does not point away from him as being the Messiah, or Coming One, but toward him (11:4–5). Moreover, from other parts of Matthew's story the implied reader, if not John, knows that there will in truth be a coming of Jesus which will result in final judgment (13:35–43; 25:31–46). But however that may be, for the time being Jesus' reply to John also serves as a word of caution to him not to take offense at him, that is, not to lose trust that he is in fact the Coming One John thinks him to be and the one whose ministry will indeed achieve its divinely appointed purposes.

The Baptism of Jesus

The crown of the first part of Matthew's story, which treats of Jesus' identity (1:1—4:16), is the baptismal scene. Here God, himself participating as "actor" in the story, empowers Jesus for messianic ministry and solemnly declares "who Jesus is." Apart from the introduction (3:13), the unit falls neatly into two sections: the dialogue between John and Jesus (3:14–15) and the two revelatory events that follow (3:16–17).

No sooner has John foretold the imminent arrival of the Coming One than Jesus appears at the Jordan river to be baptized by John (3:13). John would prevent this, objecting that he has need to be baptized by Jesus

(3:14). Jesus overrules John, however, asserting that "it is fitting for us to fulfill all righteousness" (3:15)—that is to say, that God would have them be wholly obedient and do all that he requires of them.[8] Accordingly, the reason Jesus insists on being baptized at the Jordan is that it is God's will that John should baptize him and that he should submit to such baptism. Then, too, although Jesus does not undergo baptism because he, like Israel, has need to repent of sin, the fact remains that in being baptized by John, he voluntarily identifies himself with sinful humankind (cf. 1:21; 26:28).

Matthew does not describe the baptism of Jesus itself. The focus is on the two revelatory events that follow (3:16–17). After Jesus' baptism, Matthew remarks that "immediately he went up from the water" (3:16). If in the preceding scene Jesus and John stood alone in private conversation (3:14–15), now Jesus removes himself also from John to step unaccompanied into the presence of God (3:16a). No one other than Jesus himself, therefore, sees the Spirit descend upon him (cf. 3:16: "he saw"), and only he, along with such transcendent beings as Satan (4:3, 6), hears the voice from heaven (3:17).

Retrospectively, later developments in Matthew's story corroborate this observation. Had the crowds heard the voice from heaven, it is inexplicable why one segment of the public does not at least entertain the idea that Jesus is the Son of God.[9] And had John heard the voice from heaven, it is odd that his question of 11:2–3 contains no hint of this but, on the contrary, reflects the selfsame view of Jesus he had expressed in 3:11–12, namely, that Jesus is the Coming One. To repeat, Jesus alone of the human characters in Matthew's story sees the Spirit descend in 3:16 and hears the voice speak in 3:17.

The first revelatory event is one of sight: "And behold, the heavens were opened and he [Jesus] saw the Spirit of God descending like a dove, coming upon him" (3:16). The purpose of the opening of the heavens is both to permit the Spirit to descend and to signal that divine revelation is about to take place (Ezek. 1:1). The descent of the Spirit upon Jesus denotes the divine act whereby God empowers him to accomplish the messianic ministry he is shortly to begin (Matt. 4:17). Such empowerment, of course, is not to be construed as Jesus' initial endowment with the Spirit, for he was conceived by the Spirit. Instead, it specifies in what way Jesus proves to be the mightier One John had said he would be (3:11). It also serves as the reference point for understanding the "authority" with which Jesus discharges his public ministry (7:29; 11:27; 21:23–27). Empowered by God's Spirit, Jesus speaks as the mouthpiece of God (7:28–29) and acts as the instrument of God (12:28).

8. Cf. Schweizer, *Good News*, 53–56.
9. Cf. 12:23; 16:13–14; also 13:55; 14:1–2.

The second revelatory event is one of sound: "And behold, a voice from heaven said, 'This is my beloved Son, in whom I take delight!' " (3:17). Important as is the first revelatory event, this one is more important still, for Matthew has accorded it the position of stress.

The voice from heaven is the voice of God.[10] The words God speaks are drawn from Ps. 2:7; Isa. 42:1; and Gen. 22:2. In Isa. 42:1, the servant in whom God delights is the one God has "chosen" for ministry. In Gen. 22:2, Abraham's beloved son Isaac is his "only" son. And in Psalm 2, God is described as solemnly addressing the words "My son are you" to the king-designate from the house of David, his anointed ("messiah"), who on the day of his coronation assumes the throne of Judah. Together, these several emphases combine in Matt. 3:17 to form a solemn affirmation in which God declares that Jesus, the Anointed One (Messiah-King) from the line of David, is his only, or unique, Son whom he has chosen for eschatological ministry.

This declaration of 3:17 is one that God makes within the world of Matthew's story. As noted, God speaks it over Jesus (3:17) but also in the hearing of transcendent beings, such as Satan (4:3, 6). In affirming that Jesus is his royal Son, God states "who Jesus is" according to his evaluative point of view, that is, how he "thinks" about Jesus (16:23e). Because Matthew so constructs his story that God's evaluative point of view is normative, the implied reader knows that in hearing God enunciate his understanding of Jesus, he or she has heard the normative understanding of Jesus, the one in terms of which all other understandings are to be judged. In Matthew's story, God himself dictates that Jesus is preeminently the Son of God.

As I observed at the outset of this chapter, God's empowerment of Jesus with his Spirit and especially his declaration from heaven bring the entire first part of Matthew's story (1:1—4:16) to its culmination. This is the case on two counts. For one thing, God's designation for Jesus ("my Son") both overlaps in meaning the other designations we have encountered thus far ("Messiah" ["Coming One"], "Son of Abraham," "Son of David," and "King of the Jews") and transcends them. And for another, although there are indications prior to the baptism that Jesus is the Son of God, including narrative comments made directly to the implied reader (1:22–23; 2:15), Matt. 3:17 is the first place where this truth, uttered by God as "actor," assumes the form of an event that occurs within the story itself.

In what way does God's designation of Jesus as "my Son" in 3:17 both overlap in meaning the other designations encountered thus far and transcend them? The expression "my Son" stems from Ps. 2:7. In Psalm 2, the one from the house of David (= "son of David") whom God decrees is "my

10. Cf., e.g., 17:5; Gen. 15:4; Deut. 4:36; Dan. 4:31.

son" is likewise said to be God's "king" (2:6) and God's anointed (LXX: *christos* ["messiah"]; 2:2). In other words, Psalm 2 reflects in prophetic, rudimentary form the highly developed portrait of Jesus one finds in the first part of Matthew's story. The Jesus whom God declares in Matt. 3:17 to be "his royal Son" is none other than the Jesus whom Matthew, as narrator, has presented as "Messiah," "Son of David," and "Son of Abraham" (1:1) and whom the Magi have reverently called "King of the Jews" (2:2) and John the "Coming One" (= "Messiah"; 3:11; 11:2–3). In short, God's designation of Jesus in 3:17 overlaps these other designations in meaning because the Jesus who God says is "my Son" is, in fact, the Davidic Messiah-King, the descendant of Abraham.

By the same token, God's designation of Jesus as "my Son" also transcends these other designations in meaning. It does so because Matthew imbues it with a quality the others do not possess in like measure. This quality is that it attests to the unique filial relationship that exists between God and Jesus: Jesus is conceived by God's Spirit (1:18, 20) and empowered by God's Spirit (3:16) so that he is Emmanuel, or "God with us" (1:23); as such, he is the one in whom God reveals himself to humankind (11:27) and who is God's supreme agent of salvation.[11] While it is the case that through the call to discipleship others enter into fellowship with God and hence become "sons of God,"[12] Jesus alone is "the Son of God." For this reason, he speaks of God as "my Father"[13] or, with an eye to the disciples, as "your Father,"[14] but never as "our Father." The Lord's Prayer is no exception to this, because "our Father" (6:9) are words the disciples as a group are to utter in their approach to God. To reiterate, by virtue of the unique filial relationship he has to God, the Jesus of Matthew's story is preeminently the Son of God.

But although God's declaration of Jesus as his Son in 3:17 constitutes the climax of the first part of Matthew's story, this is not to say there are no indications prior to the baptism that Jesus is God's Son. On the contrary, there are numerous such indications, of which the following are but a selection: (a) In 1:16 of the genealogy, Matthew casts the verb "to be born" in the passive voice (the "divine passive") to alert the implied reader to the fact that "Jesus is born [by an act of God]." (b) In 1:18–25, Matthew points out that Mary's conception of Jesus is not through Joseph, who makes no attempt to have relations with her during her pregnancy, but "by the Holy Spirit." (c) In the "aside" of 1:23, Matthew tells the implied reader that Mary is a virgin when she gives birth to her son and that her son is Emmanuel, or "God with us" (i.e., the Son of God). (d) Throughout 2:7–23, Matthew, by

11. Cf. 1:21; 4:17, 23; 11:27; 26:28; 27:54; 28:5, 18b.
12. Cf. 4:18–22; 5:9, 45; 9:9; 13:38.
13. Cf., e.g., 7:21; 10:32–33; 12:50; 16:17; 26:39.
14. Cf., e.g., 5:16, 45, 48.

consistently designating Jesus as "the child" and repeatedly employing the expression "the child and [with] his mother," effectively prevents the implied reader from thinking of Jesus as the son of Joseph and instead reminds him or her that because the virgin Mary has given birth to a son who was conceived apart from Joseph son of David by the Holy Spirit, this son of Mary is at the same time the Son of God. (e) In the "aside" of 2:15, Matthew quotes an OT passage to the implied reader and applies it in such fashion that God is made to refer to Jesus as "my Son." (f) And by juxtaposing the baptismal pericope to the pericope on the ministry of John, Matthew gives the implied reader to understand that the "Coming One" of whom John prophesies is Jesus precisely as the Son of God whom God empowers with his Spirit (3:11, 13–17).

Accordingly, it is apparent that prior to the baptism, Matthew gives ample indication in his story that Jesus is the Son of God. Nevertheless, this recognition in no wise mitigates the contention that it is in God's declaration of Jesus as his Son in 3:17 that one reaches the climax not only of the baptismal pericope itself, but also of the entire first part of Matthew's story (1:1—4:16). In this part, Matthew presents Jesus to the implied reader. The evaluative point of view concerning Jesus' identity which Matthew sets forth is that Jesus, the Messiah-King from the line of David and of Abraham, is uniquely the Son of God. The crucial element in this evaluative point of view—that Jesus is the Son of God—Matthew as narrator does not state in the opening verse of his story. Perhaps the reason for this silence in 1:1 is that what immediately follows is a genealogy that begins with Abraham (1:2). By beginning as it does with Abraham and not with Adam and God (Luke 3:34, 38), this genealogy can bear no direct witness to the divine sonship of Jesus. But be that as it may, Matthew's procedure prior to the baptism is to allude to the truth of the divine sonship of Jesus with circumlocutions (1:16, 18, 20), with metaphors,[15] or with a term ("son") that is susceptible to dual meaning,[16] and, in the "asides" he gives to the implied reader (1:23; 2:15), even to permit it to be stated explicitly in words of prophecy. Still, all such hints or statements of this truth are merely anticipatory of that climactic moment following the baptism when God himself enters the world of Matthew's story as "actor" and proclaims over Jesus (3:17) and in the hearing of such transcendent beings as Satan (4:3, 6) that Jesus is his unique Son.

The Temptation of Jesus

By the end of the baptismal pericope, the Jesus of Matthew's story stands before the implied reader preeminently as the Son of God who has been

15. Cf. 2:8–9, 11, 13–14, 20–21; 3:11.
16. Cf. 1:20, 23, 25: the "son" of Mary is at the same time the "son" of God ("God with us").

empowered with the Spirit of God. So identified, Jesus is led by the Spirit into the desert to engage the devil, or Satan, in conflict in the place of his abode (4:1–11). The form this conflict takes is that three times Satan puts Jesus to the test.[17] Ultimately, the substance of each test has to do with Jesus' devotion, or obedience, to God. The intent of Satan in each test is to entice Jesus to break faith with God, his Father, and thus disavow his divine sonship. Should Satan succeed at this, he succeeds in effect in destroying Jesus. In testing Jesus, Satan cunningly adopts God's evaluative point of view according to which Jesus is his Son (4:3, 6).

Satan's testing of Jesus is also antitypical to the testing Israel faced in its desert wanderings from Egypt to Canaan (Deut. 6:10–19; 8:1–10). Israel, too, was designated by God as "his son" (Exod. 4:22–23). Nevertheless, when Israel son of God was put to the test, it failed.

Approaching Jesus three times in Matthew's story, Satan urges him to place concern for self above allegiance to God. In the first test, Satan suggests that Jesus miraculously still his hunger. But were Jesus to do so, he would be forcing, solely for his own benefit, a change in the circumstances into which God has brought him (4:2–4). In the second test, Satan suggests that Jesus cast himself down from the pinnacle of the temple. But were Jesus to do so, he would make himself guilty of endeavoring to coerce God into serving him by wondrously preserving Jesus' life from destruction (4:5–7). In the third test, Satan suggests that Jesus, to secure control over the substance of the nations of the world, fall down and worship him. But were Jesus to do so, he would be placing lust for the wealth of the world above fealty to God (4:8–10). The outcome of the three tests is that Jesus withstands the enticements of Satan and therefore bests him (4:11a). Unlike Israel son of God, Jesus Son of God is perfect in his devotion, or obedience, to God, his Father.

Jesus' conflict with Satan is the first true conflict of his career, since he was but an infant when Herod threatened his life. Occurring as it does prior to Jesus' public ministry, it possesses fundamental significance for both his ministry and the rest of the history of salvation. In Matthew's scheme of things, the world is the scene where two kingdoms, or spheres of power, are locked in cosmic battle (13:36–43).

On the one hand there is the Kingdom of Heaven, which has by God's design become a present, though hidden, reality in Jesus Son of God. Through the ministries of Jesus and of his pre-Easter and post-Easter disciples, Jesus summons first Israel and then also the Gentiles to repentance and to discipleship, sonship, brotherhood, and life in the sphere where God, through Jesus, rules. Such summoning to life in the sphere of

17. For a discussion of the pericope on the temptation, cf. Gerhardsson, *Testing of God's Son*.

God's Rule will continue until Jesus' return in splendor for judgment at the consummation of the age.

On the other hand, there is the kingdom of Satan (12:26). In this sphere of power Satan himself rules, and he has at his command both angels (25:41) and demons (10:8; 12:24), or unclean spirits (10:1). In both Israel and the world, Satan is at work to bring humans under his control (13:24–30, 38–39). The mark of those who serve him is that they are evil (13:49) and lawless (13:41), for they live contrary to the will of God.

By withstanding the testing of Satan following his baptism, Jesus Son of God demonstrates that he is stronger than Satan. In the long term, therefore, Satan, the implied reader knows, is doomed (25:41). But short of the consummation, Satan continues to wield power in the world (13:36–43). Throughout the ministry of Jesus, he enlists Israel and, at times, disciples of Jesus in his cause. Israel, in fact, has become "this evil generation."[18]

Especially do the leaders of the Jews have affinity with Satan. Satan is the "Tempter" who put Jesus to the test (4:3), and they, too, put Jesus to the test (16:1; 19:3; 22:18, 35). Satan is the "Evil One" par excellence (13:19, 38), and they, too, are evil (12:34–35, 39, 45). Satan is the personal "Enemy" of Jesus (13:25, 39), and they, too, are the enemies of Jesus, bent on destroying him (12:14; 26:3–4).

But the Jewish crowds also stand under the influence of Satan. True, they trail after Jesus (4:25), are astonished at his teaching and miracles and praise God for the latter,[19] and hold him to be a prophet (16:14; 21:46). Still, they never receive him for the one he is, Israel's Davidic Messiah and God's Son. Instead, they repudiate him (11:16–19; 27:25), and as he hangs upon the cross, they put him to the test (27:40). To the crowds, too, Jesus ascribes the epithet "this [evil] generation" (11:16).

Nor does the circle of the disciples escape the machinations of Satan. Peter "stands in" for Satan as he rejects the notion that Jesus should submit, in obedience to God, to suffering and death (16:21–23). In addition, those who follow Jesus are continually in danger of becoming servants of "lawlessness" and "evil," of which Satan is the root source.[20] To meet this danger, Jesus instructs the disciples in the Lord's Prayer to petition God, ". . . but deliver us from the Evil One" (6:13).

In sum, following God's baptismal declaration Jesus Son of God proves, in conflict with Satan, that he is perfect in obedience to God and superior in strength to Satan. Although Satan, the transcendent fountainhead of evil, continues to vie with Jesus Son of God in this age for the allegiance of

---

18. Cf. 11:16; 12:39, 41, 42, 45; 16:4; 23:36.
19. Cf. 7:28; 9:33; 15:31.
20. Cf. 5:37; 7:16–20; 13:49; 15:19; 18:32; 20:15; 25:26; 7:21–23; 24:12.

humans, at the consummation he, his angels, and all those who give him their fealty will be consigned by Jesus to perdition.

The Relocation of Jesus

To conclude the first part of his story (1:1—4:16), Matthew tells of Jesus' return to Galilee and the completion of his "preliminary" travels. If Joseph settled in Nazareth after the return from Egypt (2:22–23), Jesus now leaves Nazareth and moves to Capernaum (4:12–13), which becomes "his own city" (9:1). He is thus poised to begin his public ministry.

SUMMARY

Matthew employs the first part of his story (1:1—4:16) to present Jesus, the protagonist, to the implied reader. Through the device of the genealogy, Matthew advances an initial evaluative point of view concerning Jesus' identity, namely, that God has so guided Israelite history that it might reach its culmination in the birth of Jesus, the Messiah-King from the line of David and Abraham (1:1–17).

Preeminently, however, Jesus is the Son of God. In 1:1, Matthew makes no mention of this, perhaps because the genealogy begins not with God and with Adam (Luke 3:38), but with Abraham (Matt. 1:2). Still, although Abraham, not God, is the first link in the genealogy, the "origin" of Jesus is nonetheless to be traced to God. Conceived in Mary by the divinely wrought act of God's Holy Spirit, Jesus is without human father (1:16, 18, 20). As Matthew says in an "aside" to the implied reader, Jesus is "God with us," that is, the Son of God (1:23; cf. 2:15). What "Son of God" connotes is the unique filial relationship Jesus has with God, his Father (3:16–17; 11:27). In Jesus Son of God, one encounters God (11:27).

After Jesus has been born, Herod the Great threatens his life (Matthew 2). In his conflict with Jesus, Herod is the precursor of both Pilate and the leaders of the Jews.

To prepare for the ministry of Jesus, John the Baptist undertakes his ministry to Israel (3:1–12). As the forerunner of Jesus, he typifies in his person and work the person and work of Jesus. The division in Israel that John occasions foreshadows the division Jesus, too, will at first encounter: the favorable response of the people contrasts with the obduracy of the Jewish leaders.

The climax of the first part of Matthew's story occurs in the baptismal pericope (3:13–17). In the revelatory events that follow Jesus' baptism, God empowers Jesus with his Spirit and declares over him and in the hearing of the world of transcendent beings that Jesus is his unique Son whom he has chosen for messianic ministry (3:16–17; 4:3, 6). Here God himself enters the world of Matthew's story as "actor" and enunciates that evaluative point of view concerning Jesus' identity which is normative for all other evaluative points of view.

Declared by God to be his Son, Jesus enters into cosmic conflict with Satan (4:1–11). Withstanding the testing of Satan, Jesus Son of God proves himself to be perfect in obedience to God and superior in power to Satan. Although Satan will contend with Jesus for the allegiance of humans until the end of time, Jesus' victory over Satan assures the implied reader that the Son of God and the Kingdom of God will ultimately prevail.

On hearing news that John the Baptist has been "delivered up" and taken into custody, Jesus returns to Galilee and completes his preliminary travels by moving from Nazareth to Capernaum (4:12–16). All is now right for him to embark on his ministry to Israel.

3
The Ministry of Jesus to Israel and Israel's Repudiation of Jesus (4:17—16:20)

IF in the first part of his story Matthew presents Jesus to the implied reader, in the second part (4:17—16:20) he tells of Jesus' ministry to Israel (4:17—11:1) and of Israel's repudiation of him (11:2—16:20). In describing the repudiation of Jesus, Matthew also treats the wonderment and speculation about his identity evoked by his public activity in Israel.

THE MINISTRY OF JESUS TO ISRAEL

The ministry of Jesus Messiah, the Son of God, to Israel (4:17—11:1) is one of teaching, preaching, and healing. To apprise the implied reader of this, Matthew punctuates the narrative with three summary-passages (4:23; 9:35; 11:1). To launch his ministry, Jesus openly proclaims, "Repent, for the Kingdom of Heaven is at hand!" (4:17). Through this message, Jesus proffers salvation to Israel. He, like John the Baptist before him (3:2), looks on Israel as a people that has lost its way. The crowds are "harassed" and "helpless," like sheep left to fend for themselves (9:36). The leaders have become evil (12:34–35), unable to discern the will of God. Jesus summons both crowds and leaders to turn about and to live in the sphere of God's Rule by becoming his followers and, through him, sons of God (5:45; 13:38) and brothers of himself and of one another (12:48–50; 23:8). Next, Jesus calls particular individuals to become his disciples, in so doing surrounding himself with eye- and ear-witnesses (4:18–22). Followed by them and attracting huge crowds (4:23–25), he ascends a mountain and there programmatically teaches the will of God (5:1—7:29). Then, wandering in the area of Capernaum and traveling across the Sea of Galilee and back, he performs ten mighty acts of deliverance, at the same time setting forth the nature and cost of discipleship (8:1—9:34). At the height of his activity, he commissions the twelve to a ministry of their own in Israel, one of preaching and healing though not of teaching (9:35—10:42). This ministry of the disciples is an extension of his own ministry (10:5b–6; 15:24).

Because Jesus' ministry of teaching, preaching, and healing is a proffering of salvation to Israel, the element of conflict does not dominate the plot of Matthew's story in 4:17—11:1. Nevertheless, the implied reader is made to sense tension between Jesus and the Jewish leaders and, in fact, become witness to their first disputes.

Thus, in Matt. 4:17—8:34 the implied reader is led merely to anticipate conflict. Scenes or statements occur that tell of persecution after the manner of the prophets (5:10–12); of the scribes and Pharisees as practicing a righteousness that falls short of what is necessary for gaining entrance into the Kingdom of Heaven (5:20); of the "hypocrites" in the synagogues as performing their acts of piety so as to enhance their personal prestige in the public eye (6:1–18); of the teaching of the scribes as being without authority and therefore unlike that of Jesus (7:29); of the sons of the Kingdom as being cast into the darkness outside while Gentiles sit at table in the future Kingdom with Abraham, Isaac, and Jacob (8:11–12); and of a scribe as being turned away by Jesus because he would arrogate to himself the authority to become Jesus' disciple (8:19–20).

In Matthew 9, the conflict the implied reader has been led to anticipate materializes between Jesus and the Jewish leaders. This conflict, however, is carefully orchestrated so that Jesus is not directly attacked for something he himself does. Instead, one observes that scribes, watching Jesus forgive a paralytic his sins, declare "within themselves" that Jesus is guilty of committing blasphemy (9:3–4); that Pharisees, in seeing Jesus sit at table with toll-collectors and sinners, approach the disciples and complain to them about Jesus (9:10–11); that disciples of John, siding on one occasion with the Pharisees, take exception to the fact that Jesus' disciples are not observing the custom of fasting and question Jesus about this (9:14); and that Pharisees, after witnessing the exorcism of a demon by Jesus, cast aspersions on Jesus' feat by claiming that he could do this only because he is in collusion with demonic forces (9:32–34).

Finally, in Matthew 10 Jesus reinforces, in ominous words he addresses to the disciples, the growing sense of the implied reader that the trend of Matthew's story is toward irreconcilable conflict between Jesus and the Jewish leaders. In his missionary discourse, Jesus describes for the disciples the bitter conflict they can expect to encounter as they go out to preach and heal in Israel (10:5b–42). With the conclusion of this discourse, the implied reader no longer doubts that the time is fast approaching when the Jewish leaders will confront Jesus personally and attack him directly.

The Preaching of Jesus

As I noted, Jesus begins his ministry to Israel by preaching *(kēryssein)*, and his message is about the Kingdom of Heaven (4:17, 23; 9:35). Before him, John the Baptist proclaimed the Kingdom (3:2), and after him the pre-

Easter and the post-Easter disciples will do the same (10:7; 24:14). This is significant in Matthew's story, because it is in the proclamation of the Kingdom that there is continuity of ministry and message among John, Jesus, the earthly disciples, and the post-Easter church. To put it differently, what Matthew wants the implied reader to observe is that throughout the entire "time of Jesus (earthly—exalted)," which extends from his birth to his Parousia and encompasses the successive ministries of John, Jesus, the disciples, and the post-Easter church, the message of the Kingdom has been, is being, and will be proclaimed.

Matthew designates the message of both Jesus himself and the post-Easter church as "the gospel of the Kingdom" (4:23; 9:35; 24:14). What does the term "gospel" mean? To get at this, the passage 26:6–13 is helpful, for it reveals that the gospel is inextricably bound up with Jesus (what he has said or done or what has happened to him) and begs to be proclaimed to the world. Accordingly, the term "gospel" in the expression "the gospel of the Kingdom" may be defined as the news about the Kingdom (which saves or condemns) which is revealed in and through Jesus Messiah, the Son of God, and is announced first to Israel and then to the Gentiles.

What is the meaning of the term "Kingdom"? To begin with, the absolute designation "the Kingdom" is simply an abbreviation of the fuller idiom "the Kingdom of Heaven." Although statistics show that Matthew prefers the latter to "the Kingdom of God," the two expressions are virtually synonymous. Because the genitive "(of) Heaven" is subjective in nuance and a metonym for "God," the purpose of the expression "the Kingdom of Heaven" is to assert the truth that "God rules (reigns)." Hence, "the Rule of God," or "the Reign of God," is a proper paraphrase.

Jesus announces, as do John the Baptist and the disciples, that "the Kingdom of Heaven is at hand (ēggiken)" (3:2; 4:17; 10:7). The Greek verb ēggiken in these capsule statements connotes a "coming near," an "approaching," that is spatial or temporal in nature. Consequently, what John, Jesus, and the disciples proclaim to Israel is that the Rule of God has drawn near.

On balance, then, what is the meaning of the expression "the gospel of the Kingdom"? As has been seen, the focus of the term "gospel" is on Jesus Messiah, the Son of God. The focus of the term "Kingdom" is on God. Still, even the term "Kingdom" is not without christological import, for Matthew states in words of the OT in 1:23 that it is in the son born to the virgin that God draws near to dwell with his people. In line with these emphases, therefore, the entire expression "the gospel of the Kingdom" may be defined as the news (that saves or condemns) which is revealed in and through Jesus Messiah, the Son of God, and is proclaimed first to Israel and then to the Gentiles to the effect that in him the eschatological Rule of God has drawn near to humankind.

To define the expression "the gospel of the Kingdom" is already to have begun scrutiny of the broad concept of "the Kingdom of Heaven" or the Rule of God. The manner in which this concept is used in Matthew's story presupposes that the implied reader has knowledge of its OT rootage. Although it does not occur in the OT as a fixed phrase, the idea that "God rules," that he is "King," is one of Israel's elemental affirmations.[1]

According to first-century Jewish thought, God's kingly Rule is "eternal" and encompasses the entire world and all its nations and powers. In the present age, however, God's sovereignty is fully acknowledged only in Israel. Nevertheless, the day is rapidly approaching when God will suddenly break into history, openly manifest himself in splendor as the ruler of all, and in so doing free his people from heathen bondage and subject all nations to his holy will.

Within his own world of thought, Matthew highlights three dimensions of the Kingdom of Heaven: the "salvation-historical," the "cosmic," and the "existential." The "salvation-historical" dimension refers to the fact that the Kingdom is a transcendent, eschatological reality that confronts people already in the present but will be consummated only in the future. John, Jesus, and the disciples, it was said, proclaim to Israel that the Kingdom of Heaven is at hand (*ēggiken*). The verb *ēggiken* connotes, as I observed, a "coming near," an "approaching," that is spatial or temporal in nature. "Spatially" the Kingdom has drawn near because God in the person of his Son Jesus even now resides with those who live in the sphere of his Rule (1:23; 18:20; 28:20). Under the aegis of the earthly and exalted Son of God, the will of the Father who is in heaven is not hidden but known on earth, and the disciples of Jesus respond to it with lives that reflect the greater righteousness.[2]

"Temporally," too, the Kingdom of Heaven has drawn near. Although the Kingdom belongs to the future, in the person of Jesus Son of God it has come upon the present so as radically to qualify it.[3] Consequently, the present is to be viewed in light of the future and everything seen as moving toward the consummation and the Parousia of Jesus in his role as the Son of man.[4]

The "spatial" and the "temporal" aspects of the drawing near of the Kingdom of Heaven are part and parcel of its "eschatological" nature. Associated with this adjective are notions about both the time and the ultimate significance of the Kingdom. For example, the Kingdom of Heaven is an eschatological reality because the proclamation of its nearness occurs

1. Cf. Exod. 15:18; Deut. 33:5; Pss. 47:2; 93:1; 96:10; 103:19; 145:13.
2. Cf. 5:17–20; 6:10; 11:25–27; 12:50; 13:38, 43; 16:19; 18:18; 28:18.
3. Cf. 3:2, 11–12; 4:17; 10:7; 11:2–6; 13:16–17.
4. Cf. 5:3–10; 13:39–40, 49; 24:3; 28:20.

in the "time of Jesus (earthly—exalted)," that is, the "last times" that precede the consummation and are inaugurated by the birth of Jesus.[5]

But the Kingdom is also an eschatological reality because the proclamation of its nearness is of ultimate significance for both Israel and the Gentiles. The nub of this proclamation is, after all, that God with his Rule has in fact drawn near to humankind in his Son Jesus. In such proclamation, Israel and the nations encounter the Rule of God, a Rule that, again, is tending toward its consummation. God's will is that the proclamation of his Kingdom be received with repentance and faith, and that people enter the sphere of his sovereignty to their salvation (4:17; 24:14). They can, however, reject this proclamation and at the last perish (12:41).

As is apparent, the Kingdom of Heaven is a reality that can only be described in terms of both the present and the future. Indeed, the verb *ēggiken* harbors within it this very tension between present and future. On the one hand it connotes that the Kingdom is indeed near, so near that in the person of the earthly and exalted Son of God the authority, or power, of God impinges on and decisively qualifies the present. On the other hand, it connotes that the Kingdom has not yet arrived, for God has not yet miraculously consummated his Rule in all visible glory and might. When will this take place? As the apocalyptic Son-of-man sayings stipulate, this will take place at the end of the age when Jesus returns for judgment.

If the verb *ēggiken* embodies a tension between the present and future modes of the Kingdom, in numerous places in Matthew's story the stress is more clearly on either the one pole or the other. Thus, in a wide variety of ways the conviction comes to expression that God has been, or is presently, at work in his Son Jesus to visit people with his Rule. It is this conviction, for instance, that lies at the basis of the whole schema of prophecy and fulfillment and that explains why Jesus stands forth as a figure of such authority that he delivers the Sermon on the Mount as one who stands above Moses (Matthew 5—7) and also dares to forgive sins (9:2–6). It is also this conviction that surfaces in such sayings of Jesus as these: "From the days of John the Baptist until now the Kingdom of Heaven has suffered violence, and violent ones plunder it" (11:12);[6] and ". . . if I by the Spirit of God cast out demons, then the Kingdom of God has come upon you" (12:28). And it is furthermore this conviction that informs the use Jesus makes of the term *makarios* ("blessed"), whereby he portrays the present in

5. Cf. 1:22–23; 3:1–2; 4:17; 10:7; 24:3, 14.

6. Who, specifically, are these "violent ones"? From Matthew's perspective, they are the devil and all the false disciples, Israelites, and Gentiles who are his "sons" ("the sons of the Evil One"): those who resist the Rule of God and "plunder" it in that through various means they lead the "sons of the Kingdom" astray and bring them to fall (cf., e.g., 7:15–23; 12:45d; 13:19–21, 38–39, 49; 23:13; 24:9–11; 25:41–46).

light of the future and gives expression to that unique religious joy that springs from those who even now share in the salvation God will bestow on all who live in the sphere of his Rule.[7]

While due emphasis is placed in Matthew's story on the fact that God is presently at work in his Son Jesus to bring his eschatological Kingdom to people, a more vivid picture emerges of the future consummation of the Kingdom. In this regard, Jesus Son of God assumes the role of the Son of man of OT prophecy, and the event that marks the coming of the future Kingdom is described as unfolding in the following sequence: the forces of nature will suddenly fall into disarray; Jesus will be seen coming on the clouds of heaven in power and great glory; all the nations will be gathered before him, he will separate them into two groups, and he will pronounce judgment on them, thus determining who will "inherit the Kingdom" that has been prepared from the foundation of the world and who will "go away into eternal punishment."[8]

Matthew is at pains in his story to show that the Kingdom of the future is continuous with God's kingly activity in the present. Jesus' parables of the tares (13:24–30), mustard seed (13:31–32), leaven (13:33), and net (13:47–50) illustrate this well. Matthew is also concerned to show that the future Kingdom means, for Jesus and the righteous, vindication and the perfect realization of hope. With respect to Jesus, the irony is that he who suffers crucifixion at the hands of Jew and Gentile and is utterly rejected is the very man (i.e., the Son of man) whom God has chosen to return at the consummation as the judge and ruler of all.[9] To Jesus as well the saying applies: "For there is nothing hidden which shall not be revealed . . ." (10:26).

With respect to the righteous, one encounters a wide variety of word-pictures that characterize the future Kingdom as the perfect realization of hope. For example, the future Kingdom is portrayed as a realm the righteous will "enter,"[10] "go into" (21:31), or "inherit" (25:34); and what these idioms signify is evident from parallel passages that tell of "entering life" (18:8–9; 19:17), "entering the joy of your Lord" (25:21, 23), or "inheriting eternal life" (19:29). Of course the contrary is equally true: one can "not enter,"[11] be shut out (25:10), or be "thrown out"[12] and therefore excluded from the latter-day Kingdom.

Accordingly, one of the dimensions of the Kingdom of Heaven Matthew highlights is the "salvation-historical." A second dimension is the "cosmic." The "cosmic" dimension of the Kingdom has to do with its growth. The

---

7. Cf. 5:3–11; 11:6; 13:16–17; 16:17; 24:45–47.
8. Cf. 25:31–46; 13:40–43; 16:27; 24:29–31, 37–39, 44, 50.
9. Cf., e.g., 16:21, 28; 17:22–23; 20:18–19; 13:41–43; 25:31–46.
10. Cf. 5:20; 7:21; 18:3; 19:23–24; also 23:13.
11. Cf. 5:20; 18:3; 13:42, 50; 22:13; 25:30.
12. Cf. 8:12; 13:42, 50; 22:13; 25:30.

notion that the Kingdom grows relates to Matthew's understanding of the course of the Kingdom in the world as a present reality that confronts people in the "time of Jesus (earthly—exalted)." God in heaven reigns over all things (11:25), but he has determined in the last times to draw near to humankind in the person of Jesus Messiah, his Son. Still, the nearness of God in the person of his Son, and by extension in the church's post-Easter proclamation of the gospel of the Kingdom, is not something unambiguous. On the contrary, it is something that can be perceived only by means of divine revelation (13:11; 16:16–17). Nevertheless, as the church in post-Easter times proclaims the gospel of the Kingdom to the nations,[13] persons will in truth be led to acknowledge the Rule of God in Jesus, his Son, and as they become disciples of Jesus, the Kingdom can in fact be described as growing. Finally, at the consummation of the age, God in the person of Jesus, as the Son of man of OT prophecy, will wondrously establish his Rule in glory over all the "tribes of the earth" (24:30). Thus, the course of the Kingdom in the world during the "time of Jesus" is that from the "small beginnings" of Jesus Messiah, the Son of God, and his initial disciples, the Kingdom, through the agency of the post-Easter church,[14] "grows" as the gospel is proclaimed to the nations, and, at the last, when Jesus shall burst into history as the Son of man, this Kingdom will visibly be established over all and hence be cosmic in scope.[15]

Along with the "salvation-historical" and the "cosmic" dimensions of the Kingdom of Heaven, Matthew also stresses the "existential," or the personal, dimension. This dimension I have already touched on in connection with the beginning of Jesus' ministry to Israel, for it concerns the new life that can result from one's encounter with the Rule of God. The occasion for such encounter is, of course, the presence of the Kingdom in the person and words and deeds of Jesus Messiah, the Son of God. Encounter with Jesus places a person in a crisis of decision.[16] The choice is between "repenting" and "entering" the gracious sphere of the Kingdom[17] and rejecting Jesus as the Messiah (cf. Matthew 11—12). In Matthew's own time following the resurrection, encounter with the church's proclamation of the gospel of the Kingdom precipitates the same crisis of decision.[18] One either "understands" the word (13:23) and is "baptized" and observes all that

---

13. Cf. 24:14; 26:13; 28:18–20.

14. Cf. 13:47; 28:18–20.

15. This view of the growth of the Kingdom is documented particularly well in several of the parabolic units in Matthew, to wit: the parables of the mustard seed (13:31–32), of the leaven (13:33), of the net (13:47–50), of the last judgment (25:31–46), and the interpretation of the parable of the tares (13:36–43).

16. Cf. 4:17; 10:34–35; 11:3–6, 20; 12:41; 13:9, 43b.

17. Cf. 4:17; 11:20; 12:41; also 21:31.

18. Cf. 10:18; 24:14; also 10:13–15, 20, 27, 40; 23:34.

Jesus has commanded (28:19–20), or one does "not understand" the word and consequently falls under the power of Satan (13:19, 38d–39). Whoever receives Jesus may be likened to a "good tree" that produces "good fruit"[19] or to a "good man" who brings forth "good things" out of his "good treasure" (12:35)—that is to say, this person, like Jesus Son of God himself, "does the will of the heavenly Father."[20] Such a person abounds in righteousness more than the scribes and Pharisees (5:20) and will, at the coming of Jesus, be identified by him as one of the "righteous"[21] who will "inherit eternal life" (25:46) and "shine [in perfection] as the sun in the Kingdom of their Father" (13:43).

On the other hand, those who have fallen under the power of Satan are "evil ones"[22] who may be likened to a "bad tree" that produces "bad fruit"[23] or to an "evil man" who brings forth "evil things" from his "evil treasure" (12:35). At the latter day Jesus will designate these people as the "accursed" (25:41), and they will be cast into the "fiery furnace" (13:42; 25:41) or into the "outer darkness" (8:12), where they will experience "eternal punishment" (25:46), such as the "weeping and gnashing of teeth" (8:12; 13:42, 50). So again, encounter with the Kingdom means that a person must decide: will he or she enter the "narrow gate" and take the "hard way" that leads to "life," or will he or she enter the "wide gate" and take the "broad way" that leads to "destruction" (7:13–14)?

To conclude, at the center of Jesus' preaching in Matthew's story is the Kingdom of Heaven, or God's eschatological Rule. In Jesus' preaching, the Kingdom is salvation-historical, cosmic, and existential in nature. Salvation-historically, the Kingdom is a present, though hidden, reality in Jesus Son of God which is tending toward its consummation at the future coming of Jesus in his role as the Son of man. Cosmically, the Kingdom can be said to grow as God guides it from seemingly insignificant beginnings in the ministry of Jesus and his disciples to the point where he determines that it will, at the end of time, embrace the world and all the nations in it. And existentially, the presence of the Kingdom in the person and words and deeds of Jesus and in the gospel the post-Easter church will preach impels persons to decision: will they repent, become followers of Jesus, and enter the sphere of God's Rule or will they refuse such entrance and live in the sphere where Satan rules?

The Teaching of Jesus

In his ministry, Jesus Messiah, the Son of God, summons Israel to repentance and to entrance into the sphere of God's eschatological Rule.

19. Cf. 7:16–20; 12:33.
20. Cf. 26:42; 6:10; 7:21; 12:50.
21. Cf. 13:43, 49; 25:37, 46.
22. Cf. 13:19, 38d–39.
23. Cf. 7:17–18; 12:33.

Fundamentally, the teaching of Jesus envisages human conduct as it comports itself amid life in this sphere. By citing teaching *(didaskein)* ahead of preaching and healing in the summary-passages (4:23; 9:35; 11:1), Matthew gives it the position of stress and invites the implied reader to attach special importance to it.

Surprisingly, Jesus' teaching occasions less conflict in Matthew's story than one would expect. The reason is that the Jewish leaders are the recipients of none of the great discourses of Jesus (Matthew 5—7; 10; 13; 18; 24—25), and even Jesus' speech of woes is not delivered to the scribes and Pharisees but to the disciples and the crowds (Matthew 23). It is in certain of the debates Jesus has with the Jewish leaders that his teaching generates conflict. Almost always at issue is the correct interpretation of, or the proper adherence to, the Mosaic law or the Pharisaic tradition of the elders. Cases in point are those debates that deal with the practice of having table fellowship with toll-collectors and sinners (9:10–13); the non-observance of the custom of fasting (9:14–15); alleged violations of the sabbath law (12:1–8, 9–14); the disparagement of the tradition of the elders sparked by the charge of non-compliance with the ritual obligation of washing the hands before eating (15:1–20); the dispute over the question of divorce (19:3–9); the problem of the legality of paying taxes to Caesar (22:15–22); the argument (with the Sadducees) over the reality of the resurrection (22:23–33); and the questions relating to the greatest commandment of the law (22:34–40) and to the Davidic sonship of the Messiah (22:41–46). These issues constitute an index of the "flash points" that motivate the Jewish leaders not only to oppose Jesus but also to conspire to take his life (12:14; 22:46). In their eyes, Jesus is a threat to the continued existence of Jewish society, for he places himself above law and tradition. In Jesus' perspective, the debates concerning law and tradition are all to be resolved by the proper application of one basic principle, or better, of a single attitude of the heart, namely, utter devotion to God and radical love of the neighbor (5:48; 22:37–40).

Taken as a group, the debates Jesus has with the Jewish leaders are glaring indication that the distance between him and them is unbridgeable. A more subtle indication of this distance is the manner in which Matthew makes use of the synonymous terms "rabbi" and "teacher." When the true disciples and those minor characters who exhibit faith call on Jesus, they do so as "Lord," acknowledging thereby that he is one of exalted station who exercises divine authority.[24] By contrast, when the Jewish leaders, a stranger, or the traitor Judas address Jesus, it is as "rabbi" or "teacher."[25] On one occasion Jesus himself refers to himself as "teacher," but he points out

24. Cf. e.g., 8:2, 6, 8, 21, 25; 9:28; 14:28, 30; 15:22, 25, 27; 16:22; 17:4, 15; 18:21; 20:30, 31, 33; 26:22.

25. Cf. 8:19; [9:11]; 12:38; [17:24]; 19:16; 22:16, 24, 36; 26:25, 49.

in this connection that it is as "the Messiah" that he is teacher (23:8–10). And on one occasion Jesus instructs the disciples to refer to him as "teacher," but this is in connection with a conversation they are to have with a stranger in which "teacher" expresses the way this man will regard Jesus (26:17–19). The thing to notice in all this is that the designations "rabbi" and "teacher" attribute to the person so addressed human respect, but nothing more. Hence, in addressing Jesus as "teacher," the leaders of the Jews accord Jesus the honor they would accord any teacher, but that is the extent of it. To their mind Jesus' station is not that of the Messiah Son of God, his authority is not divine, and they in no sense follow him or have faith in him.

In substance, Jesus' teaching is the exposition of the will of God in terms of its original intention (19:4, 8). Three examples in particular illustrate this. In debate with the Pharisees and scribes from Jerusalem, Jesus introduces his quotation of the law not with the words "For Moses said . . . ," but with the words "For God said . . ." (15:4). Again, in debate with the Pharisees on divorce Jesus flatly declares that the will of Moses is to be looked on as having been transcended by the will of God (19:4, 7–9). Last, in debate with the Sadducees over the question of the resurrection, Jesus refutes their argument with the telling question, ". . . have you not read what was said to you by God . . ." (22:31). Plainly, Jesus advances the claim in his teaching that he is the supreme arbiter of the will of God.

Integral to this claim of Jesus is yet another claim that is no less weighty, namely, that what he teaches is of permanent validity. As far as the activity of preaching goes, Jesus does this, but so do John, the pre-Easter disciples, and the post-Easter church. But when it comes to teaching, Jesus alone is the one who undertakes this. Never is it even intimated that John or the pre-Easter disciples teach, and when the exalted Jesus commissions the post-Easter disciples to go to the nations, it is no accident that what they are given to teach is "all that *I* have commanded you" (28:20). As Jesus says in his eschatological discourse, "Heaven and earth shall pass away, but my words shall not pass away" (24:35).

Part and parcel of Jesus' teaching of the will of God is his teaching of the law of Moses. For purposes of clarification, the term "law" (*nomos*), when used by itself in Matthew's story,[26] does not refer merely to the so-called Ten Commandments but, more broadly, to the five books of Moses, or the Pentateuch. Similarly, the expression "the law and the prophets" denotes quite simply the whole of the OT as it is known to Matthew, the implied author, and functions as scripture.[27]

To determine Jesus' attitude toward the law of Moses in Matthew's story,

26. Cf. 5:18; 12:5; 15:6; 22:36; 23:23.
27. Cf. 5:17; 7:12; 11:13; 22:40.

the place to begin is with the programmatic statements Jesus makes in the Sermon on the Mount concerning the law and the prophets (5:17–20).[28] As Jesus sees it, the law and the prophets serve two purposes: they function ethically as a norm of human behavior,[29] and they function salvation-historically in that they prophesy the time of fulfillment (11:13). In the passage 5:17–20, Jesus attests to both these purposes. He asserts in 5:17 that, salvation-historically, he has come not to annul the law or the prophets, but to fulfill them—that is to say, to bring them to completion. In what way does Jesus accomplish such fulfillment, or completion? He does so by being who he is (the Messiah Son of God) and through what he both says and does. Here in the Sermon on the Mount, the focus is, as the introduction stipulates (5:2), on the words, or teaching, of Jesus. Hence, as far as the law and the prophets as functioning ethically as a norm of human behavior are concerned, a primary way in which this norm receives its final revelation is in the teaching of Jesus.

Following v. 17 in the passage 5:17–20, Jesus no longer speaks of law and prophets but solely of the law. The law is, as I mentioned, the law of Moses. But again, it is the law of Moses as it is being taught by Jesus. In the final analysis, therefore, what Jesus says about the law applies to it as something being authoritatively reinterpreted by his teaching. It is not the Mosaic law in and of itself which has normative and abiding character for disciples, but the Mosaic law as it has passed through the crucible of Jesus' teaching.[30]

To continue with 5:17–20, Jesus affirms that until heaven and earth pass away at the consummation of the age, the law will retain its validity so that all the things of the law might be done (5:18). Exactly how one is to construe all the things of the law as being done comes to light, as will soon be seen, in Jesus' teaching of love as that which lies at the heart of the whole of the law (and the prophets) (22:37–40). With this in mind, not even the most insignificant commandment is to be broken, by what a disciple does or by what a disciple teaches (5:19). Indeed, so serious is the breaking and keeping of commandments that it will affect a disciple's "ranking" in the consummated Kingdom of Heaven (5:19). In sum, the righteousness the disciples are to evince in their lives is a conduct that shows itself to be superior to ("greater" than) that which typifies the scribes and Pharisees (5:20).

28. More recent investigations of Matt. 5:17–20 and, in general, of Jesus' attitude toward the law are those of Banks ("Matthew's Understanding," 226–42), Sand (*Gesetz und Propheten*), Meier (*Law and History*, esp. 41–171), Gerhardsson ("Hermeneutic Program," 129–50), Luz ("Erfüllung des Gesetzes," 398–435), Broer (*Gesetz und Radikalisierung*, 11–74), Guelich (*Sermon on the Mount*, esp. 134–74), Martin ("Christ and the Law," 53–70), Strecker (*Bergpredigt*, 55–64), and Betz ("Hermeneutical Principles," 37–53).

29. That the law and the prophets (i.e., the scriptures) do function in this manner is plainly indicated in Matt. 7:12 and 22:40.

30. Cf. 5:18, 21–48; 22:37–40; 24:35; 28:20.

In the portion of the Sermon on the Mount which follows 5:17–20, Jesus expounds on the "greater righteousness" that the disciples, as those who live under his aegis in the sphere of God's eschatological Rule, are to practice. It is radical in nature and has to do with conduct toward God and toward the neighbor. As conduct toward God, it comes to expression in such fundamental acts of piety as almsgiving, prayer, and fasting when they are done not for public show, but in the spirit of true worship (6:1–18). As conduct toward the neighbor, the greater righteousness is epitomized in the antitheses (5:21–48), those authoritative sayings of Jesus which appear as variations of the formula "You have heard that it was said to the men of old . . . but I say to you. . . ." As the antitheses prescribe, the disciple is not only not to kill, but not even to become enraged (5:21–26); not only not to commit adultery, but not even to lust (5:27–30); not merely to comply with the law in obtaining a divorce, but not to divorce at all (5:31–32);[31] not merely to obey the law and not swear falsely, but not to swear at all (5:33–37); not merely to adhere to the law in securing retribution, but to offer no resistance at all to one who would harm or exploit the disciple (5:38–42); and not merely to love the neighbor while hating the enemy, but not to hate the enemy at all but instead to love him (5:43–48).

Is there a center to Jesus' radical teaching concerning the life of the greater righteousness, the law, and, in general, the will of God? The answer is yes, and this center is "love." In the pericope on the Great Commandment (22:34–40),[32] Jesus declares that the first and greatest commandment is that "You shall love the Lord your God with all your heart, and with all your soul, and with all your mind" (22:37–38; Deut. 6:5). Wholly to love God as Jesus here enjoins is (a) to give to him one's total allegiance; (b) to serve him even to the point of surrendering one's life if necessary; and (c) so to administer one's substance (position and property) that it attests to one's complete devotion to him. And the second commandment, which is like the first, is, Jesus asserts, that "You shall love your neighbor as yourself" (22:39; Lev. 19:18). By finding in these two commandments the ground, or the intention, of all the precepts of the law and, indeed, of the entire will of God as set forth in the whole of the OT scriptures (cf. Matt. 22:40), Jesus advances no less a claim than that keeping the law or doing the will of God is always, in essence, an exercise in love.

That "love" is the deepest intention of the will of God as taught by Jesus is also apparent from other passages in Matthew's story. In the verse that concludes the antitheses in the Sermon on the Mount, Jesus mandates that disciples be "perfect" (teleios), that is, give demonstration of their love of

---

31. For a survey and critique of various ways in which this antithesis on divorce has been interpreted, cf. Vawter ("Divorce Clauses," 155–67), Meier (Law and History, 140–50), and Martin ("Christ and the Law," 55 n. 12).

32. Cf. Gerhardsson, "Hermeneutic Program," 129–50.

God by rendering to God wholehearted devotion (5:48; Deut. 18:13). At the end of the Sermon on the Mount, Jesus enjoins love of neighbor by citing the "golden rule": "So whatever you wish that men would do to you, you do so to them" (Matt. 7:12). In the pericope on the rich young man, Jesus proffers the man eternal life by summoning him to discipleship, at the core of which is, again, love of neighbor (19:16–21). In his speech of woes against the scribes and Pharisees, Jesus designates "mercy" (i.e., love), along with justice and faithfulness, as comprising the weightier matters of the law (23:23). In the pericopes on plucking grain on the sabbath and on healing the withered hand, Jesus twice suppresses the sabbath law in favor of the law of love (12:7, 12). And in the pericope on the call of Matthew, Jesus has table fellowship with toll-collectors and sinners, thereby showing that mercy, or love, takes precedence over Pharisaic rules regarding ritual uncleanness (9:10–13).

A word is yet in order about Jesus' attitude toward the Pharisaic tradition of the elders. This tradition was, historically, oral in form. It consisted of a vast number of regulations, regarded as obligatory for the individual Jew, the purpose of which was to make the law of Moses applicable to new times and new circumstances. As was indicated in passing above, Jesus appears to take a dim view of this tradition as giving expression to the will of God. In 16:11–12, he warns the disciples to beware of the teaching of the Pharisees and Sadducees, for it is, like leaven, corrupting. In chapter 23, it is with bitter sarcasm that he attacks Pharisaic theology and practice.[33] In 15:3–6 he declares that on the matter of "Corban" (in this instance, dedicating to God and thus craftily keeping for oneself the "gift" that otherwise should have been set aside for the support of one's parents), the tradition of the elders nullifies the word of God itself. In 15:20, Jesus sets aside the stipulated ritual of the tradition of the elders of not eating with unwashed hands. And in 9:10–13, Jesus ignores Pharisaic regulation that would impute ritual uncleanness to him for eating with toll-collectors and sinners in order to symbolize hereby the forgiveness of sins he grants them and the future fellowship they will enjoy with him in the consummated Kingdom of Heaven. But if all these words and deeds of Jesus suggest a wholesale rejection on his part of the tradition of the elders, it cannot be denied that at 23:2–3 he gives the crowds and the disciples to understand that "the scribes and the Pharisees sit on Moses' seat, so practice and observe whatever they tell you"; and that in 23:23 he seems to speak approvingly of the Pharisaic rule concerning the tithing of mint and dill and cummin ("but these things one ought to have done"). To date, no scholarly proposal for resolving these apparent contradictions has proved itself entirely satisfactory. Nonetheless, one thing is certain: in the world of Matthew's story, the norm for

---

33. On the exposition of Matthew 23, cf. Garland, *Intention of Matthew 23*.

judging whether the observance of any aspect of the tradition of the elders fosters the doing of the will of God is whether such observance expresses wholehearted devotion to God or radical love of the neighbor.

In summary, Jesus' teaching in Matthew's story sets forth the will of God in terms of its original intention. For disciples, this teaching has both normative and abiding character.

The Healing of Jesus

Along with teaching and preaching, healing *(therapeuein)*, too, is singled out in the summary-passages as being typical of Jesus' ministry to Israel (4:23; 9:35). Also through healing Jesus summons Israel to repentance and to entrance into the sphere of God's eschatological Rule (11:20–24; 12:28).

Jesus heals, just as he likewise preaches and teaches, in his capacity as the Messiah Son of God (4:17, 23–25).[34] Still, Jesus Son of God is at the same time the servant of God (12:18), and the Greek verb *therapeuein* can mean to "serve" as well as to "heal." Indeed, it is to cast Jesus' activity of healing in the mold of "serving" that Matthew informs the implied reader in a formula-quotation that Jesus, through healing, fulfills the words of the Servant Song of Isaiah: "He took our infirmities and bore our diseases" (8:16–17; Isa. 53:4). In healing, Jesus Son of God assumes the role of the servant of God and ministers to Israel by restoring persons to health or freeing them from their afflictions (Matt. 11:5). Through serving in this fashion, Jesus "saves" (9:22).

The miracles themselves Jesus performs are termed "deeds of power" *(dynameis,* plural of *dynamis).*[35] The use of the term *dynamis* ("power") is itself revealing. *Dynamis* is associated with God (22:29) and can even be used, as Jesus does in the words of the psalmist, as a metaphor for "God" (26:64). Contrariwise, "power" in the sense of *dynamis* is not something that is predicated to Satan, demons, or the opponents of Jesus. On one occasion it is said of false prophets that they will perform deeds of power, but these are followers of Jesus who will do their miraculous, but lawless, works in his name and at the latter day be condemned by him (7:21–23). Otherwise, when the prediction is made that false messiahs and false prophets will arise and perform miracles, their acts are not termed deeds of power but "signs and wonders" (24:24). With respect to the latter, the doing of "wonders" *(terata)* is never ascribed to Jesus or to the disciples, and the "sign" *(sēmeion)* is characterized as a miraculous feat that the Jewish leaders demand of Jesus as they tempt him to prove he is not in collusion with Satan (12:24, 38; 16:1). The sign Jesus does give them, a word prophesying his death and resurrection (12:39–40), is not what they have in mind. When the

---

34. Cf. 8:29; 11:2–6; also 11:27; 14:22–33.

35. Important studies of the miracle-stories in Matthew are those of Held ("Matthew as Interpreter," 165–299) and of Gerhardsson *(Mighty Acts).*

death and resurrection occur, the leaders refuse to acknowledge them (27:62–64). But be that as it may, the logic of Matthew's world of thought is plain as regards Jesus' miracles: God, the source of "power," has empowered his Son Jesus with the Spirit; in consequence of this, the miracles Jesus performs are "deed of power" and not false "signs and wonders."

Jesus' activity of healing is the source of intense conflict between him and the Jewish leaders. It also creates division between the leaders and the crowds. The crowds witness Jesus' healings and glorify God because of them (9:8; 15:31) or exclaim that "Never was anything like this seen in Israel!" (9:33). The leaders witness Jesus' healings and charge him with exorcising demons on the authority of the prince of demons (9:34; 12:24) or accuse him of breaking the sabbath law (12:9–14). In point of fact, it is following Jesus' healing on the sabbath that Matthew reports for the first time that the Pharisees go out and take counsel against him, how to destroy him (12:9–14).

Whether extolled by the crowds or denounced by the leaders, Jesus' healings still do not move Israel to repentance and to recognition of him as its Messiah (11:20–24, 25). On this score, the healing ministry Jesus carries out specifically as the Son of David assumes significance.[36] In the pericopes that portray this ministry, those who appeal to, or hail, Jesus as the Son of David are blind men,[37] a Gentile woman (15:22), and children (21:15). These are minor characters in Matthew's story, disfranchised and counting for nothing in Jewish society. For them to approach or acclaim Jesus as Israel's Davidic Messiah is for them to "see" and to "confess" the truth with which the crowds only toy[38] and which the Jewish leaders will not even so much as entertain.[39] Accordingly, discernible in Jesus' healing as the Son of David is a polemical strain: such healing underlines the guilt that is Israel's for repudiating its Messiah.

The miracles Jesus performs in Matthew's story divide themselves rather neatly into two groups: (a) therapeutic miracles (miracles of healing), in which the sick are returned to health or the possessed are freed of demons (cf. esp. Matthew 8—9); and (b) non-therapeutic miracles, which have to do with exercising power over the forces of nature.[40] In the summary-passages devoted to Jesus' healing, it is exclusively the therapeutic miracles to which Matthew makes reference.[41] This has the effect of highlighting their promi-

36. Cf. 9:27–31; 12:22–23; 15:21–28; 20:29–34; 21:14–15.
37. Cf. 9:27–31; 20:29–34; also 12:22–23.
38. The question the crowds raise in 12:23 as to whether Jesus is the Son of David anticipates a negative answer, and in 21:9–11 the irony is that the crowds who hail Jesus as the Son of David understand him to be no more than a prophet.
39. Cf. 9:34 to 9:33; 12:24 to 12:23.
40. Cf. 8:23–27; 14:13–21, 22–33; 15:32–39; 17:24–27; 21:18–22.
41. Cf., e.g., 4:24; [11:5]; 15:30–31; 21:14.

nence as a part of Jesus' ministry. Moreover, it is also these miracles that create the stir in public: astonishment among the crowds[42] but disapprobation among the leaders (9:34; 12:24). In short, an essential mark of the therapeutic miracles is that they picture Jesus as being active in the full view of Israel.

As a group, the therapeutic miracles are remarkably uniform in structure and thematic.[43] The focus is squarely on Jesus and the suppliants, and the liberal use of direct speech lends immediacy to the encounter. For their part, the suppliants appeal to Jesus in great faith and with prayer-like petitions on behalf of themselves or of others for healing. Jesus, in turn, grants their requests of faith, doing so in a manner that corresponds to what was asked of him and that demonstrates the compassion, the will to heal, and the unparalleled authority that are his.

The non-therapeutic miracles are less uniform in structure and differ in thematic.[44] Here the focus is on Jesus and the disciples, and the characteristic feature is that Jesus reveals, in the midst of situations in which the disciples exhibit "little faith," his awesome authority. Then, too, the way in which Jesus reveals his authority is by exercising power over the forces of nature: he calms wind and wave (8:23–27), twice feeds the multitudes (14:13–21; 15:32–39), walks on water and rescues Peter from drowning (14:22–33), and curses a fig tree (21:18–22).[45] The reason Jesus gives the disciples these startling revelations is to bring them to realize that such authority as he exercises he makes available to them through the avenue of faith.[46] In the later situation of their worldwide mission, failure on the part of the disciples to avail themselves of the authority Jesus would impart to them will be to run the risk of failing at their tasks (28:18–20; 24—25).

To recapitulate, through healing Jesus summons the people of Israel to repentance and to the Kingdom, and he "serves" them by curing illnesses and releasing persons from their afflictions. Also, in exercising power over the forces of nature, he enables the disciples to catch a glimpse of the divine authority he is ever ready to share with them.

The Ministry of the Disciples to Israel

Thus far, Jesus has been calling Israel, through his ministry of teaching, preaching, and healing, to repentance and to entrance into the sphere of God's eschatological Rule. In extension of his ministry, Jesus now commissions the disciples to a ministry in Israel of their own (9:35—10:42). Except for the activity of teaching, which Jesus reserves for himself, the disciples are to do exactly as he has done. Like him, they are to restrict their activity

42. Cf. 9:8, 33; 12:23; 15:31.
43. Cf. Held, "Matthew as Interpreter," 241–46.
44. Cf. Gerhardsson, *Mighty Acts*, 52–67.
45. Cf. further 17:14–20, 24–27.
46. Cf. 8:25–26; 14:15–16; 15:33; 17:19–20; 21:18–22.

to Israel: "Go nowhere among the Gentiles," he commands them, "but go rather to the lost sheep of the house of Israel" (10:5–6; 15:24). Like him, they are to summon Israel to the Kingdom by proclaiming, "The Kingdom of Heaven is at hand!" (10:7; 4:17). And like him, they are to "heal every disease and every infirmity" among the people (10:1; 9:35; 4:23).

Peculiarly, Matthew never reports that the disciples actually undertake the ministry to Israel about which Jesus instructs them. Mention is made neither of their departure nor of their return (cf. 10:42—11:1). Instead, the bulk of Jesus' missionary discourse to the disciples dwells on the fierce conflict they can expect to encounter. As they discharge their ministry, they will be like sheep in the midst of wolves (10:16). Just as it has been said of Jesus that he acts in collusion with Satan (9:34; 12:24), so the same will be said of them (10:25). Indeed, in carrying out the mission with which Jesus is entrusting them, they must even be prepared, should this be necessary, to surrender their lives (10:17–18, 28, 38–39). In other words, the purpose that Jesus' speech to the disciples here in Matthew 10 serves within the plot of Matthew's story is by no means conventional: it does not tell of a ministry the disciples are subsequently described as actually carrying out. Instead, the purpose of this speech is to foreshadow the repudiation by Israel that Jesus himself is about to endure and that the disciples, in Matthew's own time following Easter, will also endure (22:1–10; 23:34–35).

ISRAEL'S REPUDIATION OF JESUS

The motif that dominates Matthew's story throughout 4:17—11:1 is Jesus' ministry to Israel of teaching, preaching, and healing (4:23; 9:35; 11:1). Through this ministry, Jesus summons Israel to repentance and to life in the sphere of God's eschatological Rule (4:17; 5:45). In 11:2—16:20, which comprises the latter half of the second part of Matthew's story (4:17—16:20), Israel's response to Jesus' ministry becomes the dominant motif. This response is one of repudiation, yet even as Israel repudiates Jesus, it wonders and speculates about his identity. The matter of Jesus' identity, then, surfaces as the second motif of importance in 11:2—16:20.

The pericopes that alert the implied reader to the centrality of these twin motifs are John the Baptist's question and Jesus' answer (11:2–6) and Jesus' rejection at Nazareth (13:53–58). These two pericopes stand out for two reasons: they are strategically located as far as the latter half of the second part of Matthew's story is concerned (11:2—16:20); and each one contains both a question having to do with Jesus' identity (11:3; 13:55) and a prominent reference to "taking offense" at him (11:6; 13:57).

The Repudiation of Jesus

As a result of Jesus' widespread activity of teaching, preaching, and healing, his fame spreads, throughout Palestine and even Syria.[47] The

47. Cf. 4:23–25; 9:26, 31, 33, 35; 11:2, 4; 13:54; 14:1.

crowds stream to him and follow him,[48] and the Jewish leaders place him under surveillance.[49] Still, the spread of Jesus' fame and the thronging to him of all manner of people are no indication that Israel has accepted him. Quite the contrary, Israel repudiates him (11:2—12:50), as the implied reader has well been forewarned.[50]

Thus, John the Baptist, perplexed because Jesus has not carried out the final judgment as he had anticipated (3:10–12), questions whether Jesus is in fact the Coming One (Messiah) he and his disciples have awaited (11:2–6). The Jewish crowds, decried by Jesus as "this [evil] generation," reject both John and Jesus: John, because they believe him to be possessed of a demon; and Jesus, because they take him to be a glutton and a drunkard, a friend of toll-collectors and sinners (11:16–19). The cities of Chorazin, Bethsaida, and Capernaum, in which Jesus has done most of his miracles, refuse to be moved to repentance (11:20–24). And how is the implied reader to understand that Jesus should meet with such rejection? In private prayer, Jesus explains his rejection by invoking the will of his Father (11:25–26).

Next, the leaders of the Jews clash with Jesus, and the level of tension in Matthew's story increases perceptibly. Two incidents occur, each for the first time. The one incident is that the Jewish leaders (the Pharisees), in charging the disciples with breaking the law by plucking grain on the sabbath and hence working, do what they heretofore have not done: they engage Jesus himself in direct debate (12:1–8). And the second incident is that the leaders not only engage Jesus himself in debate, but they do so for an action that they correctly anticipate he himself is about to take: Jesus is set to heal on the sabbath and therefore to make himself guilty in their eyes of breaking the law (12:9–14). In giving reply to the Jewish leaders, Jesus bases the defense of both the disciples and himself on the principle that mercy, or love, takes precedence over casuistry (12:7, 12). But as far as the plot of Matthew's story is concerned, it is at this latter juncture, where the Jewish leaders confront Jesus personally over an act of healing which he himself subsequently performs and which they hold to be a violation of the law, that Matthew somberly remarks, " . . . the Pharisees went out and took counsel against him, how to destroy him" (12:14). Given this narrative comment, the implied reader knows that the Jewish leaders' repudiation of Jesus has now become irreversible.

In the face of danger from the side of the Pharisees, Jesus temporarily withdraws (12:15). This, however, effects no reduction in the level of tension in the story: In the following scene the Jewish leaders for a second

48. Cf. 4:24–25; 8:1, 10; 9:33; 12:15; 13:2; 14:13; 15:30–31.
49. Cf. 9:3, 11, 34.
50. Cf. 2:3; 3:7–12; 9:3, 11, 14, 34; 10:5–42.

time accuse Jesus in their thoughts of exorcising demons on authority of the prince of demons; Jesus, knowing their thoughts, excoriates them as being evil (12:22–37). But this skirmish, in turn, only produces another. The Jewish leaders next demand of Jesus that he perform a sign so as to prove to them that he is not the agent of Satan but the agent of God (12:38–45). Jesus does give them a sign, but one they cannot immediately test, namely, the announcement of his death and resurrection (12:39–40). And last, like the others in Israel, even the family of Jesus deserts him, which leaves the disciples as the only ones who still adhere to him (12:46–50).

Repudiated by all segments of Israel, Jesus reacts by declaring that Israel has become hard of heart (13:13–15). Moreover, he gives public demonstration of this by addressing the crowds in parables, that is, in speech they cannot comprehend (13:2–3, 10–13). By contrast, he pronounces the disciples "blessed" (13:16–17) and instructs them in the mysteries of the Kingdom of Heaven (13:11, 36, 51).

Nor does Jesus fare any better in his home town of Nazareth. When the people hear him teach in the synagogue, his words astonish them but they take offense at him (13:54, 57). Even more ominously, news reaches Jesus that Herod Antipas has beheaded John the Baptist, his "forerunner" (14:1–13a; 11:10). This once again prompts Jesus to withdraw: embarking on a series of journeys, he travels to deserted places, back and forth across the sea, and into gentile lands.[51] Against this background of travel, Matthew brings the second part of his story to a close (4:17—16:20). The notion that Jesus, sensing mortal danger, takes evasive action[52] serves the larger motif that Israel has responded to his ministry (4:17—11:1) by repudiating him (11:2—16:20).

Conflicting Views About the Identity of Jesus

As I stated, entwined with the motif of repudiation in 11:2—16:20 is the motif of wonderment and speculation in Israel about the identity of Jesus. This motif of Jesus' identity serves the plot-device of conflict in Matthew's story because Israel shows itself to be ignorant of who Jesus is. Not only this, but Israel's ignorance is also made to contrast with the knowledge on this score of the disciples, the only group in Israel which still holds to Jesus.

The questioning begins with John the Baptist. Sitting in prison and wondering about Jesus' identity because he has not inaugurated the final judgment, John inquires of Jesus through his disciples, "Are you the Coming One, or do we await another?" (11:2–3). The Jewish crowds, amazed at a healing Jesus performs, ask even as they anticipate a negative reply, "This can't be the Son of David, can it?" (12:22–23). The townspeople of

---

51. Cf. 14:13, 22, 34; 15:21, 29 (33), 39; 16:4c–5, 13.
52. Cf. 12:14–15; 14:13—16:20; also 2:12, 13, 14, 22; 4:12.

Nazareth, astonished at the teaching of Jesus, question one another at the same time they take offense at him, "Isn't this the son of the carpenter?" (13:55). Herod Antipas, having heard news of Jesus, speculates about him: "This is John the Baptist, he has been raised from the dead, and therefore these powers are at work in him" (14:1-2). In contradistinction to the preceding, the disciples, having been caught in a storm at sea and having watched Jesus walk on water, rescue Peter from drowning, and calm the wind, worship him and confess, "Truly, you are the Son of God!" (14:24-33). Retrospectively, the disciples, in making this confession, are giving answer to the earlier question they had raised in an equally perilous situation at sea: "What sort of man is this, that even winds and sea obey him?" (8:27).

From all these conflicting thoughts about Jesus' identity, Matthew fashions two evaluative points of view which he juxtaposes to each other in the pericope with which he brings the entire second part of his story to its culmination—namely, Peter's confession near Caesarea Philippi (16:13-20). The one evaluative point of view is that of the various segments making up the Jewish public. The disciples, asked by Jesus who people imagine him to be, reply, "Some say John the Baptist, others say Elijah, and others Jeremiah or one of the prophets" (16:13-14). In other words, the evaluative point of view concerning Jesus' identity which the Jewish public takes is that he is a prophet of some stature or other (cf. 21:11, 26, 46). This evaluative point of view is, the implied reader knows, false, on three counts: (a) Jesus cannot be John the Baptist, Elijah, Jeremiah, or one of the prophets because John, himself "Elijah," is the forerunner of Jesus (11:10, 14), and it is the task of Jeremiah and the prophets to "foretell" of Jesus (2:17; 11:13; 13:17). (b) The answer that Jesus is a prophet evokes no "blessing" from Jesus. (c) And, what is most important, to think of Jesus as a prophet does not tally with God's "thinking" about Jesus (3:17; 16:23e).

The second, contrasting evaluative point of view is that of Peter, who speaks on behalf of the disciples. In response to Jesus' question as to who the disciples understand him to be, Peter asserts, "You are the Messiah, the Son of the living God!" (16:16). This evaluative point of view is correct, for two of the same reasons the other one is false: (a) It evokes from Jesus a "blessing" (16:17) and (b) it tallies with the way God "thinks" about Jesus (3:17; 16:17; 23e). Accordingly, to bring the second part of his story to its culmination, Matthew shows that whereas the public in Israel does not receive Jesus and wrongly conceives of him as being a prophet, Peter, as spokesman for the disciples, confesses Jesus aright to be the Son of God and so reveals that the disciples' evaluative point of view concerning Jesus' identity is in alignment with that of God.

Climactic as Peter's confession is, it nonetheless meets with a command from Jesus that the disciples tell no one that he is the Messiah, that is, the

Messiah Son of God (cf. 16:20 with 16:16). Why this prohibition? Because although the disciples correctly understand who Jesus is, they do not as yet know that integral to Jesus' divine sonship is death on the cross. Hence, they are in no position at this point to go and make disciples of all nations. Then, too, because Jesus forbids the disciples to make known their realization that he is the Son of God, this continues to remain a secret as far as the Jewish public is concerned. On balance, however, the second part of Matthew's story ends on this note: Israel is ignorant of Jesus' identity but the disciples know who he is.

SUMMARY

In the second part of his story (4:17—16:20), Matthew tells of Jesus' ministry to Israel (4:17—11:1) and of Israel's response to him (11:2—16:20). Jesus' ministry to Israel consists in the main of teaching, preaching, and healing (4:23; 9:35; 11:1). Through this ministry, Jesus summons Israel to repentance and to life in the sphere of God's eschatological Rule (4:17; 11:20–24; 12:28, 41). In extension of his own activity, Jesus also commissions the disciples to a ministry in Israel modeled on his own, one of preaching and healing though not of teaching (9:35—10:42). Despite warning signs and the occurrence of the first debates, during which some scribes charge "within themselves" that Jesus is guilty of blasphemy (9:3), the element of conflict does not control this segment of Matthew's story (4:17—11:1).

In the latter half of this part of Matthew's story, however, things change noticeably (11:2—16:20). To all intents and purposes, Jesus' efforts in Israel are without success. Israel's response to his ministry is one of repudiation. Indeed, the tension between Jesus and the Jewish leaders escalates to the point of irreconcilable hostility as the leaders directly attack Jesus himself over matters that pertain to the Mosaic law and then take leave of him to conspire how to take his life (12:1–8, 9–14). But although Israel repudiates Jesus, it nonetheless also wonders and speculates about his identity (11:2—16:20). Whereas the Jewish leaders dismiss him outright as an agent of Satan (9:34; 12:24), the Jewish crowds look on him, also falsely, as a prophet of one type or another (16:13–14). In contrast to the crowds and the leaders, the disciples are led to confess him to be the Messiah Son of God (16:16; 14:33). Their evaluative point of view thus coincides with that of God himself (3:17). Still, despite the correctness of the disciples' confession, Jesus commands them to silence as regards his identity (16:20). The reason is that although they know who he is, they do not as yet know that the central task lying before him is death on a cross. But this notwithstanding, the distance between the disciples on the one hand and Israel on the other is readily apparent: Israel is ignorant as to who Jesus is, but the disciples rightly perceive him to be the Son of God.

4

The Journey of Jesus to Jerusalem and His Suffering, Death, and Resurrection (16:21—28:20)

MATTHEW devotes the third part of his story to Jesus' journey to Jerusalem and to his suffering, death, and resurrection (16:21—28:20). Here the conflict between Jesus and Israel (especially the Jewish leaders), which was foreshadowed in the first part of the story and which, in the second part, burst into the open (Matthew 9) and then crystallized into irreconcilable hostility against Jesus (Matthew 12), runs its course to resolution in the passion and resurrection of Jesus (Matthew 26—28). As regards the resolution of the conflict, the opening verse of 16:21 is revealing in two respects: (a) It calls attention to the three principals involved in Jesus' passion, namely, God (*dei:* "it is necessary"), Jesus, and the Jewish leaders. And (b) it informs the implied reader that all three desire Jesus' death, even though the implied reader already knows that the objective the leaders pursue, which is destructive (12:14), is the opposite of that intended by God and Jesus, which is to save (1:21). Secondarily, Jesus also enters into conflict with the disciples in this part of Matthew's story, as he leads them to appropriate his evaluative point of view concerning servanthood.

To lend this third part of his story cohesion, particularly up to the point where Jesus enters Jerusalem in chapter 21, Matthew employs two literary devices. The one device is that of the "journey." In 16:21, Matthew reports that it is God's will that Jesus go to Jerusalem. As far as the travels of Jesus are concerned, 16:21 stands out as a watershed. Already prior to 16:21, Jesus has begun those travels that will ultimately bring him to Jerusalem (12:15; 14:13). But these "prior" travels are of a decidedly different nature from those that follow. As I observed, prior to 16:21 Jesus' travels have the character of "withdrawal in the face of danger," whether it be a conspiracy on the part of the Jewish leaders to kill him (12:14–15) or Herod's beheading of John the Baptist (14:13a). From 16:21 on, Jesus' travels assume the character of a "divinely ordained journey to Jerusalem." To be sure, not until 19:1 does Jesus actually leave Galilee and head for Jerusalem. But this notwithstanding, the force of 16:21 is that it alerts the implied reader to the circumstance that the entire section of 16:21—20:34, including the portion that consists of Jesus' continued wandering in Galilee (16:21—19:1), is to be understood as part and parcel of Jesus' "journey to Jerusalem."

The second literary device that lends cohesion to the third part of Matthew's story is the passion-prediction. There are three such predictions (16:21; 17:22–23; 20:17–19), supplemented by a verse in the passion-account itself which calls the three to mind (26:2), and they serve as the counterpart to the major summary-passages found in the second part of Matthew's story (4:23; 9:35; 11:1). The function of the passion-predictions is at least twofold. On the one hand, they invite the implied reader to view the whole of Jesus' life-story following 16:21 from the single, overriding perspective of his passion and resurrection. On the other hand, they also invite the implied reader to construe the interaction of Jesus with the disciples throughout 16:21—28:20 as controlled by Jesus' concern to inculcate in them his understanding of discipleship as servanthood (16:24–25; 20:25–28).

THE JOURNEY OF JESUS TO JERUSALEM AND HIS ACTIVITY IN THE TEMPLE

The Journey of Jesus to Jerusalem

Jesus' first passion-prediction begins the third part of Matthew's story (16:21). As I noted in the last chapter, although Peter's confession on behalf of the disciples that Jesus is the Messiah Son of God is correct (16:16), Jesus commands the disciples to silence concerning it (16:20). The reason for this, it was said, is that although the disciples know who Jesus is, they do not as yet know about the central purpose of his ministry. To apprise them of this, the first thing Jesus does in the third part of the story is to tell them that he is divinely appointed to go to Jerusalem and there to suffer, die, and be raised (16:21). In response to this new word, Peter rebukes Jesus, rejecting out of hand the notion that such a fate should ever befall him (16:22). This act on the part of Peter is stark evidence of the conflict that henceforth colors Jesus' relationship with the disciples owing to the fact that they contest his evaluative point of view concerning his mission and therefore also concerning discipleship. Jesus reacts to Peter's remonstrance by reprimanding him: he censures Peter for placing himself in the service not of God, but of Satan (16:23). Then, addressing all the disciples, Jesus asserts programmatically that the corollary to suffering sonship is suffering discipleship (16:24).

Jesus' words to the disciples are followed by his transfiguration in the sight of Peter, James, and John (17:1–9) and his ensuing conversation with them about the suffering of John the Baptist as foreshadowing the suffering he must soon endure (17:10–13). Taking the three disciples with him, Jesus ascends a high mountain. Atop this mountain he is suddenly transfigured before them (17:2), and from a bright cloud they hear a voice exclaim, "This is my beloved Son, in whom I take delight; hear him!" (17:5). The voice is that of God, and for the second time God bursts into the world of Matthew's story as "actor" and expresses his evaluative point of view concerning Jesus' identity. Whereas the announcement ("This is my beloved Son, in whom I take delight") repeats the baptismal declaration (3:17), the injunction ("hear him!") is new. Within the context of Matthew's story, the purpose of the announcement is to confirm to the three the truth of the confession Peter had made on behalf of all the disciples near Caesarea Philippi that Jesus is God's Son (cf. 17:5 with 16:16; 14:33). The purpose of the injunction is to exhort the three to receive and not to reject, as Peter had done, the new word Jesus had delivered to the disciples: that he, whom they rightly perceive to be the Messiah Son of God, has been ordained by God to submit to suffering and death in Jerusalem (cf. 17:5 with 16:21–23). As Jesus and the three descend from the mountain, Jesus commands them to silence concerning their experience (17:9). The importance of this command is dual: With respect to the plot of Matthew's story, Jesus' command informs the implied reader that not until the resurrection will the disciples comprehend that death is the essence of the ministry of Jesus Son of God. And with respect to the truth of the divine sonship of Jesus, Jesus' command serves, like the one following Peter's confession as well, to suppress knowledge of this truth so that the experience of the three disciples atop the mountain does not result in its public disclosure.

Jesus and the three descend from the mountain to the crowd and the other disciples below, and Jesus teaches the disciples of the power of faith (17:14–20). Still in Galilee, he predicts his passion to the disciples for a second time (17:22–23), which reminds the implied reader of the leitmotif of the third part of Matthew's story and conveys a sense of heightened tension. On the heels of an exchange with Peter over the voluntary payment of the "half-shekel tax" (17:24–27), Jesus delivers his so-called ecclesiological discourse (18:1–35). His message to the disciples is that loving concern for the neighbor and the spirit of forgiveness are to be the hallmarks of the community of believers in whose midst he, the Son of God, will ever be present (cf. 18:6, 10, 20, 21–22).

Leaving Galilee at last, Jesus moves toward Jerusalem, traveling into the regions of Judea across the Jordan (19:1). Huge crowds follow him, and he "serves" them by healing the sick (19:2). In debate with his opponents, he takes a radical stand against divorce, instructing the disciples in the process (19:3–12). In addition, he also acts in all of the following ways: He counters the "status–consciousness" of the disciples by blessing the children (19:

13–15). He summons the rich young man, who declines, to follow after him (19:16–22). He warns the disciples against the perils of wealth while also giving them a vision of the eschatological rewards of discipleship (19: 23–30). And he challenges the disciples through his narration of the parable of the laborers in the vineyard to be as unstintingly generous in their behavior toward others as God is toward them (20:1–16).

About to go up to Jerusalem, Jesus takes the disciples aside and, for the third time, predicts his passion (20:17–19). Again the leitmotif of 16: 21—28:20 sounds, and again the implied reader is reminded that the decisive struggle between Jesus and the Jewish leaders is inexorably approaching. To combat the disciples' desire for power and privilege, Jesus holds up himself, the man who willingly gives his life for others, as the example of servanthood they are to emulate in their lives together (20:20– 28). Then, having passed through Jericho in the company of the disciples and a great crowd, Jesus heals two blind men who appeal to him in faith as Israel's Davidic Messiah (20:29–34). The "sight" of these blind men underlines the "blindness" of Israel's sight.

The Entry of Jesus into Jerusalem

From the outskirts of Jericho, Jesus journeys up to Jerusalem, arriving at the Mount of Olives (21:1). He dispatches two disciples to obtain the "messianic mounts" he foresees are awaiting his use, the donkey and her colt (21:2–6). Riding the animals, Jesus enters Jerusalem with great ceremony (21:7–9). He "takes possession" of the city as Israel's Davidic Messiah-King, but in humility and peace and without display of military might (21:5, 9; Zech. 9:9). The crowds, spreading garments and tree-branches on the way (Matt. 21:8), pay him the homage that befits a king (2 Kings 9:13), and with their antiphonal shouts of "Hosanna," they hail him with petitions of salvation (Ps. 118:25–26).

If Jesus' entry into Jerusalem is thus enshrouded in the fulfillment of OT prophecy, it is at the same time an event that is ironic to the core. On the one hand, the Jewish crowds, and therefore Israel, do receive Jesus into Jerusalem as the Son of David (Matt. 21:9). On the other hand, when on Jesus' entry, the crowds are asked by the inhabitants of Jerusalem who this Jesus is, they reply that he is "the prophet from Nazareth of Galilee" (21:10–11). Exactly as the disciples had said when questioned by Jesus near Caesarea Philippi, the evaluative point of view of the Jewish public concerning Jesus' identity is that he is no more than a prophet (16:13–14; 21:46). In hailing Jesus as the Son of David, the Jewish crowds have spoken the truth, but they have done so unwittingly, seeing in him but a prophet.

Jesus' first act in Jerusalem marks the beginning of the penultimate stage of his conflict with the Jewish leaders and also shapes the setting for the remainder of his stay in the city prior to his passion: he cleanses the temple and briefly occupies it, and his presence there provokes the Jewish leaders, led by the chief priests, to engage him in direct confrontation. Until the destruction of Jerusalem in A.D. 70, the temple was not only the religious and cultic center of Judaism but also, as sanctioned by the Romans, the seat of domestic government for Judea and, at times, other parts of Palestine as well.[1] The High Council, or Sanhedrin, under the leadership of the high priest, met in plenary session in a hall in the temple area, and exercised, in addition to purely religious powers, legislative and judicial powers as well. Consequently, for Jesus to raise the claim through his cleansing of the temple that the temple has, under the custody of the Jewish leaders, become a "den of robbers," and that his purification of it from the desecration of merchants is its restoration to rightful use as Israel's house of prayer and worship, is for him to mount a massive assault on the authority and integrity of the Jewish leaders (21:12–13). This act on Jesus' part paves the way for the sharp debates with the Jewish leaders which follow.

As a token of these debates, Jesus heals, in conjunction with his cleansing of the temple, the blind and lame who come to him, persons otherwise forbidden entrance to the temple (21:14–17; 2 Sam. 5:8). This prompts children who are also present in the temple to acclaim Jesus with shouts of "Hosanna to the Son of David!" (Matt. 21:15). Witnessing the healings and hearing the shouts, the chief priests and the scribes, incited to indignation, call Jesus to task for his acceptance of the acclamation of children. Jesus silences them with the retort that if they could properly read scripture, they would know that the children's acclamation of him as the Son of David constitutes the fulfillment of prophecy. With this, Jesus leaves the temple and Jerusalem and spends the night in Bethany. For the implied reader, however, the irony of this scene is apparent: just as the Jewish crowds had hailed Jesus as the Son of David on his entry into Jerusalem but could not perceive the truth of their words, so now the Jewish leaders have heard the children hail Jesus as the Son of David but cannot perceive the truth of their words. The children, who count for nothing in the Jewish society of Matthew's story, "see" and "confess" what Israel cannot, namely, that Jesus is its Davidic Messiah.

But correct though it surely is to look on Jesus as being the Son of David, Matthew shows later in his story that, of itself, this evaluative point of view is insufficient. This is the thrust of the pericope on the question about David's son (22:41–46). In debate with the Pharisees, Jesus confounds them with a problem of antinomy. The question he puts to them is: How is it possible for the Messiah to be both the "son" of David and the "lord" of David when these two views are ostensibly contradictory? Although Jesus leaves the answer to be inferred, the implied reader can well supply it: The

1. Cf. Reicke, *New Testament Era*, 141–49.

Messiah is the "son" of David because he stands in the line of David (1:1, 6, 25). At the same time, the Messiah is also the "lord" of David because he is, as God's evaluative point of view concerning him dictates (3:17; 17:5), the Son of God and therefore of higher station and authority than David.

The Activity of Jesus in the Temple

Matthew continues to place Jesus—during his stay in Jerusalem prior to his delivery of the eschatological discourse and his ensuing passion—in the temple, where he teaches, debates, and speaks in parables (21:12—23:39). The tension between Jesus and the Jewish leaders increases to the breaking point, as the circle of the leaders who debate Jesus grows ever wider and as Jesus addresses his three parables against Israel to those identified with the Sanhedrin. As far as the widening circle of those who debate Jesus is concerned, he is put to the test, respectively, by the chief priests and the scribes (21:15); by the chief priests and the elders of the people (21:23); by the disciples of the Pharisees together with the Herodians (22:15–16); by the Sadducees (22:23); and by a lawyer from the Pharisees (22:34–35). Still, Jesus himself closes the entire series by himself challenging the Pharisees (22:41). The result of these confrontations in the temple is that Jesus reduces all his opponents to silence. As Matthew comments at the conclusion of the final debate: "And no one was able to answer him a word, nor from that day did any one dare to ask him any more questions" (22:46).

Unable to best Jesus in debate, the Jewish leaders leave the scene of the temple. Alone with the crowds and the disciples, Jesus seizes the offensive and himself attacks the scribes and Pharisees in his scathing speech of woes (Matthew 23). Following this speech, verbal exchanges between Jesus and the Jewish leaders are no more possible, and the leaders concentrate on destroying Jesus, not through debate, but through death on the cross.

I mentioned that Jesus, during his stay in the temple, also speaks in parables. The three parables Jesus narrates bespeak judgment on Israel owing to its repudiation of John the Baptist (21:28–32), of himself (21: 33–46), and of his messengers (22:1–10). Of particular importance to the plot of Matthew's story is the second of these parables, that of the wicked husbandmen (21:33–46).

Jesus addresses this parable to "the chief priests and the elders of the people," that is, to Jewish officialdom associated with the Sanhedrin (cf. 21:33 with 21:23). In it, Jesus sketches, with the aid of metaphors, God's dealings with Israel in the history of salvation. He identifies God with the owner of the vineyard, the Jewish leaders with the wicked tenant farmers, and himself with the son of the owner whom the tenant farmers kill but who is also vindicated. In making these identifications, Jesus boldly asserts that he is the Son of God whom the Jewish leaders will kill but whom God will vindicate through resurrection, and that his death and resurrection are the decisive events in the whole of salvation history. Then, too, as Jesus speaks of the son, or of himself, he presents the owner of the vineyard, or God, as referring to him as "my son" ("They will respect my son"; 21:37). This reference to "my son" calls to mind, of course, the words the heavenly voice uttered at the baptism and the transfiguration ("This is my beloved Son"; 3:17; 17:5). Accordingly, it is with phraseology attributable to God himself that Jesus asserts in this parable that God looks upon him as his Son. In narrating this parable, therefore, it is the aim of Jesus to make God's evaluative point of view concerning his identity his own and to confront the Jewish leaders with it.

This aim of Jesus is not lost on the Jewish leaders. They understand the metaphors he has used and the claim he has raised that he is, in the sight of both God and himself, the Son of God whom they will kill (21:45). Their response is to want to arrest him, but the reputation he enjoys in public of being a prophet causes them to hold off (21:46). Still, by wanting to arrest Jesus, the Jewish leaders show that they repudiate the message of his parable. In repudiating the parable's message, however, they likewise show that their understanding is, in reality, "obdurate understanding":[2] having grasped Jesus' message with their minds, they cannot accept it with their hearts, and so reject it. Ironically, in rejecting Jesus' message, the Jewish leaders are unwittingly rejecting the evaluative point of view of God concerning Jesus' identity (cf. 21:37 with 17:5; 3:17). The upshot is that even though they are told the secret that Jesus is the Son of God, they are unable to comprehend its truth. In the final analysis, therefore, although the secret of Jesus' divine sonship has been uttered in public, it nevertheless continues unbroken as far as the Jewish public is concerned.

As Matthew began his narration of Jesus' ministry in chapter 4, he depicted Jesus as becoming successively involved with three major groups, each of which functions as a character in his story: the *disciples* (4:18–22); the *crowds*, together with the disciples (4:25; 5:1–2); and the Jewish *leaders* (9:2–13). As an indication that only the climax of his story (i.e., the passion of Jesus) still remains to be narrated, Matthew now depicts Jesus' involvement with each of these same three groups as being successively terminated in a reverse order to the initial one—that is to say, in an order that is chiastic in nature. Thus, by reducing the Jewish *leaders* in open debate to silence, Jesus forces their withdrawal from the scene (22:46). With the leaders gone, Jesus publicly addresses the *crowds* in the temple, together with the disciples (23:1). And leaving the temple, Jesus delivers his eschatological discourse to the *disciples* alone (24:1–3). Through the use of this

2. Regarding the expression "obdurate understanding," cf. Pesch (*Markusevangelium*, 2:223) and Boucher (*Mysterious Parable*, 60, 84).

chiastic pattern, Matthew signals the implied reader that the culmination of his story is at hand.

THE BETRAYAL, CONDEMNATION, CRUCIFIXION, AND RESURRECTION OF JESUS

The Betrayal and Condemnation of Jesus

As the culmination of Matthew's story, the passion-account also constitutes the decisive stage in Jesus' conflict with Israel (Matthew 26—28). Here the resolution of this conflict works itself out in dramatic detail.

At the beginning of the passion-account, Jesus says to the disciples, "You know that after two days the Passover is coming, and the Son of man will be delivered up (betrayed) to be crucified" (26:1–2). These words remind both the disciples and the implied reader of the three passion-predictions Jesus has already given (16:21; 17:22–23; 20:18–19). In these predictions, especially the first one, Jesus made it known that he, God, and the Jewish leaders will be the three principals involved in his passion. Conversely, this also means that while such characters as the disciples (including Judas), the crowds, Pilate, and the Roman soldiers will likewise have their necessary roles to play, by comparison they will be minor.

All three principals, it was said, desire the death of Jesus, though for different reasons. Through the unfolding of Matthew's story, these reasons have become increasingly clear. God has ordained the death of Jesus because it is to be the crucial event in the whole of the history of salvation.[3] Jesus freely submits to suffering and death because he is, on the one hand, perfect in his devotion to God and, on the other hand, perfect in his service to humankind.[4] No helpless victim, Jesus knows and predicts his fate, guides events both by what he does and by what he leaves undone so that they will issue in his death, and yet will die as one completely innocent of wrongdoing who will find in death the last and greatest test of his fealty to God. By contrast, the Jewish leaders desire the death of Jesus because they understand him to be a "deceiver," or false messiah (cf. 27:63). They rightly perceive that he stands as a mortal threat to their authority and therefore to the religion and society based on that authority (15:13; 21:43). According to their evaluative point of view, Jesus blasphemously arrogates to himself the prerogative of God to forgive sins; derives his astonishing authority from having entered into collusion with Satan; places himself above law and tradition; dismisses with antagonism the legitimate request that he prove he does indeed act on authorization of God; impugns their ethics and undermines their authority as interpreters of scripture and the leaders of

3. Cf. 1:21; 20:28; 21:33–44; 22:1–10; also 26:28; 27:51.
4. Cf. 4:1–11; 5:48; 20:28; 22:37–40; also 26:26–29, 39, 42.

God's people Israel; and threatens Israel's very existence by forming his own community of disciples who do as he does and violate law and tradition.

The position other characters will take toward Jesus as he faces death is likewise not unpredictable. Although the crowds hold Jesus to be a prophet, they have never pledged him their allegiance (11:16–24), and at the last they will join in solidarity with their leaders against him. The disciples, although they have pledged Jesus their allegiance, have not appropriated the notion that suffering sonship entails suffering discipleship, and this will result in their being ill-prepared, even unable, to cope with the events surrounding his passion. Since Pilate and the Roman soldiers have not yet appeared in the story, it can simply be said that, except for those soldiers who acclaim Jesus at the foot of the cross, Pilate and the Romans will prove themselves complicit in the crime perpetrated against Jesus.

To pick up the flow of Matthew's passion-account following Jesus' recapitulation of his passion-predictions (26:2), the initial scenes are calculated to establish, respectively, the culpability of the Jewish leaders for Jesus' death, the unreadiness of the disciples to master the events that lie before them, and the inability of Judas to foresee the true nature of the act he is committing in agreeing to betray Jesus for gain. Thus, the chief priests and the elders stand forth as the ones most immediately responsible for the death of Jesus. Gathering in the palace of the high priest, they take counsel together how to have Jesus arrested by cunning and killed (26:3–4). To avoid a disturbance among the people, however, they decide not to try to take Jesus during the celebration of the feast of Passover (26:5). In the next scene, the disciples, who are with Jesus in the house of Simon the leper at Bethany, show themselves unable to comprehend the true significance of events taking place. By indignantly dismissing as a waste of money the woman's anointing Jesus with expensive ointment, they misconstrue what in reality constitutes the preparation of Jesus for burial (26:6–13). And in the subsequent scene, Judas, in hiring himself out to the chief priests and hence placing himself in the service of their desire to kill Jesus, reveals himself to be oblivious to the circumstance that he is, ironically, thereby also fulfilling scripture and facilitating with his deceit God's plan of salvation (26:14–16).

By contrast, Jesus demonstrates, by guiding and predicting events, that he is acutely aware God is, in him and his destiny, bringing to fulfillment the divine plan of salvation. In sending the disciples to make arrangements for eating the Passover meal, Jesus displays his mastery of the situation by telling them exactly where to go and with whom to speak (26:17–19). As he and his disciples recline at meal, he predicts that one of the twelve will betray him, and he indicates to Judas that he knows it is he (26:20–25). In full knowledge of the significance of his death, Jesus makes the meal itself the occasion on which he explains this to the disciples: In the bread they eat, which is his body, they have fellowship with him; in the cup they drink, which is his blood, they share in the atonement for sins which he will accomplish for all; and in the promise he gives them that he will no more drink wine until he is united with them in the Father's Kingdom, they have assurance that they will share future bliss with him (26:26–29). Following the meal and under way to the Mount of Olives, Jesus makes three further predictions, all of which relate to the disciples: All of them will desert him; Peter will deny him; but such failure notwithstanding, he will meet them in Galilee after his resurrection (and consequently reconcile them to himself) (26:30–35). On arrival at the Mount of Olives and the place called Gethsemane, Jesus attests in prayer to his perfect obedience to the Father: he goes to his death not as one who desires for himself the glory of martyrdom, but because he would do his Father's will (26:36–46). In thus wanting what God wants, Jesus freely subjects himself to what his enemies also want: his death. Then, in awareness that his hour of betrayal is at hand, Jesus goes to meet Judas and the hostile crowd with him. Although he could, if he wanted, call on his Father and receive for his defense more than twelve legions of angels, he forgoes this and submits, in order to fulfill the scriptures, to betrayal by Judas, to arrest by his opponents, and to abandonment by the other disciples (26:47–56). Moreover, later, at the very time he will stand before the Sanhedrin and confess who he is, Peter will fulfill prophecy and deny him before others (26:58, 69–75).

The climactic event in this part of the passion-account is Jesus' appearance before the Sanhedrin (26:57–68). In putting Jesus on trial, the Jewish leaders believe they will finally achieve the resolution of their conflict with Jesus which they have long desired (12:14). During the proceedings, Jesus once again faces, as constituent groups belonging to the Sanhedrin, the chief priests and the elders (26:57, 59), those to whom he had previously addressed the parable of the wicked husbandmen (21:23). As long as the testimony brought against him is false, Jesus remains silent (26:59–62). Abruptly, however, the high priest places Jesus under oath to tell the Sanhedrin whether he is the Messiah, the Son of God (26:63). In terms of the plot of Matthew's story, this unexpected query raises the problem as to the source from which the high priest has even gotten the idea to question Jesus about being the Son of God. This source is Jesus himself and his narration of the parable of the wicked husbandmen. As the presiding officer of the Sanhedrin, the high priest has knowledge of the claim to divine sonship which Jesus made in telling his parable to the chief priests and the elders. At the trial, therefore, the high priest seizes on Jesus' own claim, converts it from allegorical speech into literal speech, and hurls it back at Jesus as a weapon by which to destroy him. Because from

Jesus' standpoint false testimony at the trial has suddenly given way to a query that expresses the truth, he breaks his silence and replies in the affirmative, "(So) you have said!" (26:64; cf. 27:43).[5] In consequence of Jesus' reply, the Sanhedrin, at the instigation of the high priest, condemns Jesus to death for having committed blasphemy against God (26:65–66).

And therein lies the irony of Jesus' fate. In the case of Jesus, the irony is that although he is made to die for committing blasphemy against God, his "crime" has been to dare to think about himself as God, at the baptism and the transfiguration, has revealed he does in truth "think" about him (3:17; 17:5; 21:37). In the case of the high priest and the Sanhedrin, the irony is that in condemning Jesus to death for blaspheming God, they are alleging they know the "thinking" of God. Yet even while alleging this, they are effectively disavowing God's "thinking" and demonstrating that they have in no wise penetrated the secret that Jesus is indeed the Son of God. In resolving their conflict with Jesus as they have, the Jewish leaders have achieved the opposite of what they had intended: they have not only not pleased God, but they have also condemned to death the Son he has sent them and called forth his wrath on themselves and their nation (21:43–44; 22:7).

The Crucifixion of Jesus

Having sentenced Jesus to death, the chief priests and the elders deliver him to Pilate, the Roman governor (27:1–2).[6] Before describing Jesus' hearing before Pilate, however, Matthew digresses in order to relate the death of Judas (27:3–10). In so doing, Matthew virtually summarizes the passion-account to this point by stressing such factors as the guilt of both Judas and the Jewish leaders, the innocence of Jesus, and the circumstance that, ironically, the passion of Jesus serves the salvation-historical purposes of God. As for the guilt of Judas and the innocence of Jesus, Judas himself attests to both when he returns with the pieces of silver to the chief priests and the elders in the temple and declares, "I have sinned in betraying innocent blood" (27:4). Moreover, in going out and hanging himself, Judas also brings to fulfillment the woe Jesus had pronounced in foretelling that one of the twelve would betray him: " . . . but woe to that man by whom the Son of man is betrayed! It would have been better for that man if he had not been born!" (26:24). As for the guilt of the Jewish leaders, the chief priests are made to acknowledge this in words they themselves utter: "It is not lawful to put them [the pieces of silver] into the treasury, since they are blood money" (27:6). And concerning the irony that God is at work in the passion of Jesus to accomplish his purposes, Matthew notes that the Jewish

5. Cf. Catchpole, "Answer of Jesus to Caiphas," 213–16.
6. For a penetrating study of Matthew 27, cf. Witherup, "Cross of Jesus."

leaders, in using the blood money Judas had thrown down in the temple to purchase a potter's field for the burial of strangers, unwittingly fulfill OT prophecy (27:6–10).

Faced with the Jewish conspiracy against Jesus, Pilate makes himself complicit by acceding to the demand that Jesus be crucified (27:11–26). The role Pilate plays in the passion-account is thus not unlike that of Judas, for by abetting the Jewish conspiracy, Pilate is at the same time, ironically, facilitating God's plan of salvation. At Jesus' hearing, Pilate makes his identity the issue. He asks Jesus whether he is the "King of the Jews," and Jesus replies in the affirmative (27:11). To Pilate, Jesus' reply means, based on his evaluative point of view, that Jesus is an insurrectionist (27:37). But in spite of this, Pilate indicates by the way he conducts Jesus' hearing that he believes him to be innocent of this charge (27:11–24). Nevertheless, once Pilate can be satisfied that he has absolved himself of any guilt associated with Jesus' death and that the Jews have taken full responsibility for it, he consents to the legal plea that Jesus be crucified and delivers him to the soldiers (27:24–27). The soldiers, in turn, take Jesus to the praetorium and there make mockery of him as the King of the Jews (27:27–31). In so doing, they unwittingly show in what way Jesus truly is the King of the Jews. He is so, not as one who restores to Israel its national splendor and not as one who foments rebellion against Rome, but as the one who saves others by willingly giving himself over to suffering and death.

Matthew presents Jesus' crucifixion as a testing (27:32–56; cf. 27:40).[7] At Golgotha and on the cross, Jesus demonstrates in all he endures that his love for God is perfect, or wholehearted: what God wills, Jesus wills (26:42). In particular, Jesus does not allow concern for self to put him at odds with God's appointed plan that he relinquish his life (27:38–50). Earlier he had said to his disciples, "For whoever desires to save his life will lose it" (16:25). On the cross, Jesus exemplifies his own counsel by resisting the temptation to do as the passersby, the Jewish leaders, and the two robbers call on him to do, namely, to save himself by using his power to descend from the cross (27:39–44). Nor does Jesus endeavor to escape death by appealing to Elijah for miraculous deliverance, as some standing at the foot of the cross mistakenly think he does (27:47–49). On the contrary, as Jesus nears the moment he himself has chosen for his death (27:50), he faces his abandonment by God (". . . why have you forsaken me?"; 27:46) by crying out to God in trust ("My God, my God . . ."; 27:46). Nor is God to disappoint the "trust unto death" which Jesus places in him: on the third day, he is to raise Jesus from the dead.

At Jesus' death, Matthew tells of the occurrence of supernatural portents (27:51–54). These portents elicit from the Roman soldiers guarding Jesus

7. Cf. Gerhardsson, "Gottes Sohn," 96–103.

the acclamation, "Truly this man was the Son of God!" (27:54). As characters who appear on the scene only briefly, it is not for the soldiers but for the implied reader to grasp the full import of their words. In this regard, three things stand out.

The first thing is that this acclamation of the Roman soldiers constitutes a vindication of Jesus' claim to be the Son of God (21:37; 26:63–64). In condemning Jesus to death at his trial and in blaspheming and mocking him as he hangs upon the cross, the Sanhedrin in the one instance and the passersby and the Jewish leaders in the other repudiate Jesus' claim to be the Son of God (26:63–66; 27:39–43). Against the backdrop of this repudiation, the soldiers' acclamation becomes a counter-assertion, evoked by God himself through the supernatural portents he has caused to occur, that, on the contrary, Jesus "truly" was the "Son of God" (27:51–54).

The second thing that stands out is that the verb in this acclamation is in the past tense ("was"; 27:54). In that the Roman soldiers say that Jesus *was* the Son of God, their acclamation calls attention to the fact that the cross marks the end of Jesus' earthly ministry. In the eyes of the Jewish leaders, the significance of this end is that Jesus, a false messiah who has infected Israel with perilous error (27:63–64), has, as necessity dictated, been destroyed (12:14; 26:4; 27:1). In divine perspective, however, the end of Jesus' ministry is at the same time its culmination, for the cross is the place where Jesus "pours out" his blood for the forgiveness of sins (26:28) and consequently "saves" his people from their sins (1:21). In the cross, Jesus atones for sins (26:28) and, in fact, supersedes the temple and the Jewish cult (27:51) as the "place" of salvation.

And the last thing that stands out is that with this acclamation of the Roman soldiers, Matthew brings the third part of his story (16:21—28:20) to its initial climax. In declaring Jesus to be the Son of God, the Roman soldiers "think" about him as God "thinks" about him (3:17; 17:5; 16:23e), so that their evaluative point of view concerning Jesus' identity can be seen to be in alignment with that of God. Moreover, in contrast, for example, to Peter's confession on behalf of the disciples, no comment of any kind, narrative or otherwise, which can function as a command to silence follows the soldiers' acclamation (cf. 16:20). The reason is apparent: whereas Peter and the disciples near Caesarea Philippi correctly understood who Jesus is but were as yet ignorant of his passion, the Roman soldiers acclaim Jesus to be the Son of God at that juncture where he has completed his passion and, in fact, the whole of his earthly ministry.

Two consequences flow from this. The first is that the soldiers' acclamation becomes the place in Matthew's plot where Jesus is, for the first time, both correctly and publicly affirmed by humans to be the Son of God. And the second consequence is that, as a result of the soldiers' acclamation, the way is in principle now open for the task of "going and making disciples of all nations" or, to put it differently, for the task of making the salvation Jesus has accomplished in his death owing to his conflict with Israel redound to the benefit of all humankind. Also, since the Roman soldiers are themselves Gentiles, they attest in this way, too, that the time for embarking upon this universal mission is at hand.

The Resurrection of Jesus

Central to Matthew's resurrection-narrative is the angel's declaration to the women that "he has been raised" (28:6). The passive voice here is the "divine passive," so that what the angel affirms is that "God has raised Jesus from the dead" (cf. 16:21). Earlier in Matthew's story, Jesus twice said to the disciples that "whoever loses his life will find it" (16:25; cf. 10:39), and on the cross Jesus held fast to God in trust even as he relinquished his life (27:46, 50). In raising Jesus from the dead, God certifies the truth of Jesus' words and the efficacy of his trust, which is to say that God vindicates Jesus: God resolves Jesus' conflict with Israel by showing that Jesus is in the right. Within the world of Matthew's story, however, Israel as such will not see God's vindication of Jesus until the Parousia and the final judgment (13:36–43; 25:31–46; 26:64). Still, in Matthew's story Jesus has also been in conflict with the disciples, a subject to be discussed at length in chapter 6. God's vindication of Jesus in the resurrection is the point at which Jesus' conflict with the disciples comes to fundamental resolution. Because the resolution of this particular conflict is the topic with which Matt. 28:16–20 deals, and because 28:16–20 constitutes the major climax not only of the third part of Matthew's story but also of his entire story, it is with it that this chapter's study of Matthew's story will conclude.

Prior to his death and resurrection, Jesus' conflict with the disciples was over their unwillingness to appropriate Jesus' evaluative point of view according to which suffering sonship is a call to suffering discipleship, or to servanthood (16:21, 24; 20:28). Because of such unwillingness, the disciples became apostate when confronted by the events of Jesus' passion: Judas betrayed Jesus (26:47–50), the disciples fled from him (26:56), and Peter denied him (26:69–75).

But now on the day of Jesus' resurrection and notwithstanding the apostasy of the disciples, the angel of the Lord enjoins the women at the tomb to go and remind the disciples of Jesus' earlier promise that, following his resurrection, he would precede them to Galilee where, the angel adds, they will see him (28:5–7; 26:32). Moreover, as the women obey the angel and depart from the tomb, the resurrected Jesus himself meets them, and he likewise commands them to tell the disciples to make their way to Galilee, where they will see him (28:10). In making reference to the disciples, Jesus calls them "my brothers" (28:10).

The upshot of this sequence is that when the eleven disciples do make their way to Galilee and Jesus does appear to them on the mountain there, he meets them as the "brother" who has "gathered" them from their "having been scattered" (26:31; 28:16). In other words, the resurrected Jesus meets the disciples as the one who reconciles them to himself. True, some of the disciples worship him while others of them doubt (28:17). Nonetheless, doubt is "little faith," or weak faith, but is not "unfaith" (14:32), so that the assertion stands: the resurrected Jesus gathers the scattered disciples and reconciles them to himself.

As Jesus appears to the disciples atop the mountain in Galilee, he does so as the "Son of God" whom God, he himself, the disciples themselves, and the Roman soldiers have all claimed him to be.[8] By the same token, he is both the crucified and the resurrected Son of God. Thus, he is the resurrected Son of God whose eschatological glory God revealed proleptically to Peter, James, and John on the mountain of the transfiguration (17:2, 5). Yet, even as the resurrected Son of God, he remains the crucified Son of God ("the one who has been, and remains, the crucified"; 28:5). Indeed, he is the rejected "stone-son" whom God has placed "at the head of the corner," that is, raised from the dead and exalted to universal lordship (21:37, 42; 28:18). He is, in fact, Emmanuel, or "God with us," the Son conceived of the Spirit in whom God will abide with the disciples until the consummation of the age (1:20, 23; 28:20).

The disciples, in seeing Jesus Son of God as the resurrected one who remains the crucified one, see him, but also themselves, in new perspective. Because the Jesus the disciples see is the crucified, albeit also resurrected, Son of God, they now comprehend not only what they earlier perceived as well—namely, that he is the Son of God (14:33; 16:16), but also the central purpose of his mission—namely, his death on the cross and the salvation from sins he thereby accomplished (26:28). Comprehending at last not only who Jesus is but also what he was about, the disciples necessarily gain insight into themselves as well: they finally understand and appropriate Jesus' evaluative point of view according to which suffering sonship is their call to suffering discipleship, or to servanthood (16:21, 24). Equipped with this insight, the disciples are not again commanded by Jesus, as previously, to silence concerning him (16:20; 17:9), but are instead commissioned to go and make all nations his disciples (28:19). In reconciling the disciples to himself and in giving them this commission, Jesus resolves the conflict he has had with them. With this conflict so resolved, the disciples move from Easter into the world Jesus predicted for them in his eschatological discourse of Matthew 24—25.

8. Cf. 3:17; 17:5; 21:37; 26:63–64; 14:33; 16:16; 27:54.

SUMMARY

In the third part of his story (16:21—28:20), Matthew employs the device of the "journey" (16:21—21:11) and the setting of Jerusalem and environs, including the temple (21:12—28:15 [16–20]), in order to forge a cohesive narrative from disparate materials. To inform the implied reader of the tenor of the narrative, Matthew employs three passion-predictions that tell of Jesus' suffering, death, and resurrection (16:21; 17:22–23; 20:18–19). Also, at the outset of the passion-account itself he calls to mind these three predictions (26:2).

In this third part, the conflicts Jesus has with Israel on the one hand and with the disciples on the other run their course to resolution. Jesus' conflict with the disciples is that he must lead them to appropriate his evaluative point of view that suffering sonship entails suffering discipleship (servanthood) (16:21, 24). Jesus' conflict with Israel is to the death (16:21). Whereas the Jewish leaders conspire to have Jesus killed so as to destroy him (12:14; 26:2–3), God and Jesus desire Jesus' death because it will constitute the decisive, saving event in the history of salvation. In his parable of the wicked husbandmen, Jesus confronts the Jewish leaders with the claim that he is the Son of God, that is, God's supreme agent in the history of salvation (21:33–46). At his trial, the high priest abruptly puts Jesus' own claim to him in the form of a question, and when Jesus replies in the affirmative, the high priest and the Sanhedrin condemn him to death for having committed blasphemy against God (26:57–68). Delivering Jesus to Pilate, the Jewish leaders then prevail on Pilate to have Jesus crucified as an insurrectionist (27:11–37). In this way, the Jewish leaders, with the support of the crowds, bring about the death of Jesus and believe that in so doing they have acted in a God-pleasing manner in order to put to an end a movement initiated by one who was a false messiah (27:25, 63–64). What they have done in reality, however, is to show themselves to be blind to God's revelation that this Jesus is his royal Son whom he has sent them and, in making themselves responsible for Jesus' death, to call down God's wrath on themselves and their nation (21:43; 22:7). Ironically, what also happens is that God turns Jesus' death to advantage for all humankind, for through the death of Jesus, Jesus atones for sins and becomes the one through whom God henceforth grants salvation to all humans, Jews and Gentiles alike (1:21; 26:28). In the final analysis, therefore, God vindicates Jesus in his conflict with Israel, that is to say, he shows Jesus and not Israel to have been in the right. As proof of such vindication, God raises Jesus from the dead after three days (28:6), and at the end of time he will dispatch him in glory with angels to carry out the final judgment and to establish his Kingdom in splendor in sight of all the nations of the world (24:29–31;

25:31–46). In the meantime, the disciples of Jesus, having seen Jesus in Galilee as the crucified one whom God has raised, have at last comprehended that suffering sonship entails suffering discipleship (servanthood), and have received from Jesus the commission to go and make all nations his disciples (28:16–20). Empowered by this commission, they carry out their task within the world Jesus described for them in his eschatological discourse of Matthew 24—25.

5

Jesus as the Son of Man

Thus far, the story Matthew narrates has largely been treated apart from the fact that, beginning with 8:20, Jesus not infrequently refers to himself as "the Son of man" (*ho hyios tou anthrōpou*). The purpose of this chapter is to explore the meaning and function of this designation.[1] As will become evident, the impact that Jesus' use of "the Son of man" has on the plot of Matthew's story is that it enhances two features that have already become familiar, namely, "conflict" and "vindication."

Because "the Son of man" occurs exclusively on the lips of Jesus, it is tempting to interpret this as indicating that the designation sets the tone for the understanding of Jesus which Matthew would project through the medium of his story. It was observed in chapter 1, however, that Matthew has, by authorial choice, made God's evaluative point of view normative within the world of his story. If this is correct, it follows that what will be weightiest in Matthew's presentation of Jesus is the understanding of him which God conveys. As has been noted, God twice enters the world of Matthew's story as "actor" in order to announce that Jesus is his beloved Son (3:17; 17:5). Plainly, therefore, Matthean christology must be adjudged to be preeminently a Son-of-God christology, and one dare not lose sight of this in ascertaining the meaning and function of "the Son of man."

"THE SON OF MAN" AS A CHRISTOLOGICAL TITLE

"The Son of man" may be defined as the title by means of which Jesus refers to himself "in public" or in view of the "public" (or "world") in order to point to himself as "the man," or "the human being" (earthly, suffering, vindicated), and to assert his divine authority in the face of opposition.

To the implied reader of Matthew's story, "the Son of man" presents itself

1. Cf. Kingsbury, "Figure of Jesus," 22–32. Further, cf. Lindars, *Jesus Son of Man*, chap. 7.

as a technical term or christological title. At least three factors combine to make this plain. For one thing, the use to which Matthew puts "the Son of man" is such that, overall, it reflects the peculiar contours of the ministry of Jesus: Jesus designates himself as "the Son of man" in association with his earthly activity, with his suffering, death, and resurrection, and with his anticipated Parousia. The upshot is that "the Son of man" is a term applying to Jesus in a way it cannot be applied to any other human being. For another thing, "the Son of man" is also unique because it constitutes the phraseological point of view of Jesus exclusively: it occurs solely in his mouth; it is always definite in form ("the" Son of man); and when Jesus employs it, he does so to refer to himself alone. And third, Jesus fulfills OT prophecy in his capacity as the Son of man,[2] which is further indication that "the Son of man" possesses a status comparable to that of the other major titles.

But although it is a technical term or title, "the Son of man" does not inform the implied reader of the identity of Jesus (of "who Jesus is").[3] Strange as this statement may seem at first blush, the evidence substantiating it is compelling.

How does Matthew make known the identity of Jesus? In the main, he does so through use of four titles that may be said to be "confessional" in nature: "Messiah" (christos),[4] the "King of the Jews [Israel],"[5] the "Son of David,"[6] and especially the "Son of God."[7] One tactic Matthew employs with great effectiveness is to place these titles in formulas of identification ("predication-formulas")[8] so as to advise the implied reader in words (declarations or questions) uttered by characters in the story that Jesus *is* the Messiah (cf. 16:16), or *is* the King of the Jews (Israel) (cf. 27:42), or *is* the Son of David (cf. 12:23), or *is* the Son of God (cf. 14:33). Significantly, "the Son of man" never appears in a formula of identification. The result is that no character in Matthew's story, whether transcendent being or human being, ever makes any declaration, or asks any question, concerning Jesus such as the following: "You are the Son of man!"; "This is the Son of man!"; "Are you the Son of man?"; or "Is this the Son of man?" The inference to be drawn from the circumstance that no such declarations or questions are to be found in Matthew's story is that the title "the Son of man" does not specify for the characters "who Jesus is."

2. Cf. 12:40; 13:41–43; 16:27; 24:29–31, 37–39; 25:31; 26:24, 64.

3. For a more complete discussion of this point cf. Kingsbury, "Figure of Jesus," 22–27.

4. Cf., e.g., 1:1; 16:16; 26:63–64.

5. Cf., e.g., 2:2; 27:11, 37, 42.

6. Cf., e.g., 1:1; 12:23; 22:42, 45.

7. Cf., e.g., 3:17; 14:33; 16:16; 17:5; 26:63–64; 27:43, 54.

8. A "predication-formula" is a statement (even if conditional) or question that attributes to Jesus some name, designation, or title of majesty in the interest of divulging "who he is" (cf. Kingsbury, "Figure of Jesus," 25–26).

Another, related indication that "the Son of man" does not tell of the identity of Jesus is the fact that although Jesus frequently uses it in public in order to point to himself, the thought occurs neither to the Jews nor to the disciples to construe it as a term that, again, informs them of who he is.

Consider the Jews. In the full hearing of the crowds[9] and of the Jewish leaders,[10] Jesus designates himself "the Son of man." Still, when the question of Jesus' identity arises, the leaders and the public disregard completely any Son-of-man references Jesus has made and think of him as either one who is in collusion with Beelzebul (9:34; 12:24) or "that deceiver" (27:63) or a "prophet," namely, "John the Baptist," "Elijah," "Jeremiah," or "one of the prophets" (16:14; 21:11, 46).

Or take the disciples. In their hearing, too, Jesus repeatedly speaks of himself throughout 4:17—16:20 as "the Son of man."[11] But despite this, the disciples never confess him to be the Son of man or even call on him as such. To illustrate how striking this phenomenon is, one need only glance at the passages 8:18–27; 14:22–33; and 16:13–20. In 8:18–27, Jesus, in turning away a scribe who would arrogate to himself the authority to become his disciple, refers to himself in the presence of the disciples as "the Son of man" (8:20; cf. 8:18, 21a, 23). But this notwithstanding, when the disciples are depicted only seven verses later as broaching the subject of the identity of Jesus because of the miracle he has performed in calming winds and sea, they do not draw on Jesus' reference to himself as the Son of man in order to acclaim him to be such. Far from acclaiming him to be the Son of man, they pose a question that asks, in fact, about who he is: "What sort of man is this, that even winds and sea obey him?" (8:27). Then, too, when Jesus later leads the disciples to give answer to this very question they have posed about who he is, as when they are once again in the boat on the sea or in the regions of Caesarea Philippi, the confession the disciples make is not "You are the Son of man" but "Truly you are the Son of God!" (14:33) and "You are the Messiah, the Son of the living God!" (16:15–16).

To stay with this latter passage of Peter's confession in the regions of Caesarea Philippi, the first of the two questions Jesus asks the disciples reveals in especially telling fashion that "the Son of man" does not serve in Matthew's story to specify Jesus' identity. In that Matthew has Jesus ask the disciples who "men" say that "the Son of man" is (16:13), he shows that "the Son of man" is not meant to clarify for the reader who Jesus is but that it must itself be clarified.

A final indication that "the Son of man" functions other than to set forth the identity of Jesus can also be found in the pericope on the trial of Jesus

9. Cf. 8:20 with 8:18; 9:6 with 9:8 (also 9:2); 11:19 with 11:7 and 11:16.
10. Cf. 8:20 with 8:19; 9:6 with 9:3; 12:8 with 12:2; 12:32 with 12:24; 12:40 with 12:38.
11. Cf. 8:20 with 8:18; 10:23 with 10:5; 12:8 with 12:1; 13:41 with 13:36; 16:13.

before the Sanhedrin (26:59–68). This pericope turns on the question of Jesus' identity. But although Jesus has openly referred to himself as the Son of man on several occasions heretofore in Matthew's story, the high priest does not ask him whether he is the Son of man but whether he is "the Messiah, the Son of God" (26:63).

If "the Son of man" does not function in Matthew's story as a confessional title to reveal the identity of Jesus, how does it function? It functions as a "public title." It is principally with an eye to the "world," Jews and Gentiles and especially opponents, that Jesus designates himself as the Son of man. Thus, in the earthly Son-of-man sayings, it is in view of the Jewish public (16:13) or of the world (13:36–37) or in the audience of the crowds,[12] of some of the scribes,[13] and of the Pharisees[14] that Jesus refers to himself as the Son of man. In the suffering Son-of-man sayings, it is to some of the scribes and Pharisees (12:38, 40) or to the disciples but in view of Judas,[15] of "men"[16] and "sinners" (26:45), of the Jewish leaders (20:18), of Gentiles (20:19), and of the rulers of the Gentiles (20:25, 28) that Jesus speaks of himself as the Son of man. And in the future Son-of-man sayings, it is in view of all the nations (Israel, the Gentiles, the Jewish leaders, but also the disciples)[17] that Jesus calls himself the Son of man. This orientation toward the "world" in Jesus' use of the Son of man marks it, again, as being "public" in nature.

To claim that "the Son of man" is a title Jesus uses in public without at the same time disclosing his identity necessarily raises the question of its meaning. To put it succinctly, "the Son of man" describes Jesus as "the man," or "the human being" (earthly, suffering, vindicated). In four passages in particular this comes to light. At 11:19, Jesus denounces this generation for dismissing the Son of man as the "man" who is a glutton and a drunkard, a friend of toll-collectors and sinners. At 9:6, Jesus declares that the Son of man has authority on earth to forgive sins and demonstrates this by healing a paralytic, whereupon the crowds respond by glorifying God for giving such authority to "men" (9:8). At 8:27, the question the disciples raise as to "what sort of man" (potapos) Jesus is can be seen to pick up on Jesus' reference to himself as the Son of man in the preceding pericope (8:20). And in the interpretation of the parable of the tares, Jesus first identifies the Son of man with the "man" who in the parable has sown good seed (cf. 13:37 with 13:24) and then identifies this earthly Son of man

12. Cf. 8:18, 20; 9:6, 8; 11:7, 19.
13. Cf. 9:3, 6; also 8:19–20.
14. Cf. 12:2, 8, 24, 32.
15. Cf. 26:2, 24–25, 45–46.
16. Cf. 17:22; also 17:12.
17. Cf. 10:23; 13:41–43; 16:27–28; 19:28; 24:27, 30–31, 37–39, 44; 25:31–32; 26:64.

with the future Son of man who will come at the consummation of the age to inaugurate the Great Assize (cf. 13:37 with 13:40–43).

Although "the Son of man" does in fact denote "the man," or "the human being," the question as to how one can best render it in English idiom is by no means idle. Merely to substitute the term "the man" each time "the Son of man" occurs in Matthew's story falls short of the goal. The reason is that although such a procedure would technically be correct, it would not in all cases make it as clear to the implied reader as it must be that Jesus, in making use of "the Son of man," is always referring to himself (cf., e.g., 9:6; 12:8, 32). In order, therefore, to take proper account of the twin circumstances that, on the one hand, "the Son of man" denotes "the man" (or "the human being") and that, on the other hand, Jesus employs it exclusively of himself, perhaps one does best to think of the term "this man" as capturing most adequately in English the force and intention of the Greek original underlying "the Son of man." In illustration of this, note the following three examples: 8:20: "Foxes have holes, and birds of the air nests; but *this man* has nowhere to lay his head"; 17:22–23: "*This man* is to be delivered into the hands of men, and they will kill him, and he will be raised on the third day"; and 26:64: "But I tell you, hereafter you will see *this man* seated at the right hand of power and coming on the clouds of heaven."

Should it be correct that "the Son of man" points to Jesus simply as "the man," or "the human being," how, specifically, is the implied reader to construe the identity of Jesus Son of man? On this score, Matthew is unambiguous, directing the reader to the words of Peter. Who, then, is Jesus, the Son of man (i.e., Who is this man Jesus? 16:13)? He is the Son of God (16:16). And lest one object that this answer is but the words of Peter, one will recall that the evaluative point of view Peter expresses in his confession is in accord with the evaluative point of view God has expressed at the baptism (3:17) and the transfiguration (17:5). Then, too, for the reader to recognize that the Son of man in Matthew's story is to be identified as the Son of God is also of benefit for gaining insight into yet another problem area. In Matt. 16:27 and 25:34, the expressions "his Father" and "my Father" occur with reference to Jesus as the Son of man. Seen properly, these expressions likewise attest to the identity of Jesus, the Son of man: Jesus Son of man, in referring to God as "my Father," tacitly bears witness thereby that he is the Son of God.

Associated with Jesus' use of the Son-of-man title in Matthew's story is the assertion on his part of "divine authority." If one leaves aside Matt. 16:13 and perhaps 12:32, Jesus assumes to himself in the earthly Son-of-man sayings the power to forgive sins (9:6), to regulate the sabbath (12:8), to have table fellowship with toll-collectors and sinners (11:19), and to raise up in the world sons of the Kingdom (13:37–38). Paradoxically, he also asserts his authority by embracing the life-style of "itinerant radicalism" (8:19–20). In the suffering Son-of-man sayings, Jesus evinces his authority by freely going the way of the cross in obedience to the will of God.[18] Indeed, as one who employs his authority not to be served but to serve, Jesus holds himself up as the example his disciples are to emulate in their life together (20:28). And in the future Son-of-man sayings, Jesus exercises his authority as the end-time judge who ushers in the consummated Kingdom and inaugurates the Great Assize.[19]

Also associated with the Son-of-man sayings in Matthew's story is a strong emphasis on the element of "opposition." In regard to the earthly Son-of-man sayings, such opposition comes to expression in numerous ways: Satan stands forth as the cosmic antagonist of Jesus (13:37–39); "men" prove themselves to be ignorant of Jesus' true identity and imagine him to be a prophet (16:13–14); "this generation" repudiates Jesus (11:19); a scribe wrongly attempts to arrogate to himself the right to become Jesus' disciple (8:19–20); and the Jewish leaders charge Jesus with blasphemy (9:3, 6), accuse him of being in collusion with Satan (12:24, 32), and take him to task because his disciples have allegedly acted unlawfully on the sabbath (12:2, 8). In the suffering Son-of-man sayings, Jesus speaks directly of the opposition he faces by predicting his death (12:39–40), by telling his disciples what his enemies will do to him,[20] and by contrasting his will to serve to the will of the rulers of the world to lord it over others (20:25–28). And in the future Son-of-man sayings, Jesus sounds the note of opposition (but also of hope) by portraying himself as the judge who will hold the entire world accountable, consigning some to condemnation and inviting others to share in the bliss of God's presence.[21]

JESUS AS THE SON OF MAN:
CONFLICT AND VINDICATION

Before this discussion is summarized, a final question begs for consideration: What impact does Matthew's use of the title of the Son of man have on his story? To answer this question, it is instructive to compare the overall role of this title with that of the family of titles at the head of which stands the "Son of God."

Briefly, the title Son of God serves to identify Jesus for the implied reader. Thus, the first part of Matthew's story culminates in God's announcement that Jesus is his Son (3:17), and the second part culminates in the confession by Peter which is in alignment with God's understanding of Jesus, that Jesus is God's Son (16:16–17). In the third part of Matthew's

18. Cf. 17:22–23; 20:18–19; 26:24, 45, 56; also 16:21.
19. Cf. 13:40–43; 16:27–28; 24:29–31; 25:31–46; 26:64.
20. Cf. 17:12, 22–23; 20:18–19; 26:2, 24, 45–46.
21. Cf. 10:23; 13:40–43; 16:27–28; 19:28; 24:29–31, 37–39, 43–44; 25:31–46; 26:64.

story, Jesus appropriates God's understanding of him as his Son in the parable of the wicked husbandmen he addresses to the Jewish leaders (21:37–39), and from this parable, in turn, the high priest derives the question concerning Jesus' divine sonship on which Jesus' trial turns and for which he is condemned to death for blasphemy (26:63–64a). Beyond this, on Jesus' death the Roman soldiers, also uttering words that are in alignment with God's understanding of Jesus, likewise declare Jesus to be God's Son (27:54). The significance of their declaration is that with it Matthew has, in terms of narrating his story, guided it to a point where knowledge of the identity of Jesus also embraces, as far as the implied reader is concerned, a mature knowledge of the purpose of Jesus' earthly ministry. Finally, on a mountain in Galilee the disciples, to whom Jesus' identity had earlier been revealed (16:16; 14:33), see the resurrected Jesus as the crucified one (28:5–7) and hence comprehend at last not only who he is but also what he was about (26:28). Accordingly, they receive from the resurrected Jesus not a command to silence (16:20), but the commission to go and make all nations his disciples (28:16–20).

Roughly parallel with this line of development (from 8:20 on), Jesus refers to himself in Matthew's story as the Son of man. In so doing, he does not divulge his identity but instead characterizes himself as "the man," or "the human being" (this man, or this human being). The purpose for which Jesus employs this title is multiple: to assert his divine authority in the face of public opposition; to tell his disciples what the "public," or "world" (Jews and Gentiles), is about to do to him; and to predict that he whom the world puts to death God will raise and that, exalted to universal rule, he will return in splendor as judge and consequently be seen by all as having been vindicated by God. Through Jesus' use of the public title the Son of man, therefore, Matthew calls the reader's attention to the twin elements of "conflict" and "vindication." In Matthew's purview, these mark the interaction of Jesus with the public, or world, that does not receive him as the one he is, namely, the Son of God.

SUMMARY

The objective of the preceding discussion has been to explain the meaning and function of "the Son of man" in Matthew's story. As has been indicated, "the Son of man" does not function "confessionally" to inform the implied reader of "who Jesus is" but instead characterizes Jesus as "the man," or "the human being" (this man, or this human being). But although "the Son of man" does not denominate the identity of Jesus, it is nonetheless a christological title, for it bears the unique stamp of Jesus' life and ministry: earthly, suffering, and vindicated. In nature, the designation Son of man is a "public title," which is to say that Jesus employs it "in public" or in view of the "public," or "world," and especially of his opponents. Typical of Jesus' use of this title is the assertion on his part of divine authority in the face of opposition.

6
The Disciples of Jesus

THE main story-line of Matthew's Gospel concerns Jesus, since he is the protagonist. Jesus, however, calls disciples to be with him. They, too, have a story-line that can be traced. Because in the first part of his story Matthew presents Jesus to the implied reader (1:1—4:16), the disciples do not appear. By contrast, in the second and third parts of the story they have a prominent role to play.[1] Still, only marginally does their role determine the plot of Matthew's story.

Matthew's story of the disciples follows the contours of his story of Jesus. In the second part (4:17—16:20), Matthew tells of Jesus' ministry to Israel of teaching, preaching, and healing (4:17—11:1). Parallel to this, Matthew tells of the disciples' call and of their mission to Israel (4:17—11:1). Also in the second part, Matthew tells of Israel's response to Jesus, which is one of repudiation (11:2—16:20). Parallel but contrasting to this, Matthew tells of the disciples as being the recipients of divine revelation (11:2—16:20). In the third part of his story (16:21—28:20), Matthew tells of Jesus' journey to Jerusalem and of his suffering, death, and resurrection. Parallel to this, Matthew shows how the disciples are led to appropriate Jesus' evaluative point of view according to which suffering sonship is a summons to suffering discipleship, or to servanthood.

Jesus has conflict not only with Israel but also with the disciples. In each case, however, the nature of the conflict is fundamentally different. Jesus has conflict with Israel because it repudiates the evaluative point of view he espouses and judges that because of this point of view, he must be put to death. Jesus has conflict with the disciples because although they aspire to appropriate his evaluative point of view, they falter at times or fail badly. Through his conflict with the disciples, Jesus aims to instruct them or to mediate to them new insight or perception.

1. For a redaction-critical study of the disciples, cf. Luz, "Disciples in the Gospel," 98–128.

The level of conflict between Jesus and the disciples is, of course, not the same throughout Matthew's story. In the second part (4:17—16:20), for example, conflict is by no means the feature that dominates Jesus' relationship to the disciples. Nevertheless, it does surface, as when the disciples prove themselves to be persons of little faith, or do not understand at once what Jesus endeavors to teach them, or leave untapped the authority Jesus would make available to them because they forget that it is at their disposal. In the third part of Matthew's story (16:21—28:20), however, the conflict that arises between Jesus and the disciples becomes intense. Here it has to do with the disciples' imperceptiveness, and at times resistance, to the notion that servanthood is the essence of discipleship. As has been seen, the resolution of this conflict does not occur until the final pericope of Matthew's story, where it is indicated that Jesus at the last brings the disciples to adopt his evaluative point of view on this crucial matter.

THE CALL OF THE DISCIPLES AND
THEIR MISSION TO ISRAEL

As Jesus begins his public activity in Israel (4:17), he stands before the implied reader as the Son of God whom God has chosen and empowered for messianic ministry (3:16–17). Almost immediately Jesus calls his first disciples, two pairs of brothers (Peter and Andrew; James and John), thus taking to himself eye- and ear-witnesses (4:18–22). In the calling of each pair of brothers, the pattern is the same: Jesus sees, Jesus summons, and at once those summoned leave behind everything—nets, boat, and father—in order to follow him (4:18–20, 21–22). The force of this stereotyped pattern is clear: Jesus authoritatively calls those whom he himself chooses to be his disciples, and those who obey his call abandon their former way of life with all its commitments of family, goods, and occupation and join themselves to him by giving him their total allegiance.

In calling disciples, Jesus thus forms a new community, which he elsewhere designates as "my church" (16:18; 18:17) or alludes to as a "(new) nation" (21:43). What are the nature and purpose of this new community? Its purpose is plainly stated by Jesus: to be "fishers of men," that is, to engage in mission in line with the broad schema of first Israel (10:5b–6) and then the nations (28:19). The nature of this new community derives from the call Jesus extends: through Jesus, who is God's unique Son in whom God's Kingdom is a present reality, those who make up this community live in the sphere of God's eschatological Rule where God is their Father (6:9) and they are sons of God,[2] disciples of Jesus (10:1; 26:18), and brothers of Jesus (28:10) and of one another (23:8). In a word, the new community Jesus forms is a brotherhood of the sons of God and of his disciples.

2. Cf. 5:9, 45; 13:38.

Integral to this description of Jesus and the new community he forms are two elements that Matthew is at pains to emphasize throughout his story in scenes that depict Jesus as interacting with the disciples: on the one hand, the uniqueness of Jesus as the Son of God and, on the other hand, his close association with the disciples as sons of God and brothers. Thus, Jesus stands out from the disciples as the obvious figure of authority. The relationship he has with them is characterized as that of "teacher and learner," of "master and slave" (10:24–25). Consistently, they address him as "Lord" and acknowledge thereby his exalted station and his divine authority.[3] Moreover, it is he who summons, dispatches, commands, and teaches, and it is they who follow, go, obey, and heed.

By the same token, Matthew also highlights the close association the disciples have with Jesus. This comes to clear expression in the concept of "being with Jesus."[4] The Greek preposition translated as "with" (*meta* + genitive case) is frequently employed to denote accompaniment (cf., e.g., 12:3: "David . . . and those who were 'with him' "). Noteworthy is the way Matthew carefully restricts the circle of those who share in the presence, or the company, of Jesus. Except for Mary his mother (2:11) and toll-collectors and sinners (9:11), the list of those who are "with Jesus" or of whom it is said that Jesus is "with them" includes only Peter (26:69, 71), one of Jesus' followers (26:51), Peter and the two sons of Zebedee (27:37–38, 40), and the twelve or eleven disciples (26:18, 20, 36; 28:20). Noticeably absent from this list are such as the Jewish crowds or their leaders. Indeed, Judas does not so much as eat with Jesus (Mark 14:18) but merely dips his hand with him in the dish, in this manner marking himself as the one who will betray Jesus (Matt. 26:23). In point of fact, Jesus is only "with Israel" as with a "faithless and perverse generation" from whom he will withdraw his presence (17:17), and the critical principle obtains: "he who is not with me is against me, and he who does not gather with me scatters" (12:30).

In Matthew's story, then, Jesus grants the privilege of his company almost without exception only to his own. Before the resurrection, these are his disciples. After the resurrection, they are his church (16:18). The disciples before the resurrection follow along "with Jesus" as he leads them to the cross (16:21; 20:17–19). The church after the resurrection makes its way toward the consummation of the age and the Parousia on the promise of the exalted Jesus that he will surely be "with them [you]" (28:20).

What such close association with Jesus means theologically, Matthew explains in the key passages Matt. 1:23 ("Emmanuel . . . God [is] with us"), 18:20 ("there am I in the midst of them"), and 28:20 ("I am with you always"). It means, as the central thought of Matthew's story also states,

---

3. Cf. 8:21, 25; 14:28, 30; 16:22; 17:4; 18:21; 26:22.
4. Cf. Frankemölle, *Jahwebund und Kirche Christi*, chap. 1.

that through his presence Jesus Messiah, the earthly and exalted Son of God, mediates to his disciples or church the gracious, saving presence of God and his Rule. Now if, in line with this truth, these three passages are examined in context, it becomes apparent that they relate the presence and therefore the authority of the earthly and exalted Son of God to the basic activities characterizing not so much the ministry of the earthly disciples as that of the post-Easter church: baptizing (28:19), teaching (28:20), prayer (18:19), church discipline (18:18), and, in general, the mission to the nations (28:19). In addition, Matthew likewise reveals that the church's celebration of the Last Supper is done not only in commemoration of the shedding of the blood of the Son of God for the forgiveness of sins (26:28), but also in anticipation of that day to come when he will again drink wine "with them [you]" in the glorious Kingdom of his Father (26:29). In short, Matthew utilizes the concept of "being with Jesus" and the related idiom of his "being with them" in order to restrict close association with Jesus almost exclusively to the circle of the disciples and, theologically, to set forth the truth that the church worships and carries out its ministry to the close of the age in the presence and on the authority of the exalted Son of God, through whom God exercises his gracious, saving Rule.

The final feature in the pericope 4:18–22 which begs to be considered is the fact that Peter is cited as being the first of the disciples to be called (4:18). Later, at 10:2, Matthew makes specific mention of this: "The names of the twelve apostles are these: first Simon, who is called Peter. . . ." By depicting Peter as the first of the disciples to be called and by making reference to this in listing the names of the twelve, Matthew informs the implied reader of the manner in which he conceives of Peter's "primacy": it is temporal, or better, "salvation-historical," in nature. What impact does such "salvation-historical primacy" have on Peter's relationship to the other disciples throughout Matthew's story? Ruled out is the notion that it elevates Peter to a position of authority over the other disciples, for at 23:8 Jesus himself says to the disciples: "But you are not to be called rabbi, for one is your teacher [the Messiah], and all you are brothers." Peter's primacy is consequently that of being "first among equals," and this explains why he functions as the "spokesman" of the disciples and is also, in his behavior, "typical" of them, both positively and negatively. It is in line with Peter's salvation-historical primacy that he makes confession of Jesus near Caesarea Philippi and is promised in return that he will be the rock on which the church will be built and that he will be given the keys of the Kingdom, which are the authority to bind and to loose (to decide matters of church doctrine and of church discipline), an authority, incidentally, that Peter shares with the other disciples (16:16–19; 18:18). So again, Matthew in his story pointedly ascribes primacy to Peter, but this primacy is one of being first among equals (4:18; 10:2; 23:8–12).[5]

5. Cf. Kingsbury, "Peter in Matthew's Gospel," 67–83.

Accordingly, through the call of Jesus, the disciples enter into the sphere of God's eschatological Rule. In the Sermon on the Mount, Jesus describes the kinds of persons his disciples are and the quality of life they lead in the sphere of God's Rule. The kinds of persons Jesus' disciples are comes to light in the beatitudes he pronounces (5:3–10). For example, "the poor in spirit" are those who may or may not be economically deprived but who in any case stand before God with no illusions of self-righteousness or self-sufficiency. "Those who mourn" are those who grieve over sin and evil in the world. "The meek" are those who are lowly and powerless, those whose only hope is God. "Those who hunger and thirst for righteousness" are those who yearn for the final salvation that only God can effect. "The merciful" are those who eschew judgment and forgive. "The pure in heart" are those who are undivided in their allegiance to God. "The peacemakers" are those who work for the wholeness and well-being that God wills for a broken world. And "those who are persecuted for righteousness' sake" are those who incur tribulation because, as disciples of Jesus, they serve God.

The quality of life which is indicative of disciples who live in the sphere of God's eschatological Rule is designated by Jesus as the "greater righteousness" (5:20). "Righteousness" (*dikaiosynē*) is a term that Jesus predicates to both God and humans. The righteousness of God is his justice, which will issue at the consummation of the age in salvation or condemnation for humans (5:6). The "greater righteousness" to which Jesus refers envisages to be sure human conduct ("your righteousness"; 6:1), but a human conduct that contrasts sharply with that of the scribes and Pharisees (5:20). The conduct Jesus imputes to the scribes and Pharisees is "hypocrisy," which he further defines as "lawlessness" (23:28). As the antithesis of lawlessness, the greater righteousness is doing the will of God, including the law (5:17), as Jesus teaches this (6:10; 7:21; 12:50; 18:14). One does God's will when one is perfect, or wholehearted, in one's devotion to God (5:48), and one is such when one loves God with heart, soul, and mind and the neighbor as self (22:37–40). At the center of the greater righteousness, then, is undivided fealty toward God and selfless love of the neighbor (5:21—6:18).

The community Jesus forms in calling disciples to follow him and to reflect in their lives the ethic of the greater righteousness has an ethos all its own. The passage 8:18–22 captures well some of the flavor of this ethos. This passage comprises an introduction (8:18) and two contrasting scenes. In the first scene (8:19–20), a scribe approaches Jesus and offers to become his disciple: "Teacher," he says, "I will follow you wherever you go." Jesus, however, turns the scribe away with the remark, "Foxes have holes, and birds of the air have nests; but the Son of man has nowhere to lay his head."

Is there proof to substantiate the contention that Jesus turns the scribe away? The proof lies in the fact that the words of the scribe fracture the pattern one finds in pericopes that portray the call of so-called true disciples. In these pericopes, the pattern is such as to place the initiative squarely with Jesus: Jesus sees, Jesus summons, and those who are summoned follow him (4:18–20, 21–22; 9:9). In the verses 8:19–20, however, the scribe arrogates to himself the authority to make of himself a disciple of Jesus. He believes that he has within him the capacity to embark on, and to sustain, the life of discipleship. In his reply to the scribe, Jesus asserts in effect that so rigorous is the life of discipleship that no one, apart from his enabling call, is capable of embarking upon this life and sustaining it.

Is there further evidence to support the contention that Jesus turns the scribe away? It is noteworthy that the scribe addresses Jesus as "teacher" and that Jesus refers to himself in his reply to the scribe as "the Son of man." "Teacher" is not the term of address employed by those in Matthew's story who approach Jesus in "faith." These persons call on Jesus as "Lord." "Teacher" is the term of human respect that is used, for example, by the opponents of Jesus. Similarly, "the Son of man" is the term by which Jesus refers to himself in public or with a view to the public, especially his opponents. In sum, the use of the two terms "teacher" and "the Son of man" in the scene 8:19–20 has the effect of highlighting the distance that exists between Jesus and the scribe: they are not of one mind and one will. Jesus turns the scribe away.

The second scene (8:21–22) concerns a man described as already being a disciple of Jesus. The man's use of the term "Lord" and not "teacher" and Jesus' use of the pronoun "me" and not "the Son of man" are also proof of this. Earlier, Jesus had ordered the disciples to board a boat and set sail for the other side of the sea (8:18). With a view to Jesus' command, this unnamed disciple comes to him with a request: "Lord," he asks, "let me first go and bury my father." Jesus' answer to the disciple is: "Follow me, and leave the dead to bury their own dead."

The problem inherent in the request of the unnamed disciple is that he desires to suspend for a time his commitment to follow Jesus. Moreover, his request is exceedingly well founded: he has a prior obligation to which he must attend, namely, the sacred trust to go and look after the burial of his father (cf. Gen. 50:5–6). Jesus' response to the disciple's request is swift and sharp. The commitment of discipleship, he declares in essence, brooks no suspension. No obligation exists which can be permitted to take precedence over it. The resolution of this conflict is clear: the unnamed disciple boards the boat.

If the life of discipleship cannot be undertaken apart from the enabling call of Jesus but, once entered on, brooks no suspension, it is also a life always open to attacks of "little faith." The latter is the truth illustrated by the pericope on the stilling of the storm (8:23–27). Having ordered the disciples to the other side of the sea (8:18), Jesus now boards the boat and the disciples follow him in (8:23). Out on the sea, Jesus sleeps, while the disciples encounter a fierce storm (cf. 24:7–8). Fearing for their lives, the disciples awaken him and plead in prayer-like petition that he save them. Jesus grants their plea, calming winds and sea, but not before he has chided them for being cowardly and hence exhibiting little, or weak, faith. They have, in fact, allowed cowardice to frustrate his command to sail across the sea.

Two contrasting themes dominate this episode. The first theme has to do with the phenomenon of "little faith," which provokes conflict between Jesus and the disciples. Here as elsewhere in Matthew's story, little faith manifests itself as a "crisis of trust." In this instance, it thwarts the disciples' ability to carry out the task, or mission, Jesus has given them. Jesus fully expects that the disciples should obey his command and sail across the sea. They succumb, however, to the malady of little faith, which assumes the guise of cowardice, and do not complete their task. Far from showing the disciples sympathy, Jesus expresses surprise that they should have been so beset by weakness (8:26). And the second, contrasting theme is that, despite the fact that the disciples have fallen victim to a crisis of trust, Jesus does not leave them to their own devices but hears their plea and assists them in their plight. The life of discipleship is susceptible to bouts of little faith. Such little faith is not to be condoned. Nevertheless, Jesus does not abandon his disciples at such times but stands ever ready with his saving power to sustain them so that they can in fact discharge the mission he has entrusted to them.

The pericope on the call of Matthew (9:9) illustrates yet another aspect of discipleship, namely, the broad spectrum of those whom Jesus summons to follow him. The pattern governing the narration of the pericope reveals that the call of Matthew is the call of a true disciple: Jesus sees, Jesus summons, and the one summoned follows after Jesus (9:9; 10:3). In the case of the calling of Peter and Andrew and of James and John, Jesus summoned fishermen to become his disciples, persons who were accounted as being upright citizens. Matthew, however, is a toll-collector.[6] As such, he is looked on by the Jewish society of Matthew's story as no better than a robber and one whose testimony would not be honored in a Jewish court of law. Nevertheless, Jesus makes him one of the twelve (10:3). Not only the upright are called by Jesus, but also the despised.

Thus far, the focus has been on Jesus' calling of disciples. But this changes in 9:35—10:42, and the disciples' mission to Israel becomes the topic. To indicate that the circle of the twelve disciples has now been

6. Cf. Donahue, "Tax Collectors and Sinners," 39–61.

completed and that the disciples are to be "fishers of men" in Israel, Matthew recites the names of the twelve and terms them "apostles" ("ones who are sent"; 10:2–4). The mission Jesus gives them is plainly an extension of his own: he endows them with the authority on which they are to act (10:1); it is only to the lost sheep of the house of Israel that they are to go (10:6; 15:24); the nearness of the Kingdom is to be their message (10:7; 4:17); and they, like him, are to heal every disease and every infirmity (10:1; 9:35).

But this notwithstanding, the instructions Jesus gives the disciples are such that their mission to Israel becomes emblematic of their later, universal mission to the nations. The place in time of Matthew, the implied author, and of the implied reader lies between the resurrection and the Parousia (24:15; 27:8; 28:15). From that vantage point, too, this speech strikes responsive chords. Selected examples that may be noted are references to the disciples as being like sheep in the midst of wolves (10:16); as encountering persecution and hatred from both Jews and Gentiles (10:17–23); as enduring treatment after the manner of that meted out to Jesus (10:24–31); as being impelled to the fearless confession of Jesus (10:32–33); as placing allegiance to Jesus and the life of servanthood above any other good (10:34–39); and as discharging the mission entrusted to them in anticipation of the "reward" they will receive at the latter day (10:40–42). In these missionary instructions of Jesus to the twelve, "the particular" is not without the quality of "the typical."

To conclude, in the first half of the second part of his story (4:17—11:1) Matthew tells of Jesus' ministry to Israel of teaching, preaching, and healing and, in tandem with this, of Jesus' calling of the disciples and of their mission to Israel. In calling disciples, Jesus creates a new community described as a brotherhood of the sons of God and of the disciples of Jesus the purpose of which is to engage in missionary activity (4:18–22). The ethic that distinguishes the disciples of Jesus is that of the "greater righteousness" (5:20). Not only to begin but also to sustain the life of discipleship, the enabling power of Jesus is indispensable, and the commitment to which Jesus summons the disciples is enduring and takes precedence over all competing obligations (8:18–22). Called to mission as the disciples are, they are always susceptible to bouts of little faith, yet they can also always rest assured that Jesus stands ever ready to sustain them in their needs (8:23–27). This is no exclusive community of the holy; Jesus invites into the circle of the disciples the despised and the outcast as well as the upright (9:9). And commissioned to preach and to heal first in Israel, the disciples receive instructions that portend intense conflict for them and that present this mission as foreshadowing in numerous particulars the later mission they will undertake to the Gentiles (9:35—10:42).

THE DISCIPLES AS THE RECIPIENTS OF
DIVINE REVELATION

In the latter half of the second part of his story (11:2—16:20), Matthew tells of the repudiation with which Israel responds to Jesus. In contrast to Israel, the disciples stand out as the recipients of divine revelation. The incidence of conflict between Jesus and the disciples, which was low in 4:17—11:1, is more frequent in this section but still not overly prevalent.

Although the fame of Jesus has spread and the crowds throng to him, this does not mean that Israel has accepted him. On the contrary, it repudiates him. In private prayer, Jesus attributes Israel's repudiation of him to the will of God himself. Still, he couples this with the further assertion that the divine revelation, hidden by God from Israel, has nonetheless been revealed, namely, to "infants," that is to say, to his disciples. Jesus expresses himself thus:

> I thank you, Father, Lord of heaven and earth, that you have hidden these things from the wise and understanding and revealed them to infants; yes, Father, for thus it was pleasing to you (11:25–26).

In the surrounding narrative of Matthew 11—12, this prayer of Jesus is borne out, for by 12:46–50 Matthew pictures the disciples as the only ones in Israel who still adhere to Jesus. The question is: What is the nature and substance of the divine revelation imparted to the disciples?

As elaborated in the context, this revelation concerns in greatest measure two matters. The one matter is the mysteries of the Kingdom of Heaven (13:11); the other is insight into Jesus' identity as the Son of God (14:33; 16:16).

The mysteries of the Kingdom of Heaven which are made known to the disciples but hidden from Israel are contained in Jesus' parable-discourse of Matthew 13.[7] In brief, they are such as the following: The Kingdom of Heaven, or the eschatological Rule of God, confronts people in the person of Jesus as a present, though hidden, reality tending toward its consummation in the final judgment that Jesus will conduct at the end of time (13:31–32, 33). As people hear the proclamation of the gospel of the Kingdom, they are called to decision: On the one hand, those ultimately decide against this proclamation who cannot be moved by it to give God their wholehearted allegiance; or who are not prepared to endure the persecution that acceptance of it entails; or who value the pursuit of wealth more than the good news the proclamation announces. On the other hand, those (like the disciples) decide for this proclamation who receive it with understanding and are led by it to love God with heart, soul, and mind and the

---

7. On the interpretation of Jesus' parable-discourse, cf., e.g., Kingsbury (*Parables of Jesus*) and Gerhardsson ("Parable of the Sower," 165–93).

neighbor as themselves (13:3–9, 18:23). Or to take a different perspective, until the consummation of the age the entire world is the site where people live under the influence of one of two opposing spheres of power: Either people live in the sphere of God's eschatological Rule under the aegis of the earthly and exalted Jesus, or they live in the sphere of the kingdom of evil under the aegis of Satan (13:24–30, 36–43). In other respects, disciples who live in the sphere of God's eschatological Rule are summoned to be single-mindedly dedicated to the doing of God's will as taught by Jesus (13:44–46). And last, as disciples lead their lives against that time when this age will come to an end, they must guard themselves against any sense of false security, for at the latter day they, too, will undergo judgment (13:47–50).

At the end of his parable-discourse, Jesus asks the disciples whether they have understood the mysteries of the Kingdom which he has taught them. Their reply is in the affirmative (13:51–52). Yet, on other occasions conflict erupts between Jesus and the disciples when their understanding falters. Twice in deserted places Jesus expects the disciples to be cognizant of the fact that the authority with which he has endowed them (10:1) is at their disposal to feed, respectively, the five thousand and the four thousand men (14:16; 15:32–33). In the face of these expectations, however, the disciples simply stand overwhelmed, so that Jesus himself must demonstrate to them that he has not placed demands upon them incapable of fulfillment (14:13–21; 15:32–38). And in the boat on the sea, the disciples, having already forgotten that authority is available to them to satisfy human need, become agitated because they are without bread (16:5–12). For his part, Jesus desires to warn the disciples of the "leaven of the Pharisees and Sadducees." What Jesus means by this is the "(corrupting) teaching" of the Jewish leaders, and he becomes annoyed that the disciples do not comprehend this. Indeed, it is not until Jesus has explained himself that the disciples finally grasp the warning he is giving them (16:9–12). In principle, the disciples in Matthew's story do in fact possess the gift of understanding (13:11, 16–17, 51). But this does not foreclose the possibility that they can falter in making use of this gift and that such faltering can spark conflict between them and Jesus.

The other area in which the disciples are the recipients of divine revelation has to do with knowledge of Jesus' identity as the Son of God. In the pericope on the walking on water (14:22–33), Jesus compels the disciples to board the boat and to go before him to the other side of the sea. Under way on the water, the disciples witness Jesus, in sequence, walk on the water, command Peter to get out of the boat and come to him, rescue Peter from drowning when because of fear and doubt Peter begins to sink and cries out for rescue, and calm the wind. Because Peter's fear and doubt constitute a crisis of trust, or an attack of little faith, which prevents Peter from carrying out the order Jesus has given him, Jesus reprimands him and in this sense enters into conflict with him. But be that as it may, in witnessing all these events, the disciples are led to worship Jesus and to confess him to be the Son of God (14:33). They in effect give answer to the question they themselves had raised earlier in another episode out on the sea, "What sort of man is this, that even winds and sea obey him?" (8:27).

The disciples' confession of 14:33 must be seen in conjunction with Peter's confession of Jesus near Caesarea Philippi. Here Peter, on behalf of the disciples, affirms Jesus to be the Son of God (16:15–16). Noteworthy is Jesus' response to Peter's confession. He declares with no little fervor that only by divine revelation is knowledge of his divine sonship possible (16:17). To be sure, Jesus also in this connection commands the disciples to silence about his divine sonship (16:20). But this is necessitated by the fact that, at this juncture, they do not as yet know that his being the Son of God also involves death on the cross. In perceiving Jesus to be the Son of God, the disciples are in truth the recipients of divine revelation. Their perception of Jesus contrasts starkly with the notion of the Jewish public, which has rejected Jesus (11:16–24), that he is but a prophet of one sort or another (16:13–14).

In summary, at the same time Matthew portrays Israel as reacting to Jesus' ministry of teaching, preaching, and healing by repudiating him, he also marks out the disciples as the recipients of divine revelation (11:2—16:20). The revelation imparted to the disciples concerns in the main the mysteries of the Kingdom of Heaven (Matthew 13) and the knowledge that Jesus is the Son of God (14:33; 16:16). Although conflict between Jesus and the disciples flares in this latter half of the second part of Matthew's story, it does not occur with great frequency and it serves the larger purpose of enabling Jesus to instruct the disciples or to mediate new insight to them.

SERVANTHOOD AS THE ESSENCE
OF DISCIPLESHIP

The leitmotif of the third part of Matthew's story (16:21—28:20) is Jesus' journey to Jerusalem and his passion and resurrection. In harmony with this, the motif that dominates Matthew's story of the disciples in this part is that servanthood constitutes the essence of discipleship.

Matthew begins this part of his story with a narrative comment, and he follows this rather closely with a word of Jesus. In his narrative comment Matthew reports:

From that time Jesus began to *show* his disciples that he must go to Jerusalem and suffer many things from the elders and chief priests and scribes, and be killed, and on the third day be raised (16:21).

And the word Jesus speaks is this: "If any man would come after me, let him deny himself and take up his cross, and let him follow me" (16:24). The emphasis in the narrative comment on "showing" *(deiknyein)* is significant, for its use here is such that it necessarily encompasses both words and deeds, both speaking and doing. Combine these two passages while keeping this latter observation in mind, and they indicate that Jesus reveals to his disciples, in all he says and in all he does in the story following 16:21, that God has ordained he should go to Jerusalem to suffer and that his way of suffering is, as far as they are concerned, a summons to them also to go the way of suffering—that is to say, the way of servanthood (cf. 20:28). In other words, Matthew alerts the implied reader through these two passages that suffering, defined as servanthood, is the essence of discipleship and that Jesus will show the disciples in what he says and does that this is in fact the case.

Peter's immediate reaction to Jesus' prediction of his passion is to summon Jesus to him and to censure Jesus: "God forbid, Lord!" exclaims Peter, "This shall never happen to you!" (16:22). In reply, Jesus reproves Peter, warning him that in taking exception to the notion that Jesus must suffer and die he is functioning as the mouthpiece not of God, but of Satan (16:23). Then, addressing all the disciples, Jesus tells them that the corollary to suffering sonship is suffering discipleship (16:24). These words Jesus has with the disciples here at the outset of the third part of the story adumbrate the conflict Jesus will henceforth have with them: Jesus' struggle will be to wean the disciples from an evaluative point of view which can make them more akin to Satan than to God and to bring them to realize that suffering, or servanthood, is indeed the essence of discipleship.

In the pericopes on the transfiguration (17:1–9) and on the coming of Elijah (17:10–13), indication is given by no lesser authorities than God and scripture of how crucial it is in Matthean perspective for the disciples to be led to adopt Jesus' evaluative point of view concerning both his own fate and the essence of discipleship. Atop the high mountain, Peter, James, and John gaze on Jesus in transfigured splendor and hear the voice from the bright cloud declare, "This is my beloved Son, in whom I take delight; hear him!" (17:5). If this affirmation of Jesus' divine sonship is confirmation from God himself of the earlier confessions to this effect of Peter (16:16) and the disciples (14:33), the injunction to "hear him" is an exhortation, likewise from God himself, that the disciples are to attend carefully to Jesus' words regarding the necessity both of his own going the way of suffering (16:21) and of their emulating him (16:24). Then, as Jesus and the three disciples descend from the mountain, Jesus speaks of John the Baptist as also fulfilling by his suffering the eschatological expectations associated with Elijah, and he gives the disciples to understand that in this way, too, John was his forerunner (17:10–13). Thus, what Jesus tries to impress on the disciples is that, according to God's evaluative point of view, both "forerunner" and "disciples" are to reflect in their persons and lives the person and life of himself, Jesus.

Sharp conflict occurs when Jesus and the three disciples return to the crowd and the other disciples below (17:14–20). In Jesus' absence, a man had appealed to the disciples to exorcise a demon from his son, but they had been unable to do so. Taking control from the disciples, Jesus exorcises the demon and, in private, tells the disciples that the reason they failed to perform the healing is that they were hampered by "little faith" (17:20). Much earlier, Jesus had endowed the disciples with authority to exorcise demons as part of their mission to Israel (10:1, 8). Consequently, he expects them to draw on this authority. But if they approach the tasks of their mission forgetful of their empowerment and encumbered by a crisis of trust, they render themselves ineffectual. Says Jesus: "For truly I say to you, if you have faith as a grain of mustard seed . . . nothing will be impossible to you" (17:20).

Gathered with his disciples in Galilee before leaving for Jerusalem, Jesus predicts his passion a second time (17:22–23). His prediction "grieves" the disciples: what he has said they understand, but why he does not turn aside from the events he has foretold escapes them (cf. 16:21–22).

In the house at Capernaum a final time, Jesus first engages Peter in dialogue (17:24–27) and then delivers his ecclesiological discourse to all the disciples (18:1–35).[8] In the latter, Jesus instructs the disciples regarding their life together as a community. Toward those on the outside, the disciples, as sons of God and his followers, are in principle free and responsible only to God. At the same time, they do not lead lives in society that are less than exemplary or employ their freedom to give needless offense to others and hence foreclose the possibility that others may become his followers. Toward one another, the disciples lead lives that comport themselves with a community presided over by Jesus: in recognition of their total dependence on God, they deal with one another in the spirit of loving concern, of circumspection, of mutuality, and of forgiveness.

Guided by his divinely appointed goal to reach Jerusalem (16:21), Jesus at last departs from Galilee and enters the regions of Judea beyond the Jordan (19:1). Concomitantly, the extent to which he moves closer to Jerusalem is also the extent to which his conflict with the disciples becomes increasingly intense. To be sure, the disciples continue to follow him and to function as eye- and ear-witnesses to his activity, to be instructed by him, and to carry out obediently assignments he gives them (cf. 21:1–7; 26:17–19). Nonetheless, it likewise becomes ever more apparent that the evaluative point of view Jesus advocates differs in obvious respects from the one the disciples

8. On the ecclesiological discourse, cf. Thompson, *Divided Community*.

advocate. The basis of Jesus' evaluative point of view is devotion to God and love of the neighbor, which lead him to suffering and death. The basis of the disciples' evaluative point of view is self-concern, which is the opposite of servanthood: it counts as important having status in the eyes of others, possessing wealth, exercising authority over others, overcoming might with might, and "saving one's life" no matter what the cost. The end to which the disciples' evaluative point of view leads them is apostasy.

Examples abound of the conflict incited by the disciples' evaluative point of view. For one thing, the disciples rebuke those who bring children to Jesus and would turn them away, for children are "no-accounts" and without status in the society of Matthew's story (19:13–15). For another thing, the disciples, like the world around them, look on the possession of wealth as a sign of God's favor. Consequently, they are nonplussed when Jesus tells them not only that the rich do not have any advantage over others in attaining eternal life, but also that it will be difficult, indeed impossible, for them to do so. But if those who enjoy God's favor are unable to be saved, the disciples wonder, who, then, can be? For all humans alike salvation is an impossible attainment, is Jesus' reply, because salvation is of God (19:23–26). But if this be granted, what, then, do the disciples ultimately have to look forward to, Peter wants to know. Answers Jesus: the hope in which the disciples live lies, finally, in anticipation of the reward, or gift, of eternal life (19:27–30). Again, immediately following Jesus' third prediction of his passion (20:17–19) the mother of James and John approaches Jesus with the request that he award her sons the positions of first and second honor when he comes into his Rule (20:20–23). As the other ten disciples hear of this request, they become indignant, not because their motives are purer, but because they covet these same positions of honor for themselves (20:24). And last, on the day following Jesus' entry into Jerusalem, as he is returning to the city from having spent the night in Bethany, he curses and causes to wither a fig tree that had failed to produce fruit (21:18–19). Wrongly, the disciples are astonished at this feat, so that Jesus must remind them yet again that if only they will trust and not give place to doubt, or little faith, they will be able to do far greater things than this (21:20–22; cf. 17:20).

As one moves on to the events of the passion (26:1–2), one can observe that the disciples stray still further from Jesus' evaluative point of view. The upshot is that they are unable to cope with these events. What Jesus says of Peter in Gethsemane, with an eye to James and John as well, is true of all of the disciples during the passion: "The spirit is willing, but the flesh is weak" (26:41). The disciples are divided in their intentions and loyalties. To be undivided, to be wholehearted, is to be "perfect" (5:48). Jesus, therefore, is perfect; the disciples are not.

Accordingly, as the disciples face with Jesus the events of his passion, they show themselves to be enmeshed in circumstances manifestly beyond either their comprehension or their control. For instance, in the house of Simon the leper in Bethany, the disciples misinterpret as a waste of money the woman's anointing Jesus with expensive ointment. They do not perceive that she is, in reality, preparing him for burial (26:6–13). More tragically, Judas, in selling his services to the chief priests to betray Jesus, unwittingly acts in a manner that is the exact opposite of "servanthood": Jesus is the servant par excellence, for he delivers himself to death in order that others might gain life; by contrast, Judas delivers Jesus to death in order that he might gain advantage for himself (26:14–16).

In other respects, at the Last Supper Jesus shares with the disciples, he predicts that one of them will betray him. The disciples are all grieved by this, but their grief is simply expressive of the false confidence that none believes he could ever do such a thing (26:20–22). Then, too, like the others Judas also asks Jesus whether he will be the one to betray him. In addressing Jesus, however, Judas calls him "rabbi" and not "Lord," which attests to the distance of heart and mind between the two. What is more, in posing his question, Judas frames it so as to anticipate the answer no, which makes of him, in the very asking of his question, a liar (26:25; cf. 26:14–16).

On another note, Jesus predicts, on the way to the Mount of Olives, that all the disciples will fall away from him in that night and that Peter will deny him. In a grand gesture of self-delusion, Peter, joined by all the disciples, solemnly affirms that he will die with Jesus rather than deny him (26:30–35). In similar fashion, while Jesus prays in Gethsemane, Peter, James, and John are unable to watch with him and instead fall asleep. Although they have boasted that they will die rather than desert Jesus, they do not possess so much as the inner strength to stay awake. Indeed, such boasting on the one hand and such falling asleep on the other bear eloquent testimony to the fact that the disciples are in truth divided in their loyalties toward Jesus.

In a different vein, in the hour of Jesus' arrest one of the disciples, forgetful of all the words Jesus has spoken concerning his passion and in an act of utter futility, endeavors to meet might with might by drawing his sword and cutting off the ear of the slave of the high priest (26:51). And to complete the entire series of the disciples' failures, once Jesus is in the custody of his opponents, the disciples all flee from him (26:56) and Peter later denies him (26:58, 69–75).

With the exception of Judas (27:3–10), Jesus' conflict with the disciples does not, however, end in failure for them. Through a series of words given to, or meant for, the eleven disciples (26:32; 28:7, 10), Jesus directs "his scattered brothers" (26:31; 28:10) to a mountain in Galilee, where he appears to them as the resurrected Son of God who remains the crucified Son of God (28:5–6, 16–17). In seeing him, some of the disciples, full of faith, worship him, whereas others, afflicted with weak faith, doubt (28:17). Nonetheless, in gathering the eleven who had been scattered, the risen Jesus cleanses them of their sin of apostasy and reconciles them to himself. By the same token, as they see him not only as the risen one but also as the crucified one, they recognize "on his person" that the central purpose of his ministry was in fact death on the cross (16:21). In comprehending at last the essence of his ministry, they comprehend as well the essence of their ministry: servanthood (16:24; 20:28). In this full knowledge of Jesus and of themselves, they receive from the resurrected and crucified Son of God the commission to go and make all nations his disciples (28:18–20). And having received this commission, they make their way from the mountain in Galilee to the world that Jesus has described for them in his eschatological discourse of Matthew 24—25. If the resolution of the conflict between Jesus and Israel results tragically in alienation, the resolution of the conflict between Jesus and the disciples results happily in reconciliation.

SUMMARY

Matthew's story of the disciples follows the contours of his story of Jesus. As Matthew tells of Jesus' ministry to Israel of teaching, preaching, and healing (4:17—11:1) and of Israel's repudiation of Jesus (11:2—16:20), he tells of the call of the disciples and of their ministry to Israel (4:17—11:1) and of the divine revelation that is imparted to them (11:2—16:20). And as Matthew tells of Jesus' journey to Jerusalem and of his passion and resurrection (16:21—28:20), he tells of the way whereby Jesus finally leads the disciples to comprehend that servanthood is the essence of discipleship (16:21—28:20).

As Jesus Son of God calls disciples to live in the sphere of God's eschatological Rule, he forms a new community (16:18; 21:43). This new community is a brotherhood of the sons of God and of the disciples of Jesus and has as its purpose missionary activity (4:18–22). The ethic that distinguishes the lives of the disciples is that of the "greater righteousness" (5:20). Sustained in person and mission by the power of Jesus (8:18–22), the disciples are nonetheless vulnerable to attacks of little, or weak, faith (8:23–27). Moreover, in their ranks are not only the so-called upright but also the despised and the outcast (9:9). As described by Jesus, the ministry of the disciples to Israel foreshadows in many respects their later ministry to the nations (10:5b–42). Then, too, against the backdrop of Israel's repudiation of Jesus, the disciples stand out as the recipients of divine revelation (11:25–26). They are given to know the mysteries of the Kingdom of Heaven (13:11) as well as the identity of Jesus as the Son of God (14:33; 16:16–17). But this notwithstanding, Jesus must also enter into intense conflict with them because they resist the related notions that he must suffer and that his suffering is a summons to them to servanthood (16:21, 24; 20:28). Their resistance even leads them to the point where they commit apostasy (26:47–50, 56, 69–75). Nevertheless, Jesus overcomes their failure, reconciles them to himself, and, in appearing to them as the risen Son of God who remains the crucified Son of God (28:5–6, 16–17), leads them to comprehend both that death on the cross was the central purpose of his ministry and that servanthood is the essence of discipleship. Thus, the resolution of Jesus' chief conflict with the disciples is that they appropriate his evaluative point of view concerning both himself and them and receive from him the great commission (28:18–20).

7

The Community of
Matthew

SINCE our discussion of the presentation of Jesus (chap. 2), the focus of attention has been the world of Matthew's story. In this chapter, attention is directed to the community of Christians for which Matthew's story was originally written. These Christians are best referred to as the "real readers" of Matthew. What kind of people were they? And what were the conditions—social, economic, and religious—in which they lived?[1]

One way to attempt an answer to these questions is to take the implied reader of Matthew's story as an index, even if only approximate, of the real readers. If one may properly do this, one can infer from Matthew's story the kind of things the implied reader is expected to know or the events or circumstances of which he or she is expected to be aware, and derive thereby information that will enable one to sketch a picture of the real readers. Also, to supplement this information, occasional glances at Mark or Luke or at other historical data will likewise prove to be of benefit.

The initial clue as to the place in history of the Matthean community comes from Matthew himself, as implied author. In such passages as 24:15 ("let the reader understand"), 27:8 ("until this day"), and 28:15 ("until this day"), Matthew bursts the bounds of the story he is telling of the life and ministry of Jesus in order to address the implied reader directly. Temporally, these passages locate the implied reader at a point after the resurrection but short of the Parousia. Matthew himself describes this point as the time of the messianic woes, which will issue in the final judgment (24:8). The time of the messianic woes, therefore, is also the time in which the real readers of Matthew's Gospel were living.

1. On the situation in life reflected in the First Gospel, cf. Kingsbury, "Matthew's View of His Community," 56–73; Kilpatrick, *Origins of the Gospel*, chap. 7; Hare, *Jewish Persecution of Christians;* Schweizer, *Matthäus und Seine Gemeinde;* Farmer, "Post-Sectarian Character," 235–47; Waetjen, *Origin and Destiny,* chap. 2; S. Brown, "Matthean Community," esp. 213–21; Brown and Meier, *Antioch and Rome,* chap. 3; Smith, *Easter Gospels,* 55–67.

CONSTITUENCY

More prosaically, the time of the messianic woes would seem to refer to the latter part of the first century and the real readers of Matthew's Gospel to Greek-speaking Christians of Jewish or gentile origin who were perhaps at home in Antioch of Syria. As for the date of the Gospel, there appears to be a clear allusion in the parable of the Great Supper to the destruction of Jerusalem (A.D. 66–70) as an event that, from the evangelist's own vantage point in history, already lies in the past (22:7; cf. 21:41). Add to this the datum that Ignatius, writing shortly after the turn of the century (ca. A.D. 110 or 115), seemingly has knowledge of the Gospel of Matthew,[2] and one arrives rather quickly at A.D. 85 or 90 as the date of writing.

The text of Matthew's Gospel itself is testimony that the language the real readers spoke was Greek, and this, in turn, suggests that the Gospel's place of origin was most probably a city; a good conjecture is Antioch of Syria. Thus, the quality of the Gospel's language is such that it is by no means "translation Greek," the secondary rendering, for example, of a Hebrew or an Aramaic original. In an analysis of the language of the Gospel, one scholar states that although the first evangelist betrays a feeling for "Semitic atmosphere" and has at times taken over Semitisms from his sources or even himself given a phrase a Semitic twist (cf. 7:28; 11:1; 13:53; 19:1; 26:1: "And it happened when Jesus finished . . ."), he can be seen on the whole to have been "an educated person commanding sound Greek with a considerable vocabulary."[3] Then, too, if the observation is even roughly accurate that in the first century Aramaic was the language of the populace in the rural regions of Syria and Palestine but Greek the dominant language of the cities,[4] then the Greek of Matthew's Gospel would place the real readers in an urban environment. This does not prove that Antioch of Syria was the place where Matthew's Gospel was written, but neither does it challenge this view.

If the language of the real readers was Greek, does this rule out the notion that they may also have spoken Hebrew or especially Aramaic? While one cannot simply deny the possibility that the real readers were bilingual, it is difficult to make a case for it. Neither the isolated instances in which the first evangelist employs a Semitic word without translating it[5] nor the Semitic idiom of his speech as such are sufficient to prove bilingualism; indeed, they prove no more than that the evangelist presup-

---

2. Cf. Ign. *Eph.* 19:2–3; *Smyrn.* 1:1; 6:1; *Pol.* 1:3; 2:2; also Brown and Meier, *Antioch and Rome,* 24–25. For a table listing the passages in Matthew and in the letters of Ignatius most commonly cited as being parallel, cf. Trevett, "Ignatian Correspondence," 62–63.

3. Moule, *Birth of the New Testament,* 219; also Turner, *Style,* 4:37–38.

4. Cf. Theissen, "Itinerant Radicalism," 133.

5. Cf., e.g., *"hraka"* (5:22), *"mamōna"* (6:24), *"Beelzeboul"* (10:25; but cf. 12:24), and *"korbanan"* (27:6).

posed the real readers would not find such words or idiom incomprehensible. By the same token, three times the evangelist does provide a translation of Semitic words (1:23; 27:33, 46), and if it can be assumed that he had Mark available as a source, he has also chosen several times not to take over Semitic words that stand out prominently in that Gospel.[6] As for the evangelist's use of the OT, only the so-called formula-quotations would suggest that the Septuagint was not his Bible, and these he could just as easily as not have appropriated from an obscure Greek version of the OT or from an early Christian collection in Greek of OT testimonies.[7]

The real readers of Matthew's Gospel appear to have been people of Jewish and of gentile background. This is suggested by the contents of the Gospel, which presuppose knowledge of Jewish thought, history, and traditions on the one hand and openness toward Gentiles on the other. Features of the Gospel suggesting that the first evangelist wrote for a sizable Jewish-Christian constituency are numerous. To begin with, many of the key terms in the Gospel are thoroughly Jewish in tone. The sanctified life of the disciple is known as "righteousness" (*dikaiosynē*; cf. 5:20; 6:1), and part and parcel of it are "almsgiving" (6:2), "prayer" (6:5), and "fasting" (6:16). The preferred designation for the Rule of God is "the Kingdom of Heaven" instead of "the Kingdom of God," which is the expression Mark and Luke employ. God is often referred to as "your heavenly Father" or as "your Father who is in heaven" (cf. the Sermon on the Mount) and the disciples as "sons of God" (5:9), "sons of your Father who is in heaven" (5:45), or "sons of the Kingdom" (13:38). The archadversary of Jesus is designated as "the devil" (4:1–11), "Satan" (4:10; 16:23), "the Enemy" (13:39), and "the Evil One" (13:19), and in his service stands "Beelzebul, the prince of demons" (12:24; 10:25). The end of time and the final day are termed, respectively, "the consummation of the age" (13:39, 40, 49) and "the day of judgment" (11:22, 24; 12:36). These are but a sampling of the evangelist's penchant for "Jewish-like" phraseology.

The first evangelist's picture of Jesus is likewise Jewish in hue. He is the "Son of Abraham," the one in whom the entire history of Israel reaches its culmination (1:1–17). He is furthermore the "Messiah" (Matthew 1), or "Coming One" (11:2–3) who has been sent specifically to the "lost sheep of the house of Israel" (15:24). He is also the "Son of David," the royal figure who stands in the line of David (Matthew 1; 21:5, 9), the "King of the Jews [Israel]" who suffers on behalf of his people (Matthew 27). Indeed, Jesus is, in sum, the "Son of God," or "Emmanuel," the eschatological "Shepherd" in whom God, in fulfillment of OT prophecy, has drawn near to dwell with

---

6. Mark 3:17; 5:41; 7:11, 34; 10:46, 51; 14:36.
7. On this question, cf. Stendahl, *School of St. Matthew*, iii–v.

his people to the end of the age (1:23; 2:6, 15; 28:20) and who will, in his role as "the Son of man," return to judge all humankind (25:31-46).

The ministry of Jesus, too, has a particularly Jewish aura about it in Matthew's Gospel. The first evangelist is at pains to show that this ministry takes place almost exclusively within the confines of Israel (15:24; 10:5-6). Galilee is the place of Jesus' activity, and he traverses the whole of it (4:23; 9:35; 11:1). It is from Galilee that news of him spreads throughout all Syria (4:24), and it is to Galilee that the crowds from the Decapolis, Jerusalem, Judea, and across the Jordan come to be with him (4:25). When Jesus leaves Galilee, it is only briefly.[8] In fact, on one occasion when he withdraws into the regions of Tyre and Sidon, it appears that he merely crosses the border, for it is said of the Canaanite woman that she "came out" toward him (15:21-28). Only once does Jesus undertake a journey during his public ministry that is actually regarded as taking him away from the environs of Galilee, and this is his fateful trip to Jerusalem (19:2).

In point of fact, the first evangelist's treatment of the region of Galilee reveals that he actually construes it as the wider setting for Jesus' activity, for he locates numerous events in and around the city of Capernaum. This seems to be the case, for instance, with all but two of the ten miracles he records in Matthew 8—9 (8:23—9:1). As for Capernaum itself, neither Mark nor Luke ever reports that Jesus "dwells" anywhere, but the first evangelist, taking up on his previous notation that Joseph "went and *dwelt* in a city called Nazareth" (2:23), documents with a formula-quotation the circumstance that Jesus "left Nazareth and went and 'dwelt' in Capernaum" (4:13-16). Indeed, Capernaum is designated as "his own city" (9:1), and it may be that the "house" there is to be thought of as belonging to Jesus.[9]

Until Easter, the disciples in Matthew's Gospel also share in Jesus' concentration on Israel. To stress this, the first evangelist devotes the whole of the section 9:35—10:42 to their projected mission to Israel, which goes beyond anything one finds in either Mark or Luke.

The attitude Jesus takes toward the Mosaic law and the tradition of the elders is yet another factor that suggests the first evangelist wrote for a strong Jewish-Christian constituency. Although the law retains its validity until the consummation of the age only as interpreted by Jesus, it is nonetheless not set aside (5:17-20). And although Jesus wages a vigorous polemic against the tradition of the elders (15:1-9), he does not simply abolish it (23:2-3, 23). The Marcan Jesus, by contrast, appears to overthrow the legal system of the Jews (cf. 7:1-23).

Finally, the manner in which the first evangelist treats certain other details also argues for the Jewishness of a large segment of the real readers

8. Cf., e.g., 3:13—4:13; 8:23—9:1; [14:22]; 15:21; 16:4c-5, 13.
9. Cf. 9:10, 28; 12:46 and 13:1; 13:36; 17:25.

of his Gospel. Unlike Mark, the first evangelist does not explain such Jewish regulations as the washing of hands before meals (cf. Matt. 15:2 with Mark 7:2–4), and neither does he explain the custom of wearing amulets and tassels (Matt. 23:5). As has been noted, if at times he translates Semitic words (1:23; 27:33, 46), at other times he leaves them untranslated (cf. *"hraka,"* 5:22; *"mamōna,"* 6:24; *"Beelzeboul,"* 10:25; *"korbanan,"* 27:6). In addition, he also assumes his readers will be familiar with a peculiarly Jewish turn of phrase (cf., e.g., "straining out the gnat," 23:24; "whitewashed tombs," 23:27).

But if the unmistakable Jewishness of much of Matthew's Gospel favors the thesis that the first evangelist wrote with a sizable Jewish-Christian constituency in mind, the attitude he takes toward the mission to the nations shows that he also wrote with a view to real readers who were of gentile origin. One looks in vain in Matthew's Gospel for traces of the fierce controversy surrounding the gentile mission which are so prominent in Paul (cf. Galatians 2) and Acts (15). On the contrary, one can detect in the Gospel from beginning to end a pronounced "gentile bias." Already in the genealogy of Jesus, four non-Israelite women are listed as the ancestors of Jesus ("Tamar," "Rahab," "Ruth," and "the wife of Uriah" [Bathsheba]; 1:3, 5–6). In Matthew 2, the "Magi from the East" are described as "worshiping" Jesus and presenting him gifts that befit a king (vv. 1–2, 11). Jesus' settling in "Galilee of the Gentiles" to begin his ministry to Israel prefigures the post-Easter return of the disciples to Galilee, from where they will undertake their mission to the nations (4:12, 15; 28:7, 16–20). As the second of a series of ten miracles, Jesus heals the servant of a centurion, and attendant to this he declares:

> Truly, I say to you, not even in Israel have I found such faith; I tell you, many will come from east and west and sit at table with Abraham, Isaac, and Jacob in the Kingdom of Heaven (8:5–13).

At 12:21, the evangelist quotes from the OT in order to proclaim Jesus as the one in whom the "Gentiles will hope," and at 13:38 he writes that it is in the "world" that "sons of the Kingdom" will be raised up. In the parables of the wicked husbandmen (21:33–46) and of the Great Supper (22:1–14), the evangelist employs figurative speech to depict the influx of the Gentiles into the church (21:41; 22:9–10), and, more directly, he has Jesus announce in 24:14 and 26:13 that it is throughout the entire world that the gospel of the Kingdom will be proclaimed.

To sum up, from what can be inferred in the text of Matthew's Gospel the real readers were Christians both of Jewish and of gentile origin. Their language was Greek, their place in history the latter part of the first century (A.D. 85 or 90), and they were probably at home in a city, perhaps Antioch of Syria.

SOCIAL STANDING

On the matter of social standing, the real readers of Matthew's Gospel were apparently well-to-do, and the evidence also reinforces the impression that home for them was in an urban area. In comparison with Mark, who uses the word "city" *(polis)* eight times and the word "village" *(kōmē)* seven times, the first evangelist uses the word "village" only four times but the word "city" no fewer than twenty-six times. The latter statistic is all the more striking when one observes that the "city" is the setting for a significant part of Jesus' life and ministry and for the ministry of the disciples as well. Thus, Jesus grows up in the city of Nazareth (2:23; 21:11); makes the city of Capernaum home base as he discharges his ministry in Galilee (4:13; 9:1), during which he travels through the cities of the region (9:35; 11:1); and brings his ministry to completion in the city of Jerusalem (21:1—28:15). In his missionary-discourse to the disciples, Jesus similarly describes them as carrying out their ministry in the setting of the city (cf. 10:11, 14, 15, 23; 23:34). Perhaps, then, the real readers of Matthew's Gospel were members of a "city church."

Indications are strong that the real readers were also well-to-do. The Lucan Jesus, for example, pronounces a blessing on "the poor" (6:20) but the Matthean Jesus on "the poor in spirit" (5:3). The Marcan Jesus commands the disciples in conjunction with their missionary journey to take with them no "copper coin"—that is, small change (6:8)—but the Matthean Jesus commands them to take neither "gold, nor silver, nor copper coin" (10:9). The Lucan Jesus tells a parable about "minas" (19:11–27) but the Matthean Jesus about "talents" (25:14–30), one of the latter being worth approximately fifty times one of the former. The Lucan Jesus says in the words of the householder in the parable of the Great Supper: "Go out quickly to the streets and lanes of the city, and bring in the poor and maimed and blind and lame" (14:21). By contrast, the Matthean Jesus makes no such explicit reference to the disfranchised but merely says in his version of these words: "Go therefore to the thoroughfares, and invite to the marriage feast as many as you find" (22:9). And in Mark (15:43) and Luke (23:50–51), Joseph of Arimathea is a member of the council who is looking for the Kingdom of God, but in the First Gospel he is a "rich man . . . who also was a disciple of Jesus" (27:57).

It seems, in fact, that the real readers of Matthew's Gospel were well accustomed to dealing in a wide range of money. Whereas Luke mentions "silver" and a few kinds of money (cf., e.g., 7:41; 12:6, 59; 19:13) and Mark mentions an assortment of what on the whole were the lesser denominations, the first evangelist makes no reference whatever to the *lepton*, the smallest unit of money cited in the Gospels (a small copper coin = ca. ⅛¢), but does refer to all the following: the *kodrantēs* ("quadrans" = ca. ¼¢), the *assarion* ("assarion" = ca. 1¢), the *dēnarion* ("denarius" = ca. 18¢), the *didrachmon* ("double drachma" = ca. 36¢), the *statēr* ("stater" = ca. 80¢), the *talanton* ("talent" = ca. $1,080); and to *chalkos* ("copper coin"), *argyrion* ("silver"), *argyros* ("silver"), and *chrysos* ("gold"). Indeed, if one takes the three terms "silver," "gold," and "talent," one discovers that they occur in Matthew's Gospel no fewer than twenty-eight times, which may be compared with the single use of the word "silver" by Mark and the fourfold use of it by Luke. Against a background of wealth such as these terms indicate, it makes sense that the first evangelist should appropriate in 13:22 Mark's warning against riches (Mark 4:19) and sharpen the saying of Jesus at Matt. 19:23 so that difficulty in entering the Kingdom is predicated not merely to "those who have means" (Mark 10:23), but to the "rich man."

Accordingly, in light of the preceding there is further reason to postulate that the real readers of Matthew's Gospel lived in or near a city, such as Antioch of Syria, and it also seems safe to infer that they were prosperous and in no sense materially disadvantaged.

SOCIAL CLIMATE

It appears certain that the social and religious climate in which the real readers of Matthew's Gospel found themselves was one of intense conflict. On the one hand, it looks as though these Christians were living in close proximity to hostile pagans. Whether or not their mission to the nations was the sole reason, they were seemingly being hauled into court by gentile authorities, judicially harassed ("handed over to tribulation"), hated "by all," and even put to death (10:18, 22; 13:21; 24:9). Plainly, these Christians were enduring persecution from the side of their gentile neighbors.[10]

On the other hand, it likewise seems that they were living in close proximity to a vigorous Jewish community. The evidence for this is multiple. For instance, the parable of the tares (13:24–30) may refer to this directly, for it is possibly with a view to the church's relationship to Israel that the first evangelist reports Jesus as saying, "Let both grow side by side until the harvest" (13:30).[11] In a similar vein, if the story of the payment of the temple tax (17:24–27) can be interpreted to mean that the Jewish Christians in Matthew's community were being encouraged, despite their "freedom," not to offend Jews by refusing to participate in the collection of contributions throughout Jewry in support of the Patriarchy at Jamnia,[12] then this unit, too, may speak for close contact between Jews and the real readers of Matthew's Gospel.

Perhaps the first evangelist's presentation of Jesus, of the disciples, and of the leaders of the Jews also indicates that the real readers were living in

10. Cf. Hare, *Jewish Persecution of Christians*, 106–8, 124.
11. Cf. Kingsbury, *Parables of Jesus*, 63–76.
12. Cf. Thompson, *Divided Community*, 66–68.

close proximity to Jews. Thus, it may secondarily be with an eye to the Jews about him that the evangelist has portrayed Jesus Son of God as the ideal Israelite (cf., e.g., 4:1–11) and has elevated him above Moses as the supreme teacher of the will of God (cf. the Sermon on the Mount). In addition, the evangelist's description of Christian piety as the righteousness "greater" than that of the scribes and Pharisees may also have the Jews "next door" in mind (5:20), and this could further be the case for the many invectives that are hurled at the Jewish leaders throughout the Gospel (cf. Matthew 23). On another level, although the primary task of the real readers was unquestionably to make disciples of the nations (28:18–20), this does not mean, as I mentioned earlier, that no missionary activity whatever was being done among Jews. The missionary discourse of Matthew 10, which has to do with evangelization especially among Jews though also among Gentiles (cf. vv. 17–18, 22–23), would not have been without relevance for these Christians, and the passage 23:34 is an unmistakable reference to missionary activity among the Jews which, seemingly, was taking place in the evangelist's own day. The Christian mission to the Jews had not met with success and the essential task henceforth was to go to the Gentiles, but continued work among the Jews points to no lack of interaction between the real readers of Matthew's Gospel and the Jewish community.

Still, if the real readers were living in close proximity to a strong Jewish community, they are not to be thought of as a "splinter group" that was nevertheless a member of the Jewish league of synagogues.[13] The place of the real readers was no longer within Judaism but outside it. Several factors support this conclusion.

To begin with, the first evangelist, more rigorously than either Mark or Luke, makes of Jesus and his disciples a group set apart from the Jewish crowds and their leaders. This comes to the fore already both in the way he has persons address Jesus and in the way he develops his ecclesiological concept of "being with Jesus." As for the latter, I observed in chapter 6 that the evangelist very carefully reserves for the disciples alone the privilege of sharing in the company, or presence, of Jesus, so that it is not said of Judas or of the crowds or of the Jewish leaders that they are "with Jesus" or that he is "with them." Correlatively, the evangelist distinguishes sharply, as I also observed, between the manner in which Jesus is approached by the disciples on the one hand and persons without faith on the other: whereas the disciples address Jesus as "Lord," opponents and persons without faith address him only as "rabbi" or "teacher." The "apartness" of Jesus and his disciples in the Gospel's story reflects, it would seem, the religious distance of the real readers of Matthew's Gospel from the Jewish community.

<hr>

13. Cf., e.g., Hummel, *Auseinandersetzung*, 28–33, 159–61.

Further indications that the real readers had already broken with Judaism are, respectively, the first evangelist's use of the expression "their [your] synagogue(s)," his massive apology against Judaism as an institution, and the apparent organizational autonomy of the community to which he belonged. To take the last point first, Matthew's community, as will be seen, was not at all under Jewish religious control but had its own form of organization which dealt with such weighty matters as those of doctrine and of church order. In addition, by regularly appending the modifying genitive "your" or "their" to the noun "synagogue(s),"[14] the evangelist attests idiomatically to the dissociation of his community from Judaism. Also, except to acknowledge that the "scribes and the Pharisees are seated on the chair of Moses" (23:2),[15] he has virtually nothing good to say of Judaism as a religious institution. Typically, there is no "friendly scribe" in Matthew's Gospel, as there is in Mark's, of whom it is written: "And when Jesus saw that he answered wisely, he said to him, 'You are not far from the Kingdom of God' " (Mark 12:34). On the contrary, the one scribe in Matthew's Gospel who requests of Jesus that he become his disciple is turned away with the words: "Foxes have holes, and birds of the air have nests, but the Son of man has nowhere to lay his head" (8:20).[16] Indeed, far from evincing affinity with contemporary Judaism, the first evangelist has mounted a massive apology against it in his Gospel. In his eyes, contemporary Judaism was, as a saying of Jesus puts it, a "plant which my heavenly Father has not planted [and] will be rooted up" (15:13). And if persecution characterized the relationship of the real readers of the Gospel to the Gentiles, this was all the more the case as far as contemporary Judaism was concerned. From what can be inferred, Matthean Christians, and especially the missionaries, were subject to abuse that was both verbal (5:11) and physical, including floggings in the synagogues and measures aimed at expulsion or resulting, apparently, even in death (10:17, 23; 23:34).[17]

Consequently, the real readers of Matthew's Gospel, a community with members of Jewish and gentile background which stood outside the orbit of official Judaism but lived in close proximity to both Jews and Gentiles, encountered from without persecution by both Jew and Gentile. What is to be said of the internal structure of this community?

14. Cf. 4:23; 9:35; 10:17; 12:9; 13:54; 23:34.

15. In light of such passages as 23:8–10 and 16:6–12, those scholars are doubtless correct who contend that the seemingly positive words Jesus utters in 23:2–3 concerning the Jewish leaders serve not so much to pay tribute to them as to highlight the cleavage between what they say and what they do (cf. 23:3c). On this view, then, the function of these positive words is to serve as a contrast to the negative judgments that follow and in this way to lend greater prominence to the latter. Cf. most recently Cook, " 'Pro–Jewish' Passages," 135–46.

16. Cf. Kingsbury, "Matthew's View of His Community," 59–60.

17. Cf. Hare, *Jewish Persecution of Christians*, 126; Stanton, "Matthew and Judaism," 275–77; Kingsbury, *Parables of Jesus*, 57–59.

ORGANIZATION

Called through baptism to follow Jesus, the risen and exalted Son of God who presides over and resides in his "church,"[18] the real readers of Matthew's Gospel knew themselves to be "sons of God"[19] and "brothers" of Jesus and of one another.[20] As sons of God, they were also "little ones," for they understood themselves to be totally dependent on their heavenly Father (18:3, 6, 10). As the brothers of Jesus and of one another, they were at the same time the "servants" and the "slaves" of one another (20:25–28). And as followers of Jesus, they were likewise "disciples" *(mathētai)*, for they had taken on themselves his yoke and they were "learning" from him.[21] Internally, therefore, the real readers of Matthew's Gospel saw themselves as comprising the church, that is to say, a community, or brotherhood, of the sons of God and the disciples of Jesus.

Within this community, two or three groups can be distinguished. One group was that of the "prophets" (10:41; 23:34). In principle, the entire community regarded itself as standing in the tradition of the OT prophets and the twelve disciples of Jesus (5:12; 13:17). It appears, however, that there were also certain Christians in the community who were specifically thought of as being "prophets." They seem to have been itinerant missionaries who proclaimed the gospel of the Kingdom to Jews[22] but especially to Gentiles.[23]

Whether these Christian prophets functioned exclusively beyond the confines of the Matthean community is difficult to say. In 7:15–23, reference is made to prophets who were, it seems, active within the community. These prophets are denounced as being "false," as being "ravenous wolves . . . who come to you in sheep's clothing" (7:15). Also, they were "enthusiasts," for it is said that in the name of Christ they have prophesied, cast out demons, and performed many miracles (7:22). Their works, however, are castigated as contravening their profession of the name of Christ (7:16–20). The result is that they are condemned in words of Jesus as "workers of lawlessness" whom the exalted Jesus will banish from his presence at the latter day (7:23). The point is, is one to infer from such reference to false prophets as active within the community that, conversely, legitimate Christian prophets, too, are to be thought of as having engaged in ministry not only as missionaries beyond the community but also as preachers of the gospel of the Kingdom within the community?[24] One can only conjecture.

18. Cf. 28:19–20; also 1:23; 16:18; 18:17, 20.
19. Cf. 5:9, 45; 13:38.
20. Cf. 12:49–50; 18:35; 23:8; 25:40; 28:10.
21. Cf. 11:29; 10:1, 24–25; 23:10.
22. Cf. 10:41 to 10:6, 17, 23; 23:34 to 23:29a.
23. Cf. 10:41 to 10:18; 24:14; 26:13; 28:19.
24. On a less cautious note, Boring *(Sayings of the Risen Jesus,* 45) asserts that "prophets" constituted the "recognized leadership" of the Matthean church.

One or possibly two groups within the Matthean community have been identified: the "prophets" and the "false prophets." Another identifiable group is those who functioned as "teachers." They were designated variously. Thus, the "righteous man" (*dikaios;* 10:41) was a teacher of righteousness,[25] and the "rabbi" (*hrabbi;* 23:8), the "scribe" (*grammateus;* 23:34), and the "wise man" (*sophos;* 23:34) were those expert in matters pertaining to the scriptures and the law.[26] The verses 10:41 and 23:34, in which three of these four terms occur, show that Christian teachers, too, served as missionaries to the Jews, perhaps conversing or debating with them about the meaning of the scriptures, the law, and the traditions in light of the coming of Jesus Messiah.

But these Christians who served as teachers were likewise active within the community, as can be presupposed from Matt. 23:8–12 (cf. 13:52). What their exact competencies were is hard to know. Still, at one point this question becomes acute, because it touches on the matter of the regulation of the life of the community.

Indications are that by A.D. 85 or 90 the Matthean community had already developed a structure for governing its communal life. The outlines of this structure can be discerned in the evangelists' portrait of the disciples. In Matt. 16:19, for example, Peter is depicted as receiving from Jesus the promise of the power of the "keys of the Kingdom of Heaven." He receives this promise, however, in his capacity as the "first" of the disciples to be called (4:18–20; 10:2; 16:16) and therefore as the one who is their "spokesman" and who is "typical" of them and of later Christians.[27] Peter's "primacy," therefore, is not that of being elevated to a station above the other disciples but is "salvation-historical" in nature: he is, again, the "first" disciple whom Jesus called to follow him. Because Peter is the first among the disciples all of whom have been called and are in this sense equal, the power of the keys Jesus promises him is perhaps best equated with the power of "binding and loosing," which the other disciples exercise as well as he (cf. 16:19 with 18:18). The power of "binding and loosing," in turn, pertains to the regulation of church doctrine and discipline.[28] Accordingly, whatever the particular contribution of those who served as teachers, it was the entire Matthean community that decided the matters of doctrine and discipline. As the passage 18:18–20 indicates, this community made such decisions gathered together in the name and hence in the presence and on the authority of the exalted Son of God. Moreover, as it did so, it was conscious of the fact that the touchstone of whatever it decided was

25. Cf. Cothenet, "Les prophètes chrétiens," 294.
26. Cf. Wilckens, "Sophia," 7:505.
27. Cf. Kingsbury, "Peter in Matthew's Gospel," 67–83.
28. Cf. Bornkamm, " 'Bind' and 'Loose,' " 1:37–50; Brown, Donfried, and Reumann, *Peter in the New Testament*, 95–101.

that it was to be in keeping with the injunction given by Jesus to "observe all that I have commanded you" (28:20).

The Matthean community, then, was without a peculiar "teaching office" such as contemporary Judaism was in the process of developing. Indeed, with an eye toward those engaged in teaching, it counteracted the problem of position and status they could well have posed by invoking sayings of Jesus. These sayings expressly forbade those who taught to arrogate themselves a station setting them above the rest of the community. They were not, for instance, to assume the title of "rabbi" or "teacher" (didaskalos, kathēgētēs), for there is only one from whom the church receives its teaching, Jesus Messiah, the Son of God (23:8, 10). Neither were they to assume the title of "Father," for there is only one who can lay just claim to this title, God himself (23:9). In point of fact, they were to be the opposite of the "scribes and Pharisees" in contemporary Judaism who had office and authority but who "shut the Kingdom of Heaven against men," neither entering it themselves nor allowing those who would enter to go in (23:13). On the contrary, in the church "all . . . are brothers" (23:8), and the eschatological maxim applied that "whoever exalts himself will be humbled, and whoever humbles himself will be exalted" (23:12).

In summary, the real readers of Matthew's Gospel thought of themselves as the church, which is to say that they understood themselves to be a community, or brotherhood, of the sons of God and of the disciples of Jesus. Within this community, two or three groups stand out: those who were, respectively, "prophets" or "false prophets," and those who served as "teachers." But though these groups can be distinguished, they did not constitute a select leadership that decided matters of church doctrine and church discipline. On the contrary, the entire community, gathering in the presence of the exalted Son of God, decided matters of this nature, in line with the injunction of Jesus to "observe all that I have commanded you" (16:19; 18:18–20; 28:20).

THE FIRST EVANGELIST

A word is in order about the evangelist himself, the real author of the First Gospel. In greatest measure, scholarly opinion does not identify the first evangelist with Matthew the apostle. One reason is that if the First Gospel is in some sense dependent on the Gospel of Mark as a source, as most scholars believe, it is difficult to explain how it could happen that the apostle Matthew, an eyewitness to the ministry of Jesus, should have taken the greater part of his Gospel from Mark, who no one claims was a disciple or eyewitness of Jesus. Another reason is that the theological outlook of the writer of the First Gospel seems to be that of the second, not the first, generation of Christians to follow Jesus. One might also ask, if it is correct that the First Gospel was written about A.D. 85 or 90, whether the apostle

Matthew could reasonably be expected to have lived long enough to write it.

It could be, however, that the apostle Matthew, although not the author of the First Gospel, was associated at one time with the church in which the Gospel arose and was esteemed as a founder or "patron disciple" of this church. This would explain why the story of the call of Matthew (9:9) substitutes in the First Gospel for the story of the call of Levi (Mark 2:14; Luke 5:27), and why the list of the disciples of Jesus has been adjusted accordingly (cf. Matt. 10:3 ["Matthew the toll-collector"] with Mark 6:18 and Luke 9:15).

Still, some scholars, while they agree that Matthew the apostle did not write the First Gospel, nevertheless hold that his association with it was more direct than this. Appealing to a notice of the second-century church father Papias which reads that "Matthew wrote [collected] the oracles [accounts] in the Hebrew language and every one interpreted them as he was able,"[29] they contend that Matthew the apostle was the author of a primitive Aramaic document subsequently taken up into the First Gospel. In its various forms, this thesis has been thoroughly debated over the years, but the results have been inconclusive.

Can, then, the real author of the First Gospel be identified? The answer is no. It is sometimes suggested that the First Gospel was produced not by an individual, but by a school.[30] Most scholars, however, prefer to think in terms of individual authorship. A few argue that the Gospel was written by a gentile Christian, basing their case on the author's alleged "distance" from Judaism, on his use of the Septuagint and treatment of certain Semitic words and other terms, and on the supposed relationship within the Gospel between tradition (= Jewish Christian) and redaction (= gentile Christian).[31] But the majority of scholars regard the author as a Christian of Jewish background, and they point to many of his theological emphases, to his oftentimes rabbinic mode of thinking and arguing, and to the architectonic structure of his work as proof of this. Perhaps, therefore, the first evangelist can best be described as a Greek-speaking Jewish Christian of the second generation after Jesus who possessed a universal missionary outlook and had most probably enjoyed rabbinical training.

SUMMARY

By the last two decades of the first century, the church of Matthew was a firmly established community. Greek was its language, and the constituency was of both Jewish and gentile origins. It was furthermore "urban" and well-to-do, located perhaps in or near Syrian Antioch, and its neigh-

29. Cf. Eusebius, *Ecclesiastical History*, 3.39.16.
30. Cf. Stendahl, *School of St. Matthew*, 30–35.
31. Cf. Strecker, *Weg der Gerechtigkeit*, 15–35; also Meier, *Vision of Matthew*, 17–25.

bors were Jews and Gentiles. The atmosphere in which it lived was one of conflict, both from within and from without. From without, it encountered gentile but especially Jewish persecution. From within, it was troubled by miracle-working false prophets, among others. Still, this community, having had its ties with contemporary Judaism severed, conceived of itself as a brotherhood of the sons of God and of the disciples of Jesus. It knew the exalted Son of God to reside in its midst, and it traced its teaching and ethics to him. Groups within the community can be distinguished, but hierarchical tendencies were resisted. There were, for example, the itinerant prophets who proclaimed the gospel of the Kingdom among Jews and Gentiles, though the primary mission of the community was to the latter. And there were those engaged in teaching, who, although they, too, undertook missionary activity, instructed the community in the will of God as taught by Jesus. But whatever the contribution of the latter, when it came to making final decisions concerning matters of doctrine and church discipline, it was the entire community, under the aegis of the exalted Son of God, that decided.

8
Concluding Remarks

THE gospel-story Matthew narrates is of the life and ministry of Jesus of Nazareth (1:18—28:20). The context in which Matthew places this story is that of the history of salvation (1:2–17; 21:33–46; 22:1–14; 24—25). Constitutive of this history are two epochs: the time of the OT, which is the time of prophecy; and the time of fulfillment, which is the time of Jesus (cf. the formula-quotations). The time of Jesus extends from conception and birth (1:23) to Parousia (25:31), and encompasses the ministries to Israel of John (3:2), of Jesus (4:17), and of the pre-Easter disciples (10:7) and the ministry to the nations of the post-Easter disciples (24:14). The focus, however, is on the ministry of Jesus, for John is the forerunner of Jesus (11:10) and the pre-Easter and post-Easter disciples receive from Jesus their commission (10:5; 28:18–20).

Matthew divides his story of the life and ministry of Jesus into three parts: (I) The Presentation of Jesus (1:1—4:16); (II) The Ministry of Jesus to Israel and Israel's Repudiation of Jesus (4:17—16:20); and (III) The Journey of Jesus to Jerusalem and His Suffering, Death, and Resurrection (16:21—28:20). In the first part, Matthew presents Jesus as the Davidic Messiah-King, the royal Son of God (1:1—4:16). To show that Jesus is preeminently the Son of God, Matthew depicts God as announcing within the world of the story that Jesus is his Son (3:17). As the Son of God, Jesus stands forth as the supreme agent of God who authoritatively espouses God's evaluative point of view.

In the second part of his story (4:17—16:20), Matthew tells of Jesus' ministry to Israel (4:17—11:1) and of Israel's repudiation of Jesus (11:2—16:20). Sent to Israel, Jesus teaches, preaches, and heals (4:23; 9:35; 11:1). He also calls disciples, and commissions them to a ministry in Israel modeled on his own (4:17—11:1). Israel's response to Jesus, however, is one of repudiation (11:2—16:20). Still, even as Israel repudiates him, it wonders and speculates about who he is. Wrongly, the Jewish leaders think of him as one who acts in collusion with Satan (9:34; 12:24), and the Jewish public imagines him to be a prophet (16:13–14; 21:46). In stark contrast to Israel, the disciples, as the recipients of divine revelation, are led by Jesus to think about him as God "thinks" about him, namely, as the Messiah Son of God (16:15–17; 14:33). Nevertheless, because the disciples do not know at this point in the story that the central purpose of Jesus' mission is death, Jesus commands them to silence concerning his identity (16:20).

In the third part of his story (16:21—28:20), Matthew describes Jesus' journey to Jerusalem and his suffering, death, and resurrection (16:21; 17:22–23; 20:17–19). Jesus' first act is to tell his disciples that God has ordained he should go to Jerusalem and there be made by the Jewish leaders to suffer and die (16:21). On hearing this, Peter rejects out of hand the idea that such a fate should ever befall Jesus (16:22), and Jesus reprimands Peter for thinking the things not of God, but of men (16:23). Then, too, Peter's inability to comprehend that death is the essence of Jesus' ministry is only part of the malady afflicting the disciples: they are also incapable of perceiving that servanthood is the essence of discipleship (16:24). Still, key to the resolution of Jesus' conflict with both Israel and the disciples is precisely his death on the cross. Guided by the Jewish leaders, Israel desires the death of Jesus (27:20–25). As the leaders see it, Jesus threatens the overthrow of law and tradition and the destruction of the nation (12:1–14; 15:12; 21:43). In claiming to be the Son of God and the decisive figure in the history of salvation (21:33–42; 26:63–64), Jesus makes himself guilty of blasphemy against God and is deserving of death (26:65–66). Accordingly, in effecting the death of Jesus, the leaders understand themselves to be purging Israel of the error with which a false messiah would pervert the nation (27:63–64). The irony, however, is that in abjectly repudiating Jesus, the leaders achieve the opposite of what they had intended: Far from purging Israel from error, they plunge it into fatal error, for they make both themselves and the people responsible for the death of the one who is in fact the Son of God and through whom God proffers salvation to Israel; thus they precipitate the very destruction of Israel they had aimed to avoid (21:37–43; 22:7; 27:20–25). But true as this may be, God and Jesus also desire the death of Jesus (16:21; 26:39, 42). Through death, Jesus accomplishes the gracious purposes of God—that is to say, he atones for sins and offers forgiveness to all humankind (1:21; 26:28; 27:51). Moreover, to demonstrate that Jesus, in enduring the humiliation of the cross, did not die as a false messiah but as the Son who did his Father's will (21:37–39), God vindicates Jesus by raising him from the dead (28:5–6). Consequently, when Jesus appears to the disciples on the mountain in Galilee (28:16–17), it is as the crucified Son of God whom God has vindicated through resurrection (28:5c–6). Although some disciples show, in doubting, that they are yet weak of faith (28:17; 14:32), they all see on the person of Jesus that crucifixion, or suffering sonship, was the essence of his ministry (21:42). Correlatively, they also grasp at last that servanthood is the essence of discipleship (16:24; 20:25–28). As ones, therefore, who comprehend, in line with God's evaluative point of view (17:5), not only who Jesus is but also what he was about and what it means to be his followers, the disciples receive from Jesus the Great Commission and embark on a mission to all the nations (28:18–20; 24—25).

In narrating in this fashion the story of the life and ministry of Jesus, Matthew advances a bold theological claim. This claim is, as the passages 1:23 and 28:20 reveal (cf. 18:20), that in the person of Jesus Messiah, his Son, God has drawn near to abide to the end of time with his people, the church, thus inaugurating the eschatological age of salvation. This claim, which lies at the heart of "the gospel of the Kingdom," is, in Matthew's view, of decisive significance for Israel and the Gentiles alike (4:23; 9:35; 24:14). The disciples, whom the risen Jesus commissions to a worldwide ministry at the end of Matthew's story, understand this, and so does the implied reader. It is apparent that the first evangelist, who wrote this story, would also have wanted the real reader both to understand this and to act on it.

Selected Bibliography

Abrams, M. H. *A Glossary of Literary Terms*. 4th ed. New York: Holt, Rinehart and Winston, 1981.

Anderson, Janice Capel. "Point of View in Matthew: Evidence." Unpublished paper, SBL Symposium on Literary Analysis of the Gospels and Acts, 1981.

————. "The Implied Reader in Matthew." Unpublished paper, SBL Group on Literary Aspects of the Gospels and Acts, 1983.

Aune, David E. *Prophecy in Early Christianity and the Ancient Mediterranean World*. Grand Rapids: Wm. B. Eerdmans, 1983.

Banks, Robert. "Matthew's Understanding of the Law: Authenticity and Interpretation in Matthew 5:17–20." *JBL* 93 (1974): 226–42.

Barth, Gerhard. "Matthew's Understanding of the Law." In *Tradition and Interpretation in Matthew*, by G. Bornkamm, G. Barth, and H. J. Held, 58–164. Eng. trans. P. Scott. NTL. Philadelphia: Westminster Press, 1963.

Bauer, David R. "The Structure of Matthew's Gospel." Ph.D. diss., Union Theological Seminary in Virginia, 1985.

Betz, Hans Dieter. "The Sermon on the Mount: Its Literary Genre and Function." *JR* 59 (1979): 285–97.

————. "The Hermeneutical Principles of the Sermon on the Mount (Matt. 5: 17–20)." In *Essays on the Sermon on the Mount*, 37–53. Eng. trans. L. L. Wellborn. Philadelphia: Fortress Press, 1985.

Booth, Wayne C. *The Rhetoric of Fiction*. 2d ed. Chicago: Univ. of Chicago Press, 1983.

Boring, M. Eugene. *Sayings of the Risen Lord: Christian Prophecy in the Synoptic Tradition*. SNTSMS 46. New York and Cambridge: Cambridge Univ. Press, 1982.

Bornkamm, Günther. "The Authority to 'Bind' and 'Loose' in the Church in Matthew's Gospel." In *Jesus and Man's Hope*, ed. D. G. Buttrick, 1:37–50. Pittsburgh: Pittsburgh Theological Seminary, 1970.

Boucher, Madeleine. *The Mysterious Parable: A Literary Study*. CBQMS 6. Washington, D.C.: Catholic Biblical Association of America, 1977.

Bourke, Myles. "The Literary Genus of Matthew 1—2." *CBQ* 22 (1960): 160–75.

Broer, Ingo. *Freiheit vom Gesetz und Radikalisierung des Gesetzes: Ein Beitrag zur*

Theologie des Evangelisten Matthäus. SBS 98. Stuttgart: Verlag Katholisches Bibelwerk, 1980.

Brown, Raymond, E. *The Birth of the Messiah: A Commentary on the Infancy Narratives in Matthew and Luke.* Garden City, N.Y.: Doubleday & Co., 1977.

————, and John P. Meier. *Antioch and Rome: New Testament Cradles of Catholic Christianity.* New York: Paulist Press, 1983.

————, Karl P. Donfried, and John Reumann, eds. *Peter in the New Testament.* Minneapolis: Augsburg Pub. House, 1973.

Brown, Schuyler. "The Matthean Community and the Gentile Mission." *NovT* 22 (1980): 193–221.

Burnett, Fred W. *The Testament of Jesus-Sophia: A Redaction-Critical Study of the Eschatological Discourse in Matthew.* Washington, D.C.: Univ. Press of America, 1981.

Catchpole, D. R. "The Answer of Jesus to Caiphas (MATT. XXVI. 64)." *NTS* 17 (1970/71): 213–26.

Chatman, Seymour. *Story and Discourse: Narrative Structure in Fiction and Film.* Ithaca, N.Y.: Cornell Univ. Press, 1978.

Cook, Michael J. "Interpreting 'Pro-Jewish' Passages in Matthew." *HUCA* 54 (1983): 135–46.

Cope, O. Lamar. *Matthew: A Scribe Trained for the Kingdom of Heaven.* CBQMS 5. Washington, D.C.: Catholic Biblical Association of America, 1976.

Cothenet, É. "Les prophètes chrétiens dans l'Évangile selon saint Matthieu." In *L'Évangile selon Matthieu: Rédaction et Théologie,* ed. M. Didier, 281–308. BETL 19. Gembloux: Duculot, 1972.

Dewey, Joanna. *Markan Public Debate.* SBLDS 48. Chico, Calif.: Scholars Press, 1980.

Donahue, John. "Tax Collectors and Sinners." *CBQ* 33 (1971): 39–61.

Donaldson, Terence L. "Jesus on the Mountain: A Study in Matthew's Theology." Ph.D. diss., Wycliffe College and the Univ. of Toronto, 1981.

Farmer, William R. *Jesus and the Gospel: Tradition, Scripture, and Canon.* Philadelphia: Fortress Press, 1982.

————. "The Post-Sectarian Character of Matthew and Its Post-War Setting in Antioch of Syria." *PRS* 3 (1976): 235–47.

Fiore, Benjamin. "Characterization in Matthew." Unpublished paper, CBA Task Force on the Literary Study of Matthew, 1984.

Forster, E. M. *Aspects of the Novel.* New York: Harcourt, Brace & World, 1954.

Frankemölle, Hubert. *Jahwebund und Kirche Christi: Studien zur Form- und Traditionsgeschichte des "Evangeliums" nach Matthäus.* NTAbh 10. Münster: Aschendorff, 1974.

Garland, David E. *The Intention of Matthew 23.* NovTSup 52. Leiden: E. J. Brill, 1979.

Gerhardsson, Birger. "Gottes Sohn als Diener Gottes." *ST* 27 (1973): 73–106.

————. "The Hermeneutic Program in Matthew 22:37–40." In *Jews, Greeks, and Christians: Essays in Honor of William David Davies,* ed. R. Hamerton-Kelly and R. Scroggs, 129–50. Leiden: E. J. Brill, 1976.

————. *The Mighty Acts of Jesus According to Matthew.* Eng. trans. R. Dewsnap. ScrMin. Lund: C. W. K. Gleerup, 1979.

————. "The Parable of the Sower and Its Interpretation." *NTS* 14 (1967/68): 165–93.

————. *The Testing of God's Son.* ConBNT 2:1. Lund: C. W. K. Gleerup, 1966.

Guelich, Robert A. *The Sermon on the Mount: A Foundation for Understanding.* Waco, Tex.: Word Books, 1982.

Gundry, Robert Horton. *The Use of the Old Testament in St. Matthew's Gospel.* NovTSup 18. Leiden: E. J. Brill, 1967.

Hare, Douglas R. A. *The Theme of Jewish Persecution of Christians in the Gospel According to St. Matthew.* SNTSMS 6. Cambridge: Cambridge Univ. Press, 1967.

Hawkins, John C. *Horae Synopticae: Contributions to the Study of the Synoptic Problem.* 2d ed. Oxford: Clarendon Press, 1909.

Held, Heinz Joachim. "Matthew as Interpreter of the Miracle Stories." In *Tradition and Interpretation in Matthew,* by G. Bornkamm, G. Barth, and H. J. Held, 165–299. Eng. trans. P. Scott. NTL. Philadelphia: Westminster Press, 1963.

Hummel, Reinhart. *Die Auseinandersetzung zwischen Kirche und Judentum im Matthäusevangelium.* BEvT 33. Munich: Chr. Kaiser Verlag, 1963.

Iser, Wolfgang. *The Act of Reading: A Theory of Aesthetic Response.* Baltimore: Johns Hopkins Univ. Press, 1978.

Johnson, Marshall D. *The Purpose of the Biblical Genealogies.* SNTSMS 8. Cambridge: Cambridge Univ. Press, 1969.

Katz, Steven, T. "Issues in the Separation of Judaism and Christianity after 70 c.e.: A Reconsideration," *JBL* 103 (1984): 43–76.

Keck, Leander E. "Ethics in the Gospel According to Matthew," *IR* 40 (1984): 39–56.

Kilpatrick, G. D. *The Origins of the Gospel According to Matthew.* Oxford: Clarendon Press, 1946.

Kingsbury, Jack Dean. *Matthew: Structure, Christology, Kingdom.* Philadelphia and London: Fortress Press and SPCK, 1975.

———. "The Developing Conflict between Jesus and the Jewish Leaders in Matthew's Gospel: A Study in Literary-Criticism." To appear in *CBQ.*

———. "The Figure of Jesus in Matthew's Story: A Literary-Critical Probe." *JSNT* 21 (1984): 3–36.

———. "The Figure of Jesus in Matthew's Story: A Rejoinder to David Hill." *JSNT* 25 (October, 1985).

———. "The Figure of Peter in Matthew's Gospel as a Theological Problem." *JBL* 98 (1979): 67–83.

———. *The Parables of Jesus in Matthew 13.* London and St. Louis: SPCK and Clayton Pub. House, 1977.

———. "The Title 'Son of David' in Matthew's Gospel." *JBL* 95 (1976): 591–602.

———. "The Verb *Akolouthein* ('to follow') as an Index of Matthew's View of His Community." *JBL* 97 (1978): 56–73.

Lanser, Susan Sniader. *The Narrative Act: Point of View in Prose Fiction.* Princeton: Princeton Univ. Press, 1981.

Lindars, Barnabas. *Jesus Son of Man.* London: SPCK, 1983.

Loader, W. R. G. "Son of David, Blindness, Possession, and Duality in Matthew." *CBQ* 44 (1982): 570–85.

Lohr, Charles H. "Oral Techniques in the Gospel of Matthew." *CBQ* 23 (1961): 403–35.

Lotman, J. M. "Point of View in a Text." *NLH* 6 (1975): 339–52.

Luz, Ulrich. "Die Erfüllung des Gesetzes bei Matthäus (Mt 5, 17-20)." *ZTK* 75 (1978): 398–435.

———. "The Disciples in the Gospel According to Matthew (1971)." In *The Interpretation of Matthew,* ed. G. Stanton, 98–128. IRT 3. Philadelphia and London: Fortress Press and SPCK, 1983.

Martin, Brice L. "Matthew on Christ and the Law." *TS* 44 (1983): 53–70.

Meier, John P. *Law and History in Matthew's Gospel.* AnBib 71. Rome: Biblical Institute Press, 1976.

———. *The Vision of Matthew: Christ, Church and Morality in the First Gospel.* TI. New York: Paulist Press, 1979.

Mohrlang, Roger. *Matthew and Paul: A Comparison of Ethical Perspectives.* SNTSMS 48. Cambridge: Cambridge Univ. Press, 1984.

Moule, C. F. D. *The Birth of the New Testament.* New York: Harper & Row, 1962.

Nolan, Brian M. *The Royal Son of God: The Christology of Matthew 1—2 in the Setting of the Gospel.* OBO 23. Göttingen: Vandenhoeck & Ruprecht, 1979.

Pesch, Rudolf. *Das Markusevangelium.* HTKNT 2. 2 parts. Freiburg: Herder, 1976–77.

Petersen, Norman R. *Literary Criticism for New Testament Critics.* GBS. Philadelphia: Fortress Press, 1978.

———. " 'Point of View' in Mark's Narrative." *Semeia* 12 (1978): 97–121.

Prince, Gerald. "Notes Toward A Categorization of Fictional 'Narratees.' " *Genre* 4 (1971): 100-106.

Reicke, Bo. *The New Testament Era.* Eng. trans. D. E. Green. Philadelphia: Fortress Press, 1968.

Reumann, John. *"Righteousness" in the New Testament.* Philadelphia: Fortress Press, 1982.

Rhoads, David. "Narrative Criticism and the Gospel of Mark." *JAAR* 50 (1982): 411–34.

———, and Donald Michie. *Mark as Story: An Introduction to the Narrative of a Gospel.* Philadelphia: Fortress Press, 1982.

Rothfuchs, Wilhelm. *Die Erfüllungszitate des Matthäus-Evangeliums.* BWANT 8. Stuttgart: W. Kohlhammer Verlag, 1969.

Sand, Alexander. *Das Gesetz und die Propheten: Untersuchungen zur Theologie des Evangeliums nach Matthäus.* BU 11. Regensburg: Verlag Friedrich Pustet, 1974.

Sandmel, S. "Herodians," *IDB* 2 (1962): 594–95.

Schweizer, Eduard. *Matthäus und seine Gemeinde.* SBS 71. Stuttgart: KBW Verlag, 1974.

———. *The Good News According to Matthew.* Eng. trans. D. E. Green. Atlanta: John Knox Press, 1975.

Senior, Donald P. *The Passion Narrative According to Matthew: A Redactional Study.* BETL 39. Louvain: Louvain Univ. Press, 1975.

Smith, Robert H. *Easter Gospels: The Resurrection of Jesus According to the Four Evangelists.* Minneapolis: Augsburg Pub. House, 1983.

Stanton, Graham N. "The Gospel of Matthew and Judaism." *BJRL* 66 (1984): 264–84.

Stendahl, Krister. *The School of St. Matthew.* Philadelphia: Fortress Press, 1968.

Strecker, Georg. *Der Weg der Gerechtigkeit: Untersuchung zur Theologie des Matthäus.* FRLANT 82. Göttingen: Vandenhoeck & Ruprecht, 1962.

———. *Die Bergpredigt: Ein exegetischer Kommentar.* Göttingen: Vandenhoeck & Ruprecht, 1984.

Suggs, M. Jack. *Wisdom, Christology, and Law in Matthew's Gospel.* Cambridge: Harvard Univ. Press, 1970.

Theissen, Gerd. "Itinerant Radicalism." *RRel* 2 (1975): 84–93.

Thompson, William G. *Matthew's Advice to a Divided Community: Mt. 17,22—18,35.* AnBib 44. Rome: Biblical Institute Press, 1970.

Trevett, Christine. "Approaching Matthew from the Second Century: The Under-Used Ignatian Correspondence." *JSNT* 20 (1984): 59–67.

Trilling, Wolfgang. *Das wahre Israel: Studien zur Theologie des Matthäus-Evangeliums.* SANT 10. 3d ed. Munich: Kösel-Verlag, 1964.

Turner, Nigel. *Style.* Vol. 4 of *A Grammar of New Testament Greek,* by James Hope Moulton. Edinburgh: T. & T. Clark, 1976.

Uspensky, Boris. *A Poetics of Composition.* Eng. trans. V. Zavarin and S. Wittig. Berkeley and Los Angeles: Univ. of California Press, 1973.

Van Tilborg, Sjef. *The Jewish Leaders in Matthew.* Leiden: E. J. Brill, 1972.

Vawter, Bruce. "The Divorce Clause in Mt. 5, 32 and 19, 9." *CBQ* 16 (1954): 155–67.

Walker, Rolf. *Die Heilsgeschichte im ersten Evangelium.* FRLANT 91. Göttingen: Vandenhoeck & Ruprecht, 1967.

Waetjen, Herman C. *The Origin and Destiny of Humanness: An Interpretation of the Gospel According to Matthew.* Corte Madera, Calif.: Omega Books, 1976.

Wilckens, Ulrich. "Sophia." *TDNT* 7 (1971): 496–526.

Witherup, Ronald D. "The Cross of Jesus: A Literary-Critical Study of Matthew 27." Ph.D. diss., Union Theological Seminary in Virginia, 1985.

Index of References
to Matthew